Sincerity's Shadow

SINCERITY'S SHADOW

*Self-Consciousness in British Romantic and
Mid-Twentieth-Century American Poetry*

DEBORAH FORBES

Harvard University Press
Cambridge, Massachusetts, and London, England

Library of Congress Cataloging-in-Publication Data

Forbes, Deborah.
Sincerity's shadow : self-consciousness in British Romantic
and mid-twentieth-century American poetry / Deborah Forbes.
p.   cm.
Includes bibliographical references (p.   ) and index.
ISBN 0-674-01188-0 (alk. paper)
1. English poetry—19th century—History and criticism.
2. Self-consciousness in literature.
3. American poetry—20th century—History and criticism.
4. Postmodernism (Literature)—United States.
5. Romanticism—Great Britain. 6. Sincerity in literature.
7. Self in literature. I. Title.
PR585.S44F67 2004
821'.709353—dc22   2003056671

Designed by Gwen Nefsky Frankfeldt

For my parents,
Janet and Stephen Forbes

Acknowledgments

Writing is fundamentally an act of communication, and its coming into being depends as much upon the presence of imagined and actual readers as on the writer. I owe an incalculable debt of gratitude to the readers who have helped shepherd this book into existence. Helen Vendler urged me to pay closer attention to the shape each poem makes on the page. The patience and detail of her criticisms, the counter-pressure of her perspectives, and the generosity of her encouragement have been indispensable to this project's evolution. Barbara Johnson raised crucial questions, encouraged me to take as few as possible terms and assumptions for granted, and pressed my thinking further than it could have gone without her. I benefited greatly from James Engell's thoughtful guidance; the care and clear-sightedness of his observations have often helped me see my way out of a tangle of ideas.

Special thanks must go to the members of Harvard's Nineteenth- and Twentieth-Century British Literature Colloquium, particularly to Ann Rowland for providing advice at key moments, and to James Von der Heydt and Kathleen Peterson for intellectual and other forms of nourishment. I am also grateful to the three outside readers for Harvard University Press, whose criticisms allowed me to see my arguments anew, and whose advice made important contributions to the final shape of this book. And I thank Margaretta Fulton for her kindness and patience in guiding me through the process of manuscript preparation, and Mary Ellen Geer for her careful attention to every page.

I gratefully acknowledge the Packard Foundation, which provided a fellowship that permitted me to focus exclusively on this project from June 2000 to July 2001.

I am also grateful to the following publishers: the selection from "Edge" in the volume *Ariel* by Sylvia Plath, copyright © 1963 by Ted Hughes, is reprinted by permission of HarperCollins Publishers Inc.; Dream Song #76 from *The Dream Songs* by John Berryman, copyright © 1969 by John Berryman, copyright renewed 1997 by Kate Donahue Berryman, is reprinted by permission of Farrar, Straus and Giroux, LLC.

Finally, I must offer two, more personal thank-yous: to my husband, Mark Lorey, for all that his love makes possible in my work and life, and to my parents, Janet and Stephen Forbes, to whom this volume is dedicated.

Contents

Sincerity's Shadow

Introduction

READING LYRIC POETRY IS, to a great extent, the art of doing without introductions. When we encounter a poem for the first time, we confront a voice unmoored from its context, isolated as if it has suffered some disaster or has risen for some special purpose of celebration. This voice may alert us to its gender, historical period, or situation, but our sense of its circumstances remains fragmented; it addresses us apart from the interpersonal relationships that ordinarily call forth speech. This voice is intimate—engaging our memories, proclivities, and associations to discover which of its disclosures will quicken our pulse in recognition and which will remain obscure—but also public, immediately raising questions of authorial intention and collective meanings. Human and artificially constructed, tangible and disembodied, personal and anonymous, the voice opens the question of what can be transacted between it and us. Who or what speaks to us in a lyric poem? What voice is this, which by its urgency, cadence, or some other indefinable quality compels us to listen?

To avoid becoming paralyzed by these unavoidable but bewilderingly open-ended questions, it will be helpful to turn immediately to a specific example: what kind of presence confronts us when we read the following lines from Coleridge's "Dejection: An Ode"? The speaker laments that each affliction of his adult life

> Suspends what nature gave me at birth,
> My shaping spirit of imagination.
> For not to think of what I needs must feel,

> But to be still and patient, all I can
> And haply by abstruse research to steal
> From my own nature all the natural man—
> This was my sole resource, my only plan:
> Till that which suits a part infects the whole
> And now is almost grown the habit of my soul.[1]

It seems obvious that the shape and momentum of these lines originate in the poet's attempt to explain, as clearly and faithfully as possible, his current state of mind. We might then describe the presence that we encounter in these lines as the presence of the poet himself, expressing his innermost feelings. But when we examine the passage more closely, we discover that the very nature of its confessions throws into doubt the existence of a creature that is able to make such confessions. The speaker's depiction of his situation depends upon a number of distinctions: between imagination and its absence, between feeling and thinking about what one should be feeling, between a natural relationship to the world and a relationship distorted by "abstruse research." And yet, almost perversely, the writing that sets out these distinctions simultaneously undoes them, until it appears that the poem possesses greater or different knowledge than the poet does.

To take the simplest instance, the speaker tells us that his "shaping spirit of imagination" has been "suspended," yet he tells us so in shapely, imaginative writing. He tells us that his analytical faculty threatens to usurp his other faculties, but the poem is not organized solely by the dictates of reason; for example, iambic pentameter and assertive end-rhymes impart to the poem a melodiousness and satisfaction that demonstrate that the poet's extra-analytical faculties remain intact. In temporal terms, the distinctions of the passage depend upon the "almost" in the closing line, demarcating a brief moment in which the speaker fears that his inclination toward investigation has "infect[ed] the whole" of his being, so become a "habit" that he can no longer either examine or describe it, but in which what he fears has not yet come to pass. We are left to wonder whether this moment is actually inhabitable, or whether "abstruse research" has not already infected every part of the passage, falsifying its claim to present, however fleetingly, a "natural man." When the poet suggests that there is a difference between what we think we should feel and what we actually feel, we cannot help asking: how can we be sure that the poet is telling us what he actually feels just now, and that he is not (deliberately or inadvertently) substituting what he thinks he should feel? As if symptomatically, the opposition between thinking and feeling breaks down on the level of syntax. Not thinking about what should be felt and being still would seem to be in opposition to the dominating analytical faculty, but they are linked to it with an "and" ("and haply by abstruse research to steal"), as if it is nearly impossible to maintain a distinction between being patient and thinking that one should be patient. In short, the analysis of himself which the speaker attempts here, and which in turn tempts us to read this passage as honest self-expression, comes to be portrayed as a kind of thievery—research into one's nature may lead to the destruction of the "natural" altogether.

So, then, what kind of presence confronts us in this poem? This question, it would seem, can only be answered paradoxically. It is the presence of various marked absences: the expressed desire not to think and (the double negative making an equivocal positive) the failure of not thinking; the absence of the "natural man" and yet the presence of a creature who remains human enough to address us; the lamented suspension of imagination in a palpably imaginative poem. We are given the sense of a living individual with a particular temperament and history, but he has conjured himself up only to tell us that he is ceasing to exist. The argument of this book is that this contradictory condition is not unique to this particular instance, but has its analogy in any poetry that claims self-expression as its goal, and especially in British Romantic poetry and the poetry of mid-twentieth-century America.

Underpinning this argument is a broader commitment to reconsider the claims of "sincerity," an old-fashioned term long fallen into critical disrepute. We began with the premise that Coleridge is offering us exactly what he seems to be offering—and indeed what lyric poetry in general claims to offer—a fellow human being speaking truthfully to us. It would be possible to argue that the discrepancies we have noticed are proof of the poet's insincerity: would a man as depressed and bereft of imagination as this one claims to be, be able to write such a masterful poem? But one feels more just in concluding that somehow the structure of the poem itself, rather than Coleridge personally, is responsible for this failure of sincerity. The poem raises the question of sincerity while making the poet's sincerity difficult to judge, which is not to say that the issue of sincerity is irrelevant to the poem. Nor can we dismiss the question of sincerity merely because on some level of generality it is possible to say that there is no "author" (no authoritative guarantor of meaning we can access), only text;[2] to read the poem at all, we have to accept at least the fiction of a truthful or mendacious speaking presence. My aim in this book is to describe the forms of sincerity invented by self-expressive poetry, in which sincerity is strictly unverifiable but still at stake. I want to preserve the question of sincerity a little longer than postmodern criticism has tended to do in order to observe the particular opportunities poetry provides for claims of sincerity to construct and undo themselves within poetry's own terms.

It may seem inauspicious, or at least quixotic, to attempt to revive a critical term that has long existed under the mark of its own failure. Ever since sincerity was claimed as a possible aesthetic goal, critics have been adept at listing all the reasons that statements insisting upon their own honesty must be treated with suspicion: no statement is made without at least an implied listener, a social context that influences its making; human feelings and perceptions are so fluid and fleeting that it is impossible to give any true static account of them; statements must be made in words, which "half reveal / And half conceal the Soul within";[3] and in literary works an author who wishes to be sincere has to contend not only with the distorting properties of language, but also with a potentially distorting imperative to make or discover beauty, coherence, or meaning.[4] The recurring problems that arise when "sincerity" is used as a term of literary analysis can be easily demonstrated. To give but one of many possible examples: Donald Davie's 1966 article "Sincerity and Poetry" attempts to revive sincerity as a meaningful analytical term,[5] but when he moves to practical suggestions, the limits of the term's usefulness become apparent.[6] He assures us that "the measure of a poet's sincerity is, it must be, inside his poem,"[7] but at the cost of redefining "sincerity" to the extent that it becomes unrecognizable:

> We were right all along to think that a poem is valuable according as the poet has control of it; now we must learn to call that control "sincerity." For after all, what is the alternative? Are we to collect gossip about his private life? Are we to believe the poet sincere because he tells us so? Or because he shouts at us? Or (worst of all) because he writes a disheveled poetry, because the poem and the experience behind the poem are so manifestly out of his control?[8]

Jerome McGann summarizes our alternatives in still starker terms: "In a sense, no product of art can be sincere precisely because it is a thing fabricated, created; it exists in an ideal order of its own, no matter how realistically oriented it may be. By the same token, all achieved art can be called sincere because its own internal harmony will suggest no irregularities in the 'poet's vision,' no disruptive contradictions."[9] He and Davie point to a genuine and seemingly insoluble problem: how is it possible to assess the sincerity of a poem without recourse to a different order of knowledge (biography, for example), recourse that discounts the possibility that poetry itself embodies a unique form of knowing? How can we avoid having to choose between McGann's alternatives of "sincerity" as extra-poetic documentary accuracy and "sincerity" as a meaninglessly general term of approbation?

We can start by accepting the premise of the necessary failure of any poet to write with perfect sincerity, and any critic to identify unimpeachable sincerity. But rather than seeing this failure as a merely practical problem—how do we manage our inevitable human failures to live up to sincerity as an ideal?—we can make use of it as a defining precondition: what responses does the structural impossibility of sincerity permit? How do claims of sincerity work in dynamic and productive relationships with their inevitable failures? In this way, sincerity can be made a useful term within the ontological boundaries of poetry itself instead of sending us out in search of extra-poetic information. In this study I understand sincerity as a destabilizing, rather than stabilizing, factor in our reading of poetry, a concept more likely to cast shadows than to illuminate. My aim is to outline a poetics of sincerity oriented not to the biographical or psychological *origins* of a poem, but to a poem's sincerity-*effects,* the often unintended consequences of a poetic commitment to self-expression.

Both the passage from Coleridge's "Dejection: An Ode" and the questions of sincerity it raises engage larger Romantic concerns about self-consciousness. The speaker of Coleridge's poem suspects that his wholeness and integrity depend upon an absence of self-consciousness—on feeling instead of thinking of what he should be feeling and on exercising his natural faculty of imagination instead of artificially mimicking its workings through "abstruse research." The premise of the poem is that, at a certain point in his life history, Coleridge lost his ability to respond directly and unself-consciously to his world. But the poem cannot delimit this loss to a particular time in a particular person's biography—instead, it continually reenacts this loss in the present tense of its own self-consciousness. To put it another way, the poem can only explicitly name the natural man who has been lost by marking its distance from him; Coleridge can only describe his authentic self by becoming something other than that self. The question of sincerity that his poem raises could thus be rephrased as follows: does self-consciousness offer any hope of self-understanding or self-possession, or does it bring only confusion and loss?

A brief look at philosophical discussions of self-consciousness demonstrates the significance and difficulty of this question. These accounts—which have a history as long as Western thought itself, from the Delphic oracle's *Know thyself* to current debates in psychology, epistemology, and ethics—move between the belief that self-consciousness is the guarantor of the coherence of an individual identity and the suspicion that self-consciousness is an experience that makes such coherence impossible. Philosophies oriented to the first, optimistic pole claim that every act of consciousness presupposes our self-consciousness, as implied by the etymology of *con-scious-ness,* which means "knowing with its self."[10] In the famous Cartesian formula, "I think, therefore I am."[11] Philosophies sympathetic to the pessimistic view emphasize the fact that self-consciousness seems to require the presence of two selves: the self being observed (the self as object) and the self doing the observing (the self that is conscious, the self as subject). This proliferation of selves appears to discount the possibility that self-consciousness produces knowledge about a single, unified self. Or, to put it another way, self-consciousness implies an infinite regress, in which the self that is conscious must be supplemented by the self that is conscious that it is conscious, and then the self that is conscious that it is conscious that it is conscious, and so forth.[12]

This study focuses on the limits that this bipolar quality of self-consciousness imposes, as well as the opportunities it affords, for any poet contending with the problem of his or her own sincerity. Philosophical writing also abounds with rhetorical complexity produced by the paradoxes of self-consciousness, but I will confine myself to one example, from the writings of the little-known British thinker Zachary Mayne. In 1728 Mayne claims to be the first person in Western history to give an account of "consciousness."[13] He understands self-consciousness to be the condition in which the self is simultaneously the subject and the object of consciousness,[14] but rather than seeing this condition as a state of self-division, he understands it as the guarantor of unity: "Consciousness hath This in it peculiar and extraordinary, *viz.* that it is the very Cause and Reason of the Unity of that Essence or Being which is endued with it."[15] But his repetitive insistence on this unity brings it into question, leaving his own argument vulnerable to the criticism he makes of Descartes:

> 'Tis, as I may take occasion to observe, exceeding strange and hardly credible, that any one, especially so renowned a Philosopher as *Descartes,* should call in question the Certainty of his own Being and Existence, and not be satisfied thereof, until he had first found out a Medium, *I think,* to prove it by. But which is indeed no Medium at all, because the Thing does not admit of any Proof, as being, of all other Knowledge, the most immediate, because in the highest Degree selfevident [*sic*]. For he could not know or be assured that he Thought, without being *Conscious* of *Himself,* as that Being or Thing which had Thought; and that it was Himself, *i.e.* his own actual Being (the very Thing that he would prove) which, in the Act of Thinking, gave Existence to his own Thought.[16]

The circularity of this argument, in which the thing that is "in the highest degree self-evident" becomes the thing most in need of defense or explanation, is one version of the persistent philosophical paradox of self-consciousness, its mixed promise of self-possession and self-alienation. Self-consciousness seems to be both inevitable (as part of the experience of being human) and impossible (as an endpoint, as a final recuperation), and thinking about self-consciousness only heightens this tension.

Indeed, this tension has been elaborated, but not resolved, in the work of philosophers who have succeeded Mayne. The closest the philosophy of self-consciousness comes to a Copernican revolution is in the work of Kant, who follows David Hume in questioning our ability to *know* ourselves as unified selves, but who holds to the commonsensical opinion that for the most part we *experience* ourselves as unified. He understands self-consciousness (or transcendental apperception) not as the relationship between a subject (the self that is conscious) and an object (the self of whom one is conscious), but as the condition that makes subject-object relationships possible.[17] As a recent commentator has put it, "Kant's notion of transcendental self-consciousness requires a subject of self-consciousness that is somehow distinct from any subject we can experience."[18] In the pages that follow we will also find selves, cast up by the impulse to lyric self-expression, that are "distinct from any subject we can experience" under other conditions, but in the sense that they are intimately and creatively concerned with the paradoxes of self-consciousness, not in the sense that they are able to transcend them.

The precarious balance that Kant attempts to maintain between self-consciousness as self-possession and self-consciousness as self-difference soon falters.[19] The oscillation of the philosophy of self-consciousness between these two ideas becomes more exaggerated in the nineteenth and twentieth centuries. To sketch a complicated history quickly: Hegel takes Kant to task for failing to extend his theory of transcendental apperception more ambitiously and argues that subjective self-consciousness can and must be subsumed into a more general principle of reflection that ultimately synthesizes the subjective and objective altogether. Rodolphe Gasché explains that, according to Hegel,

> The first moment of reflection [in our terms, self-consciousness] is found in the recognition that the object reflected by the mirroring subject is not just any object but rather this subject's symmetric Other—in other words, a representation of its alienated self. With such an alienating position of itself as object, its reflection truly becomes an act of bringing back, a recapturing recognition.[20]

Hegel's claims of radical unity have in turn been contested in postmodern philosophy by an emphasis on radical disunity. Derrida writes of reflection (or self-consciousness): "There is no longer a simple origin. For what is reflected is split in itself and not only as an addition to itself of its image. The reflection, the image, the double, splits what it doubles."[21] As is well known, Jacques Lacan goes so far as to define human consciousness precisely as this splitting,[22] and a good deal of postmodern literature and criticism works from this assumption of self-alienation.[23] Yet many of us also assume that self-consciousness offers the benefits of increased self-knowledge and in turn a more orderly, responsible, and happier life, as the explosive growth of the therapy industry in the past twenty years demonstrates.[24] The contradiction between self-consciousness as alienation and self-consciousness as self-recuperation is as central to Western culture as it has ever been.

Lyric poetry has increasingly borne the marks of this contradiction, and certain of its features suggest that it is peculiarly well designed to embody and investigate the paradoxes of self-consciousness. For example, for its entire history, but especially beginning in the Romantic period, lyric poetry presents a paradox in which the most artificial use of language (marked off from ordinary speech by formal patterning, no matter how closely these patterns are made to follow that speech) has also been claimed as the use of language that sounds the most "natural," the language that most tangibly embodies a speaking human presence. The most generic language (the lyric "I" being freighted with a long history of formal convention independent of individual biographies, and carrying an implicit claim to general authority) has been viewed as the language most appropriate for the voicing of individual feeling. Lyric poetry is a superlatively intentional use of language,[25] with its careful shaping and scrupulous attention to the valence of words, but its intention is also singularly troublesome to locate, set apart as poetry is from the interpersonal and social contexts that usually help us interpret language. Poetry seems to be the realm in which the writer can most consistently exercise her or his mastery over language, but it is also a realm in which it becomes difficult to distinguish mastery from being mastered by the muse. In other words, in a variety of ways, like self-consciousness itself poetry holds the simultaneous promise of perfect self-discovery and threat of complete alienation.

While it is true that each of these paradoxes operates in other uses of language, including memoirs, novels, and other kinds of self-reflexive prose, in poetry they operate with unique flexibility. By nature of its comparative independence from referentiality, the self-reflexivity of its language,[26] and its Romantic proposal that truth is a matter of the heart as well as the mind, poetry is able to embody and explore self-consciousness with an urgency and inventiveness unmatched by other uses of language.

If self-consciousness is characterized by its reversibility, by the ways in which self-possession gives way to alienation and alienation may surprisingly coalesce into something like self-knowledge, lyric poetry is the terrain upon which this reversibility operates with the greatest concentration, suggestiveness, and freedom. The largest ambition of this book is to map out connections between the common promises and threats that lyric poetry and self-consciousness share, as a postmodern version of the Romantic intuition that the destinies of the questions "What is poetry?" and "What does it mean to be a self?" are linked. It would be too much to claim that the problematic structure of self-consciousness can account for poetry, or that poetry is the truest expression of self-consciousness—in a complicated way the sincerest of languages. But I want to suggest that poetry can in part be theorized as an interlocking set of specialized modes of self-consciousness, and more specifically as a particularly spectacular battleground for competing notions of sincerity.

Before these bare claims take further shape, some preliminary words should be said about the poems and methodologies the reader will find in these pages. My hope is that the theory of poetic self-consciousness elaborated here will be flexible enough to help describe the form of any lyric poem. But at the same time, it is clear that a theory linking the paradoxes of self-consciousness with poetic form is more suggestive at certain points in literary history than others. This study focuses on British Romantic poetry (represented by Wordsworth, Byron, and Keats) and twentieth-century American poetry (represented by T. S. Eliot, Adrienne Rich, Robert Lowell, Sylvia Plath, John Berryman, Elizabeth Bishop, and James Merrill), in particular the period from 1950 to 1980, with special attention to the so-called confessional movement. It has been well documented that a radical shift in the status of the individual was occurring during the Romantic period, politically through the consummation of the Enlightenment in the French Revolution (the individual person becomes a conceivable political unit); economically through capitalism's reconfigurations of value (the individual person gains importance as a consumer; the self becomes marketable); scientifically through the accelerating secularization of knowledge; and religiously and philosophically through the accelerating secularization of meaning (knowledge and meaning become increasingly idiosyncratic, "personal"). At the same time, and not coincidentally, there is a radical shift in the function of poetry. Poetry's purpose is no longer to be learnèd, to present arguments and convey knowledge about history, science, politics, and theology, but to act as a form of knowledge itself.[27] In one sense, poetry has been stripped of its traditional authority, but in another sense it has gained an unprecedented opportunity to generate authority on its own terms.[28]

This book concentrates on the origin and extension of this particular moment: the moment of the newly powerful and unstable self's collision with the newly powerful and unstable genre of poetry. At this moment, both poetry and the self become problems of knowledge: the truth-claims that an individual makes for herself and the truth-claims that poetry makes are now both more vulnerable and more important. The sincerity of the poet in the poem makes a bid to address both problems of knowledge: if poetry can be made a vehicle for uniquely authentic self-expression, then both the poem's and the self's truth-claims may be secured (this is the fundamental hope that Wordsworth expresses in his Preface to the *Lyrical Ballads*). But as the span of this project makes clear, I want to claim this moment not as one limited to a specific set of dates, places, and proper names, but as a moment that repeats itself over and over, up to the present time. I understand Romanticism not as a historical period now over, but as the complex of issues just described—even as an ideology, but without believing that this ideology is something that we have the privilege of observing from the outside. If Romanticism is defined as the recognition and elaboration of self-consciousness, we would expect that it is destined to repeat itself, given what we know of the philosophical history of self-consciousness so far.[29] Instead of trying to hold the paradoxes of self-consciousness steady, I want to try to think alongside this repetition.

I move from the British Romantic period across the Atlantic to mid-twentieth-century America because at no other point in history has the question of literary sincerity been more in contention than in the celebration and derision that have swirled around the so-called confessional poets. By connecting the concerns of these poets to their Romantic forebears, I intend to highlight the complexity, seriousness, and enduring power of the idea that poetry is primarily an act of self-expression, and to argue that this idea should not, as it sometimes is, be associated with poetic weakness but instead be understood as a source of formal innovation and strength.

By attending to these two groups of poets—three of the traditional major six poets of the Romantic period and a cluster of American poets who could all be described as white middle-class northeasterners—I neglect other groups that are equally deserving of attention, and whose poetry could in different ways open up and be opened up by a consideration of lyrical modes of self-consciousness. For example, the female poets of the British Romantic period exhibit a complex self-consciousness in response to the precarious position of the woman writer at that time. And the avant-garde poets of twentieth-century America, in the various and sometimes contradictory ways that they both embrace and reject the idea that poetry is primarily self-expression, could profitably be studied for the kinds of poetic self-consciousness they invent as well as the kinds they attempt to escape. (The conclusion to this book touches briefly on some of the directions such a study might take.) But the wager of my project is that there is work yet to be done in describing the dominant modes of self-consciousness which the British Romantic poets develop and upon which their American successors expand.

Although this selection of writers could be taken to reinforce received judgments about literary value, I seek instead to interrogate the ways in which questions of poetic self-consciousness shape such judgments. There is a general, often unspoken assumption in literary criticism that the more self-consciousness a poem demonstrates, the more successful it is. In moral terms, the poet's self-consciousness about his or her faults and limitations is thought to ameliorate them, and in aesthetic terms, the self-consciousness implied by formal shaping and the sophistication of a poet's self-consciousness about poetic tradition are thought to be the standard of artistic maturity. Both of these assumptions are questioned in some of my individual readings; in particular, I criticize instances in which formal self-consciousness is conflated with moral goodness and objectivity. To my mind, a poem's success depends as much on the unruliness and tendentiousness of the subjectivity it presents as on the ways in which that subjectivity is contained by its strategies of self-consciousness.

In this study I group poets from different historical periods in order to draw attention to the consistency with which the problem of sincerity creates recurring limitations and opportunities: Wordsworth with Adrienne Rich, Robert Lowell, and Sylvia Plath; Robert Browning with T. S. Eliot, John Berryman, and Plath; Byron with Anne Sexton; and Keats with Elizabeth Bishop and James Merrill. This procedure violates many of the categories we ordinarily use to understand literature, including periodization, national affiliation, chronological influence, and literary "schools." Instead of concerning itself with divisions *between* poets and groups of poets, this project explores the structural and recurring divisions that the effort to write sincerely produces *within* individual poets and poems. Focusing on the poet's self-consciousness makes questions such as Wordsworth's influence on Byron and Keats, or the "Americanness" of American poetry, or how we should draw the lines between Romanticism, Modernism, and Postmodernism seem, at least temporarily, less important. This leveling effect of the idea of self-consciousness is to some extent a drawback: because any poem can be understood ac-

cording to the way it engages the paradoxes of self-consciousness, think-
ing in these terms sometimes blurs lines of affiliation and development,
potentially diminishing our sense of the unique contributions that indi-
vidual poets and poetic movements make. But I believe that this leveling
effect also has the benefit of allowing us to see these familiar poets with a
freshness made possible by the abandonment of some of our habitual cat-
egories. My emphasis on historical continuities is not meant to imply that
the concepts of self-consciousness and sincerity do not have histories of
their own—clearly they do—only to suggest that from the British Ro-
mantic period onward, the specific invitation to self-possession and self-
doubt tendered by the experience of self-consciousness has determined
the shape of lyric poetry with surprising consistency.

While my project is thus more formalist than historicist in its orienta-
tion, there are a couple of indirect contributions I hope to make to the
historicist project. First, I would like to suggest that we cannot judge the
extent to which a poem takes account of or responsibility for its histori-
cal context without a theory of the modes of self-consciousness a poem
presents. The concept of self-consciousness is helpful, even indispensable,
in the work yet to be undertaken toward theorizing the relationship be-
tween poetry and history. The theories of self-consciousness that I de-
velop here, particularly in the following chapter, could be applied to that
task. Second, to digress for a moment from the ways that self-conscious-
ness shapes poetic form to the ways that it shapes the rhetoric of literary
criticism, it is my impression that the more polemical versions of New
Historicism get caught up in the Romantic paradoxes of self-conscious-
ness even as they try to distance themselves from these paradoxes. Im-
plicit in the New Historicist approach is the claim that the critic possesses
(or at least admits to) a more reliable historical self-consciousness than
the poet he analyzes. But often the critic's historical self-consciousness
becomes difficult to distinguish from the other modes of self-conscious-
ness found in the Romantic poetry that he analyzes. We come to suspect
that the poem has already anticipated us. To take a classic example, in
The Romantic Ideology Jerome McGann names the "last and final illu-
sion" of self-reflective Romantic poetry as the illusion that "it can expose
or even that it has uncovered its illusions and false consciousness, that it
has finally arrived at the Truth."[30] What he names here as an "illusion" is
an apt description of his own strategy of exposing hidden motives in
seemingly ahistorical Romantic poems and reinstating historical truth.[31]
More recent New Historicist work recognizes the contradictions critics
undergo when they try to mark a division between their own conscious-
ness of history and that of the poets they examine: for example, Alan Liu

argues that the supposed Romantic denial of history "is also the strongest kind of engagement with history"; "history is the very category of denial";[32] Thomas Pfau contends that "historicism produces 'its' unified subject of history by inverting [that is, reproducing] the symbolic concision and aesthetic unity of the literary artifact";[33] and James Chandler writes that "it is precisely by our work of situating Romantic writings historically that we share their blindness, their ideology."[34] According to these perspectives, the literary critic's historical consciousness turns out to be not the repudiation of an insufficiently engaged Romantic self-consciousness, but its repetition. To the extent to which New Historicist critics fail to acknowledge or analyze this contagion of self-consciousness, criticizing the Romantic self as a falsifying replacement for history without realizing that their own historicism partakes of the Romantic problem of self-consciousness, they risk trivializing the influence and productive instability of the Romantic commitment to sincerity.

The readings that follow trace some of the different figures that poems make on the page when the poet undergoes, or alternatively attempts to resist, the pressure to express herself sincerely. At times the poet asks us to believe in her sincerity because we can recognize in her the human nature we hold in common. At other times the poet locates his sincerity in his difference from us, offering himself as an utterly unique personality. The poet sometimes attempts to suture the split inherent in self-consciousness by taking moral responsibility for herself and her creations, while at other times she parcels this split out into dramatis personae, until she herself takes on the attributes of a fictional character. The poet may come to accept the premise that his sincerity will inevitably fail, or that the self he wants to express is only representable as an absence, but this sophistication of self-consciousness will not rescue him from its contradictions. Examining lyric poetry through the lens of sincerity does not give us a poetry that is more substantial, backed by the authority of a lived life; nor does it give us a poetry that is simplified into an unmediated human cry. Instead, we discover a poetry that is "full of fine things said unintentionally,"[35] the often unexpected effects of acts of self-consciousness directed elsewhere; poetry that is a map of productive and frequently beautiful failures of self-expression, or—because poetry is the place of sudden reversals—failures to avoid self-expression. The failures outlined in the following pages are richer than any success we could imagine. Without them, poetry itself would be unimaginable.

CHAPTER ONE

The Personal Universal

Sincerity as Integrity in the Poetry
of Wordsworth and Rich

HERE WAS A TIME when the term "sincerity" was more likely to be applied to a fine wine than to an honest person. Lionel Trilling explains:

> [Sincerity] derived from the Latin word *sincerus* and first meant exactly what the Latin word means in its literal use—clean, or sound, or pure. An old and merely fanciful etymology, *sine cera*, without wax, had in mind an object of virtu which was not patched up and passed off as sound, and serves to remind us that the word in its early use referred primarily not to persons but to things . . . One spoke of sincere wine . . . simply to mean that it had not been adulterated, or, as was once said, sophisticated . . . As used in the early sixteenth century in respect of persons, it is largely metaphorical— a man's life is sincere in the sense of being sound, or pure, or whole; or consistent in its virtuousness.[1]

As strange as it may seem, this idea of sincerity as wholeness is not all that foreign to the concept of sincerity developed by William Wordsworth and Adrienne Rich. Their version of sincerity holds that the ability to speak truthfully depends upon a condition of wholeness and integrity.[2] It involves not only honest self-expression, but also the integrated state of being that makes honesty possible. A sincere poet is someone who attempts to engage and connect all of her faculties, who works either as if head and heart, and the aesthetic and the moral, are indistinguishable, or as if it is possible and necessary to make them so. Sincere poets, in this sense, are not merely those who close the distance between themselves and the speakers in their poems to create the aesthetic effect of a more direct address to the reader, but poets who close this distance by subjecting the speakers in their poems to the same moral imperatives that they themselves feel.[3] This sincerity entails a commitment to seriousness; in its pure form, it is capable of bitterness but not irony, because the poet's purpose is to unite rather than oppose style and sentiment.[4]

Wordsworth and Rich, two poets who are separated by enormous differences in temperament, values, style, and historical context, nonetheless believe that the poet's task, first and foremost, is to be sincere in this sense.[5] Wordsworth famously defines poetry as sincere self-expression ("all good poetry is the spontaneous overflow of powerful feelings"), but he almost as famously qualifies this definition: "though this be true, Poems to which any value can be attached were never produced on any variety of subjects but by a man who, being possessed of more than usual organic sensibility, had also thought long and deeply. For our continued influxes of feeling are modified and directed by our thoughts, which are indeed the representatives of all our past feelings; and, as by contemplating the relation of these general representatives to each other, we discover what is really important to men."[6] In other words, self-expression is not the expression of personal feelings alone, but also an act that requires discovering what is important to humankind in general. Wordsworth does not use the term "sincerity" here, but in his "Essay upon Epitaphs," in which he attempts to establish a "criterion of sincerity,"[7] the connection between individual and universal feeling is made more explicit. A good epitaph, that is, one that faithfully bears witness to the essence of the person who has died, includes two basic components: an appeal to "the common or universal feeling of humanity" and a rendering of "a distinct and clear conception of the individual." General sympathy and an interest in individual particulars are "two powers [that] should temper, restrain, and exalt each other."[8] Sincere poetry, then, is poetry that successfully integrates individual feeling with the generalized feelings of humankind. The question of how such an integration can be undertaken is the animating question of Wordsworth's poetry, and the refusal of the individual and the universal to fully merge leaves its record in the fissured grandeur of his poems.

Adrienne Rich also understands poetry as the integration of personal experience with collective experience, but she rejects the Romantic faith in natural connections between the personal and the universal and instead describes her task as connecting the personal and the political.[9] Rich believes that casting poetry as self-expression requires work undertaken against resistance, work necessary to counter the idea that you must "keep your private life private, [which is] the attempt to fragment you, to prevent you from integrating love and work and feelings and ideas, with the empowerment that can bring."[10] Over the course of her career, she often tells the story of the "split" she experienced as a young writer "between the girl who wrote poems . . . and the girl who was to define herself by her relationships with men."[11] She describes the long process of integrating the two as a political coming-to-consciousness, a moving beyond the conceptual barriers that separated her personal struggles as a young wife and mother from aesthetic and political concerns. The story's climax comes when "at last the woman in the poem and the woman writing the poem become the same person."[12] Though undertaken in radically different terms, this quest to integrate personal feeling and experience with a poetic voice capable of addressing humanity more generally parallels Wordsworth's quest, encountering its own stubborn obstacles and leaving in its wake the rugged formations of her poetry.

Once this common goal has been recognized, the other similarities between Rich and Wordsworth become less surprising. Both see themselves as reformers, dedicated to educating the public against a depraved taste for the pretentious and over-stimulating unreality of poetic diction (in Wordsworth's case) and the coercive and benumbing unreality of American consumer culture (in Rich's). (They undertake this education in part to create the taste by which their own work, which transgresses the aesthetic criteria of their respective times, can be understood and appreciated.) They understand themselves to be living through similar periods in history: Wordsworth laments that "a multitude of causes, unknown to former times, are now acting with a combined force to blunt the discriminating powers of the mind, and, unfitting it for all voluntary exertion . . . reduce it to a state of almost savage torpor,"[13] and Rich echoes his concern almost two hundred years later: "The society I was living and writing in . . . smelled to me of timidity, docility, demoralization, acceptance of the unacceptable. In the general public disarray of thinking, of feeling, I saw an atrophy of our power to imagine other ways of navigating our collective future."[14] Both poets turn to groups of people historically excluded from "high culture" as a method for renewing a poetic tradition that to them appears to be losing touch with humanity. Finally, both poets are on a doomed search for origins: Wordsworth for the unmediated relationship with nature that was once and he hopes will be his moral guide, and Rich for the socio-historical coordinates of her development, which she believes will permit her to take greater responsibility for her life.

Wordsworth's and Rich's formulations of sincerity as integration run counter to our post-confessional assumptions about what sincere poetry looks like: for these poets, sincerity is not synonymous with autobiographical disclosure. It seems an obvious point, but it is easy to forget that Wordsworth, with his reputation as a groundbreaking autobiographer, does not believe that what we now, post-Freud, think of as major psychological events are the proper material of poetry. Both Wordsworth and Rich in fact exhibit a palpable reticence about their personal biographies. The solitude in which most of the defining moments of Wordsworth's autobiographical epic, *The Prelude,* occur suggests that the most important parts of personal life exclude those shared with parents, guardians, siblings, childhood friends, spouses, and lovers; and sexual transgression, if it is to be included, must be fictionalized (his affair with Annette Vallon becomes the story of Vaudracour and Julia in the 1805 *Prelude* and disappears soon after), not confessed in the proto-Freudian style of Boswell and Rousseau. For Rich's part, even though she has sometimes been identified as a "confessional" poet (and it is possible to identify poems about various family members, friends, and lovers), she more often cloaks in obscurity what seem to be specific autobiographical facts. She is much more likely to address family members at one remove (a mother-in-law, grandmothers) or, even more often, to address historical figures, than to address her parents (in stark contrast to her "confessional" contemporaries).[15] Like Wordsworth, Rich finds that her main quarrel is not with her co-sufferers in the family romance, but with herself.

The refusal of Wordsworth's and Rich's work to meet our post-confessional expectations has important generic implications. Unlike many autobiographical poets of the twentieth century, Wordsworth and Rich do not encourage us to piece together a biographical narrative with recognizable characters who interact dramatically. Even though *The Prelude* presents itself as a narrative of personal development, its method of isolating emotionally concentrated and transformative experiences effectively breaks the narrative flow. Readers have long approached *The Prelude* as if it were a series of self-contained lyric poems ("the boat stealing incident," "the Mount Snowdon episode") rather than a continuous narrative. In contrast, as we read a series of "confessional" poems about identifiable family members with recognizable names, we tend to weave those poems into a narrative whole; the poems become episodes in a *bildungsroman* rather than self-contained artifacts. (A particularly clear example of this effect can be found in Robert Lowell's *Life Studies,* which includes a prose memoir at the center of the book that provides a narrative context for the personal poems that follow.) Wordsworth's and Rich's refusal of this kind of life story counters this narrative pressure, opening up new directions for the lyric in its own right and demonstrating that autobiographical self-consciousness can be a resource for formal innovation within poetry as well as a method for uncovering new stories.

The following readings describe some of the features of this innovation—the fortuitous results of Wordsworth's and Rich's failure to achieve the perfect, verifiable integration of their faculties that would make for an achieved moral sincerity. I begin with Rich because her own theory and practice, instructive in their own right, also function as a reading of Wordsworth, a reading that has the added benefit of casting the current New Historical perspective on Wordsworth's poetry in a new light. In the next section I describe the bewildering, coexisting pressures toward and away from sincerity in Wordsworth's poetry. Finally, in the closing section I raise the question: if poetry is primarily an act of imaginative integration, what happens when "poetry" encounters language? Both Wordsworth and Rich understand themselves as working to some degree in opposition to language, and this extraordinary position produces yet another constellation of sincerity-effects in their work.

Rich and the Poetics of Accountability

In his critical writings, Wordsworth implies that sincerity, like Nature, is a bedrock waiting to be rediscovered rather than a condition that must be invented. Achieving sincerity means purifying oneself of the cultural influences that have distorted one's true nature rather than extending one's cultural consciousness. To put it another way, Wordsworth believes that sincerity is to be found by recovering an unself-conscious state, rather than by expanding self-consciousness (though in practice, expanding self-consciousness is the only action available to him). In contrast, Adrienne Rich argues that an honest response to the world can only be achieved by a continual expansion of self-consciousness. After arduous effort, "at last the woman in the poem and the woman writing the poem become the same person."[16] But this integration is not a stable endpoint; it has to be won again and again through "consciousness raising," an extending of self-awareness which, according to Rich's understanding, also entails an expansion of moral accountability.[17]

But even before we turn to Rich's poetry, we can already see that her theory of sincerity as accountability suffers from a basic contradiction. The integration of private and public that makes widened moral accountability possible involves, for Rich, two contradictory imperatives: the imperative to write in a historically and biographically marked voice, and the imperative to write in an impersonal, implicitly universalizing voice. It is the tension between these two demands that defines the parameters of Rich's poetry. In answering the first imperative, Rich criticizes the universalizing assumptions of the traditional lyric "I," pointing out that its putative authority masks the "untutored and half-conscious renderings of the facts of blood and bread, the social and political forces of [one's] time and place."[18] As she puts it in a later essay, "You yourself are marked by family, gender, caste, landscape, the struggle to make a living, or the absence of such a struggle. The rich and poor are equally marked. Poetry is never free of these markings even when it appears to be."[19] Since there is no choice about these markings, it is the decision to take responsibility for them that becomes crucial. Rich suggests that the only way to avoid asserting the "I's" experiences as falsely universal is to be conscious of the facts of blood and bread that shape these experiences, and somehow to make poetry responsible to this consciousness.

But Rich's own practice indicates that such historical self-consciousness is more feasible in autobiographical prose than in poetry. She recommends fighting the false impersonality of the lyric "I" with "the experiential grounding of identity politics,"[20] which for her means finding ways to speak "as a woman, as a feminist, as a Jew, as a lesbian."[21] Summarizing a particular essay in which she undertakes this work, she writes:

> [This essay represents] a moving into accountability, enlarging the range of accountability. I know that in the rest of my life . . . every aspect of my identity will have to be engaged. The middle-class white girl taught to trade obedience for privilege. The Jewish lesbian raised to be a heterosexual gentile. The woman who first heard oppression named and analyzed in the Black Civil Rights struggle. The woman with three sons, the feminist who hates male violence. The woman limping with a cane, the woman who has stopped bleeding are also accountable. The poet who knows that beautiful language can lie, that the oppressor's language sometimes sounds beautiful.[22]

And the essay to which she refers ("Split at the Root: An Essay on Jewish Identity") does indeed attempt to recover a story of origins: in it, Rich explores the ideas about gender, race, and class that she received as a young woman poet and describes how her increasing awareness of the particular deprivations and privileges that these categories conferred has created a new sense of responsibility. But the crucial thing to notice is that Rich undertakes such work in her essays because it is less clear how it is to be undertaken in poetry. Rich's poetic practice, as we shall see, is not generally a practice of trying to create a marked voice, a voice that finds ways to let us know that the labels "woman," "Jew," "lesbian," "token woman," "mother," and so forth suit it.

Rich's own theorizing suggests one reason why. In another essay, she discusses the necessity of stripping away false assumptions about how people with backgrounds different from ours live. Rich expresses hope that "the imaginative writer could learn to write with accountability of women who are not simply of her own caste or class or background, resisting stereotypes, trying to create whole persons . . . this may mean changing her life, not just her writing."[23] This vision restates in modern terms the Romantic idea that sympathy should be an act of the imagination, not merely an experience of fellow feeling. But here, it is the specifics of a marked identity that stand in the way of sympathy. Too conscious a sense of the differences between the self and the other endangers the project of identifying with the other, of taking responsibility on behalf of the other.[24] As if in response to this insight, Rich's poetry, as opposed to her essays, predominantly presents an "I" that is an almost disembodied self-consciousness about the possibilities and limitations of imaginative sympathy rather than a historically marked and bounded voice.

Rich's many poems that attempt to create a sympathetic relationship with historical women involve occasional simplified claims to identification ("I am an American woman . . . / Foot-slogging through the Bering Strait"),[25] but in their more characteristic (and, I would argue, more effective) mode these poems elaborate a self-consciousness that constantly questions the possibility of such an identification. For example, the poem "Hunger" interrupts its identification with African women to comment, "I live in my Western skin, / my Western vision, torn / and flung to what I can't control or even fathom";[26] and the poem "Frame" (the title draws our attention to its "framing" by a white narrator) breaks its empathetic imagining of a black woman to confess, "*I don't know her. I am / standing though somewhere just outside the frame / of all this, trying to see.*"[27] Both of these poems partially mark the identity of the narrator (the narrator of "Hunger" is marked by her "Western vision," the narrator of "Frame" by her "white skin"), but this marking serves more as an emblem of the difference between the narrator and her subject (a formal distance that makes the narrator's self-consciousness necessary) than as the sign of a fully present and accountable woman, Jew, lesbian, and so forth. Rich reverses our expectations by using poetry to theorize the possibility of speaking in a marked voice, while her prose essays are the space in which she can actually put her theories into practice.

Rich's most characteristic poetry, then, may not be her poetry with the most explicitly political subject matter, but her poetry that most thoroughly explores a self-consciousness which, rather than creating a marked voice, invents new ways of speaking impersonally.[28] This self-consciousness reveals itself in its starkest form in her poem "Splittings" (1974), which raises a question central to Rich's project: is it possible to decrease suffering, or to make suffering less "useless," by becoming self-conscious about its nature and origins? The poem would seem to answer "yes" to this question, for at its close it claims to have successfully refused "the splitting / between love and action"; to have chosen "not to suffer uselessly" and "to love   this time   for once / with all my intelligence."[29] This victory takes place in terms of integration—the speaker believes that her self-awareness (her "intelligence") has permitted her to integrate love and action, creating a wholeness that resists useless suffering. But what actually takes place in the poem itself is rather different.

In the opening section of the poem, the speaker takes the occasion of a separation from her lover to speculate:

> . . . if I could instruct
> myself, if we could learn to learn from pain
> even as it grasps us   if the mind, the mind that lives
> in this body could refuse   to let itself be crushed
> in that grasp   it would loosen.[30]

Self-consciousness thus allows part of the mind (the part that is conscious) to slip from pain's grasp.[31] But the implications of this solution are not, as we might expect, that the speaker discovers a newly authentic personal voice, speaking from a healed, integrated position. Instead, pain itself is given a voice:

> *We are older now*
> *we have met before   these are my hands before your eyes*
> *my figure blotting out   all that is not mine*
> *I am the pain of division   creator of divisions*
> *it is I who blot your lover from you*
> *and not the time-zones nor the miles*
> *It is not separation calls me forth   but I*
> *who am separation   And remember*
> *I have no existence   apart from you.*[32]

This passage suggests that the speaker's attempt to integrate pain into her own psyche, to take responsibility for her pain in a moral sense that will break its power over her, can only be undertaken as the imagination of a severe dis-integration, a personification of her own experience, which comes to address her as a separate being. In terms of the poem, seeing pain as separate gives pain new powers—the power of speech and the power of independent existence—both of which undermine its message, "I have no existence apart from you." In this imagining, a self-conscious examination of suffering seems as likely to heighten suffering as to diminish it.

Once we notice that the poem operates by a logic of dis-integration instead of, as advertised, one of integration, we become sensitive to the provisionality of the poem's triumphant ending. When the speaker claims, "I refuse . . . the splitting / between love and action" and "I am choosing / not to suffer uselessly," we understand that this conclusion depends upon the very splitting that Rich repudiates. The implication is that the poet must continually start over in her refusal of splitting, because self-consciousness is the wound as well as the cure of dis-integration. This paradox is displayed less optimistically in an earlier poem, "Walking in the Dark" (1971):

> I wish there were somewhere
> actual we could stand
> handing the power-glasses back and forth
> looking at the earth, the wildwood
> where the split began.[33]

But there is nowhere "actual we could stand" that will heal the split—we can only observe it by inventing a new split between ourselves and what we see. Self-consciousness permits Rich to envision a poetry strong enough to suture this split and counter useless suffering, a vision which is utterly compelling but absolutely unrealizable on its own terms.

Rich creates a tentative solution to this problem by attempting to become the power-glasses in the passage quoted above—that is, by embodying the technologies of observation (and, by extension, of self-consciousness) themselves. "Planetarium" (1968), the poem of which Rich claims that "at last the woman in the poem and the woman writing the poem become the same person,"[34] demonstrates this strategy. We would expect that a poem that is supposed to achieve unity between speaker and poet would be spoken in the first person, a lyric "I" flexible enough to contain both the idiosyncratic experiences and the poetic and moral ambitions of Adrienne Rich. But surprisingly this poem operates mostly in the third person, and from the perspective not of Rich but of a woman astronomer. As in "Splittings," the integration of the woman and the poet entails a form of dis-integration, a splitting between Rich and the woman astronomer with whom she identifies, and a splitting between the astronomer herself and the constellations she observes.

The poem separates and juxtaposes constellations shaped like women with a woman who observes them:

> A woman in the shape of a monster
> a monster in the shape of a woman
> the skies are full of them.[35]

On the ground, separated from these hyperbolically remote images of women, is the woman observing "'in the snow / among the Clocks and instruments' / . . . riding the polished lenses."[36] The astronomer cannot even view the constellations with the naked eye; the instruments of observation separate her further from them.[37] By depicting the constellation-women as "impetuous," Rich makes a clear connection between them and the woman scientist who is doing work that generally has been reserved for men, but the poem does not envision any way for the constellations and the astronomer to be unified.

Unlike "Splittings," this poem does not end by claiming the (necessarily deferred) union between observer and observed. Instead, the speaker transforms herself into the instrument of observation itself:

> I have been standing all my life in the
> direct path of a battery of signals
> the most accurately transmitted most
> untranslatable language in the universe
> . . . I am an instrument in the shape
> of a woman trying to translate pulsations
> into images   for the relief of the body
> and the reconstruction of the mind.[38]

The speaker's position here is one of startling passivity, far removed from the poem's earlier, more activist (and more facile) solution to the distance between woman-as-observed-object and woman-as-observing-subject: "What we see, we see / and seeing is changing."[39] It is a position that does successfully connect observer and observed, and by extension passive suffering and transformative action, but crucially, it is a position that can be inhabited only metaphorically, that is to say poetically, not literally. The "I" here is a world apart from the autobiographical "I" who has a body of experiences to confess: the speaker's identity is marked in only the most generic, formal way, "an instrument in the shape of a woman."

Even more fundamentally, Rich's reverse personification creates an "I" that is not even human, let alone a morally accountable being. Instead, the speaker becomes pure form transmitting what cannot be translated into content, into autobiographical narrative.

This pattern can be seen again in another important poem of Rich's, "Diving into the Wreck" (1972), in which the speaker's body becomes equipment that she must learn to maneuver underwater. Though the poem is about a quest for origins, for "the wreck and not the story of the wreck,"[40] the speaker focuses her attention on how she must position herself in relation to her search instead of on what she may find. If we take the poem as an allegory for Rich's search for her socio-historical origins, origins that will someday anchor her claim to sincerity, the poem re-stages this search as a meditation upon the conditions of such a search, as if in implicit recognition that these origins can never completely be secured. Rich writes:

> the sea is another story
> the sea is not a question of power
> I have to learn alone
> to turn my body without force
> in the deep element.[41]

When Rich's attention moves from the contents of consciousness to the experience of self-consciousness, the questions of political power and force that frequently concern her become strangely irrelevant. There is a useful neutrality in taking the position of the instrument of consciousness instead of its possessor. Toward the poem's close, she concludes: "we are half-destroyed instruments / that once held to a course / the water-eaten log / the fouled compass."[42] The instruments that the poet here embodies have become even less analogous to individual human beings, too ruined even to provide a specific angle of perception. By becoming an instrument, Rich exchanges a falsely universalizing "I" for what might be better described as an impersonal or even a nonhuman "I."[43] Her embodiment of the tools of observation, and by extension of the mechanism of self-consciousness itself, is the most innovative sincerity-effect of her work.

Wordsworth and the Poetics of Unaccountability

Turning now to Wordsworth, it is easy to be struck in retrospect by all that he takes for granted. If integrated sincerity is continual, arduous labor for Rich, it is something that Wordsworth claims to achieve simply by refusing to substitute unfeeling and mechanical poetic diction for the natural language of his rural home. While Rich suggests that self-knowledge is the result of a difficult and lifelong archaeology of the psyche, Wordsworth struggles much less explicitly to achieve personal honesty or self-knowledge, even in his most autobiographical poetry. For example, although *The Prelude* is the poem in which Wordsworth attempts to trace "the growth of the poet's mind," self-understanding is subsumed under other priorities.[44] Addressing Coleridge, Wordsworth describes his goals:

> . . . my hope has been, that I might fetch
> Invigorating thoughts from former years;
> Might fix the wavering balance of my mind,
> And haply meet reproaches too, whose power
> May spur me on, in manhood now mature,
> To honourable toil. Yet should these hopes
> Prove vain, and thus should neither I be taught
> To understand myself, nor thou to know
> With better knowledge how the heart was framed
> Of him thou lovest, need I dread from thee
> Harsh judgments.[45]

The goal of self-knowledge is limited here to discovering and producing confirmations of the poet's vocation: this is what Wordsworth seems to mean by "understanding" himself.[46] He does not suggest that extracurricular self-knowledge has any worth for its own sake. Vocation is assured by the blessing of maternal nature, or Wordsworth's metaphorical invocation of that blessing; it is not earned, as poetic vocation seems to be for Rich, through a work-ethic of sincerity.

Wordsworth's poetry supports his reputation as our first poet of sincerity[47] because it produces the illusion of a meticulous description of the shifts in the poet's perceptions and moods. The first book of *The Prelude* is filled with such fluctuations: the poet's excitement at his escape from the city undergoes minor qualifications (the remembrance of "[t]hat burthen of [his] own unnatural self"); and the inner breeze which vitalizes the poet "vex[es] its own creation," is consciously slowed, and evaporates.[48] Such finely textured movements between hope and despair can be traced in the winding, self-qualifying clauses of virtually any sentence of *The Prelude*. Wordsworth half-playfully suggests that such mood swings are definitive of the poet's temperament:

> The Poet, gentle creature as he is,
> Hath, like the Lover, his unruly times;

His fits when he is neither sick nor well,
Though no distress be near him but his own
Unmanageable thoughts.[49]

What is striking (particularly in comparison with Rich's poetry) is
Wordsworth's willingness to let his moods flow over him without making
a conscious effort to trace their cause or ascribe intentions to them. His
coronations within and banishments from the vocation of poetry do not
necessarily accompany moral breakthroughs or lapses. Doubtful moods
do not impede the poem's confident mode of narration: the evenness of
Wordsworth's blank verse makes the poem feel consistently sure-footed
and unflustered. Time interposes itself between moods to create a sense of
layered or doubled consciousness, but these moods often are not self-con-
sciously woven into a larger structure of meaning. Wordsworth's lack of
consistency in his attempts to interpret his own moods creates an uneven
texture that permits us to read him as both sincere and evasive, uninten-
tionally candid and self-consciously manipulative (and vice versa).

It should not surprise us that Rich directly criticizes the seeming ease
with which Wordsworth moves from personal experience to universal
truth. She writes disapprovingly, "The poet achieved 'universality' and
authority through tapping his, or occasionally her, own dreams, longings,
fears, desires, and, out of this, 'speaking as a man to men,' as Words-
worth had phrased it."[50] Her criticism, and the counter-example her own
poetry provides of a historically responsible and politically engaged writ-
ing, parallels the recent systematic critique of Wordsworthian sincerity by
the New Historicists, who claim that Wordsworth's invention of the in-
trospective Romantic self is at its core a defensive denial of historical par-
ticularity.[51] By rewriting historical conflicts as personal conflicts, Words-
worth supposedly undergoes them on territory that is safer because it is
vaguer and at the same time more under his control. The link between
Wordsworth's critics and Rich's theories is underlined when Rich criti-
cizes her own earlier poetry in language that mirrors the New Historicist
critique of Wordsworth. For example, in "The Diamond Cutters" (1955)
Rich makes diamond-cutting a metaphor for writing poetry. In 1984 she
adds the following note:

> Thirty years later I have trouble with the informing metaphor of this poem. I
> was trying, in my twenties, to write about the craft of poetry. But I was
> drawing, quite ignorantly, on the long tradition of domination, according to
> which the precious resource is yielded up into the hands of the dominator as
> if by a natural event. The enforced and exploited labor of actual Africans in
> actual diamond mines was invisible to me, and therefore invisible in the
> poem, which does not take responsibility for its own metaphor. I note this

here because this kind of metaphor is still widely accepted, and I still have to struggle against it in my work.[52]

Just as Rich attempts to take responsibility for the historical contexts of the metaphors in her work, New Historical criticism of Wordsworth acquires its polemical impact by suggesting that he has failed to take moral responsibility for the metaphors in his poetry.[53]

But before we join Rich and the New Historicists in condemning Wordsworth's bad faith, we should remember what we have learned from Rich's own poetic practice. While New Historical interpretations of Wordsworth give the impression that he could have somehow done a better job of acknowledging his historical constraints and opportunities (even though this assumption is less and less frequently avowed, it is necessary to give significance to the idea of Wordsworth's "denial" of history), Rich's productive failures to take full responsibility for herself and her world suggest that such comprehensive acknowledgment is structurally impossible. Wordsworth's refusal of Rich's type of historical and political self-consciousness, then, need not be understood as a refusal of history (after all, history happens whether one is self-conscious of it or not, and what kind of self could actually take full responsibility for its historical context?). But at the same time, I believe the New Historicists are correct when they suggest that the self we receive in Wordsworth's autobiographical poetry is strangely abstract and even impersonal, an equivocal being that seems to evade biographical and historical grounding.[54] Instead of accepting that the peculiar moral unaccountability of the Wordsworthian self results solely from the absence or denial of history, I will try to show that Wordsworth makes himself uniquely vulnerable to the question of sincerity by juxtaposing personal disclosure with the impersonality inherent to poetic voice in such a way as to produce a crisis of interpretation. More specifically, Wordsworth makes both his self-confidence and the reasons to doubt that confidence so apparent to his reader that it becomes impossible (and yet remains urgent) to determine which of his revelations are intentional and which are unintentional.[55]

This indeterminacy can be viewed with exceptional clarity in the poem "Nutting," which tells a story of sexual violence which the poet partially and unsuccessfully overlays with a benign story of Mother Nature's gentle intervention. The young Wordsworth is sent out to harvest hazelnuts, and we witness his progress:

> I forc'd my way
> Until, at length, I came to one dear nook
> Unvisited, where not a broken bough

Droop'd with its wither'd leaves, ungracious sign
Of devastation, but the hazels rose
Tall and erect, with milk-white clusters hung,
A virgin scene![56]

The sexualized language continues as the boy-poet "[b]reath[es] with such suppression of the heart / As joy delights in; and, with wise restraint / Voluptuous, fearless of a rival" plays with flowers.[57] Eventually the adult poet steps in to judge that his younger heart is "[w]asting its kindliness on stocks and stones / And on the vacant air."[58] As if in response, the narrative continues:

. . . Then up I rose,
And dragg'd to earth both branch and bough, with crash
And merciless ravage, and the shady nook
Of hazels, and the green and mossy bower,
Deform'd and sullied, patiently gave up
Their quiet being.[59]

This ruthless rape ("merciless ravage") or castration of nature literally rips open the pastoral scene, but the poet-speaker expresses no shock and little remorse. Instead he implores his companion, "Then, dearest Maiden! move along these shades / In gentleness of heart; with gentle hand / Touch,—for there is a Spirit in the woods,"[60] as if he has overlooked his own violation of gentleness entirely.

Anyone with a passing acquaintance with Freud will see a number of possible analyses here. Perhaps the most straightforward would explain that a primal fear of castration has led the boy to project violence onto a female principle (here, Nature, a phallic Mother), his rape of nature serving as a preemptive strike. (A second projection occurs at the poem's close, when the speaker represses the fact that it is his violence that requires the correction of gentleness, and instead implores his female companion to be gentle.)[61] But the problem with this reading of Freudian subtext is that the sexual content of the poem is not subtext—it is clearly on the surface of the poem. Missing is the gap between the manifest and latent (repressed) content that a Freudian analysis would have predicted. The speaker is neither hiding himself (he is open about his violence and its analogy to sex, if not its sexual nature), nor is he exposing himself (nowhere does the poem recognize or take responsibility for its sexual violence as such). The speaker's selective and self-justifying interpretation of his own experience leaves the reader impatient to point out his insincerity, and yet the disclosures that lead to our impression of insincerity are disarmingly candid.

One way the poem achieves this double sense of hiddenness and openness is by its (strategic? unwitting?) miscalculation of the reader's responses. Apparently oblivious to the connotations of his own language, to the stark contrast of "happiness beyond all hope" with the "merciless ravage" for which he, after all, is responsible, the poet confesses:

> . . . unless I now
> Confound my present feelings with the past,
> Even then, when from the bower I turn'd away,
> Exulting, rich beyond the wealth of kings—
> I felt a sense of pain when I beheld
> The silent trees and the intruding sky.[62]

The reader's and the poet's senses of what has just happened are strikingly different—it takes a moment to absorb the understatement of this passage. Yet it does not seem as if the speaker's interpretation of what has just happened is a misrepresentation, for he does finally make the admission that the reader feels he must: he confesses that he feels remorse. But "a sense of pain," which the speaker presents as an unexpected response, a response he even worries that the reader may doubt ("unless I now / Confound my present feelings with the past"), is wildly incommensurate to the mutilation just described. It falls far short of the shock and remorse the speaker's actions would seem to require. This incommensurability, though, is not the same thing as a lie; at least in one way, it makes the speaker seem more sincere rather than less. If he is trying to manipulate our responses by pitching his description toward our belief, he has failed entirely. Wordsworth opens the question of sincerity (could this really be how he felt?) without permitting doubt to disrupt the surface of his narrative. He occupies a position in which he can be accused of naiveté and a lack of self-understanding, but he has so reliably planted clues of his own doubts, and they remain so completely on the surface, that the critic feels as if she has been anticipated. In this sense, Wordsworth's sincerity is not a stable claim; instead, the most distinctive sincerity-effect of Wordsworth's poetry is the way in which his poetry makes the question of his own sincerity urgent but undecidable.

"Nutting" may be the most dramatic example of this effect, but it can be seen in any of Wordsworth's autobiographical poems. For example, "Lines Composed a Few Miles Above Tintern Abbey" raises similar issues more subtly. Here, rather than presenting a contrast between a violent sexual narrative and the story the poet wishes to tell about a "Spirit in the woods," the poem presents a contrast between a relatively straight-forward story about nature's tutelage of the poet and the convoluted writing used to relate this story. The poem's abstractions, repetitions, and double negatives, which are put forward in densely textured, syntacti-cally overstitched blank verse, open the possibility of doubt as effectively as the poet's occasional explicit avowals of anxiety. Again, Wordsworth's confidence in interpreting the meaning of his experience ("Nature never did betray / The heart that loved her")[63] works as a challenge to the reader to doubt him. And once again, the poet has left evidence of his own doubts close enough to the surface of the poem that the reader can-not be sure that Wordsworth was not aware of them himself.

The most open expression of doubt in "Tintern Abbey" comes at the beginning of the third verse paragraph. The rhythm of blank verse en-closes the expression of doubt between two strong expressions of faith, so that doubt literally cannot give us pause. Here is how the lines read, run together: "We see into the life of things. // If this / Be but a vain be-lief, yet oh! how oft—" (the thought eventually completes itself, that the poet often has turned to the Wye river for inspiration).[64] This recognition of the possible mistakenness of the poet's own belief that he "sees into the life of things" threatens the entire poem, for he is not only questioning whether or not his belief in nature's inspiration is justifiable, but whether his own subjective perception reflects reality—if it does not, the entire poem is in danger of becoming the mere record of a hallucination. By opening up a gap between what he believes and what may or may not be true, the poet undermines the unification that sincerity claims to achieve between subjective experience or belief and objective truth. The insistent pulsing of the rhythm of these lines, which washes over this possibility, nonetheless leaves it intact—Wordsworth easily could have chosen to write, "We see into the life of things. // How oft," leaving his blank verse undisturbed without the extra clause. We are left with the question: which counts more, the presence of an expression of doubt or the rapid, unfazed abandonment of it? Do we focus on the (false?) ease with which Wordsworth repairs the gap of doubt in his poem, or on his opening of the gap in the first place? How do we decide whether this expression of doubt is real, or a canny substitute for genuine self-questioning? How loose do the edges of the poem have to come, how raw and obvious do repression and the return of the repressed have to be in order to count as sincerity?

These questions are left unanswered and unanswerable, and they are made more troublesome by the fact that doubt seems to be the very stuff

Wordsworth's poem is made of, if one attends to the minute fluctuations of each line of his blank verse. A number of Wordsworth's stylistic habits reinforce our sense of seeing the wrong side of a tapestry, with its loose threads and seams visible—for example, his use of negatives and double negatives. Here is how he communicates the idea that he has carried images from Tintern Abbey in his mind during his absence: "These forms of beauty have not been to me, / As is a landscape to a blind man's eye."[65] The double negative of "not" and "blind" suggests a possible absence of perception and then blots it out, which in turn suggests a blind spot in perception itself, or at least a doubt in language's ability to present perception; it raises the question of why, in a poem about the intimate link between visual perception and memory, a blind man has been mentioned at all. Negatives thread through the poem, producing the impression that part of it has been crossed out: we have "uncertain," "unremembered" (twice, in quick succession, almost as an afterthought in a poem about memory), "unintelligible," "unprofitable," "unborrowed," and "unwearied," each reminding the reader of its opposite even as this opposite is under the mark of erasure. As William Galperin puts it, "The reader knows very well that the negative syntax . . . signifies doubt; yet it is difficult at this juncture for the reader to consider this without feeling he or she is being unfair, both to the speaker and to him or herself."[66] At the same time, the poem is structured as a whole around such negatives: Tintern Abbey is the not-city; the poet's experience now is not his experience as a child; Dorothy will remember his experience of nature when he is not there. Even Wordsworth's use of abstraction works as a version of the double negative. When he explains that the difference between his childhood and adulthood experiences of nature is that now he can hear "[t]he still, sad music of humanity,"[67] this expression works a little bit as "not unhuman" might. Humanity takes its place in the poem, but not in any substantial or concrete sense; even when Dorothy enters the scene, the poem remains one that is emphatically about a particular person's experience of a landscape, protected by a palpable solitude. This poem insistently haunts itself with its own doubts without committing these doubts to sustained examination.

There is yet another way in which the poem registers doubt, or at least the possibility of failure, even when the speaker refuses to: through its structure of repetition. The second verse paragraph, which will culminate in the moment when "[w]e see into the life of things," includes at least two false starts before we reach this point. The speaker informs us that the mental image of the landscape near Tintern Abbey has given him "sensations sweet, / Felt in the blood, and felt along the heart, / And

passing even into my purer mind."⁶⁸ "Purer" suggests a familiar Enlight-
enment hierarchy—the body and the feelings must be transcended in or-
der to reach the mind (reason, or in Platonic terms, the soul). But this hi-
erarchy or valuation apparently is unsatisfying to the poet, and several
lines later he begins again:

> To them I may have owed another gift,
> Of aspect more sublime; that blessed mood,
> In which the burthen of the mystery,
> In which the heavy and the weary weight
> Of all this unintelligible world,
> Is lightened:—⁶⁹

Like the ineffectual crossings-out seen in the negative constructions
above, the kinetics of the body haunt this passage that tries to erase the
body—the final metaphor relies upon the physical sense of a weight
lifted. When "the burthen of the mystery . . . / Is lightened," this phras-
ing, rather than communicating the clarity that comes with the reduction
of unintelligibility, suggests a literal light-headedness. Furthermore, in
this repetition, the faculties of perception and experience have been
crossed out—we no longer have blood (body), heart (emotion), and
mind; they have been replaced, in characteristic fashion, by the vaguer
word "mood." But again, this version of transcendence is brought into
question by the final repetition, which is successful to the extent that it
closes the verse paragraph and allows the writer to move on to another
thought (though this new thought will be his direct confrontation with
doubt). In the final version (also a "mood"):

> . . . the affections gently lead us on,
> Until, the breath of this corporeal frame,
> And even the motion of our human blood
> Almost suspended, we are laid asleep
> In body, and become a living soul:
> While with an eye made quiet by the power
> Of harmony, and the deep power of joy,
> We see into the life of things.⁷⁰

Here we move directly from the body to what before was called the
"purer mind," with the heart working as the engine of this process in-
stead of occupying the same level as the other faculties. The final image

still needs the body that is putatively asleep: it is the eye that permits the transcendence of mere vision. We can put aside the question of why this formulation is more satisfying than the others; the important question for our purposes is whether these repetitions indicate a confession of the failure of the earlier formulations, or an admission of doubt about the possibility of expressing the experience the poet wishes to describe in words. Again, it seems that failure is not being admitted, but neither is it being concealed—this reading of Wordsworth's uncertainty does not need to look very far beyond the clues he has left on the surface of his poem.

Jerome McGann praises "Tintern Abbey" for its candor even as he understands it as a poem of denial: "The greatness of this great poem lies in the clarity and candor with which it dramatizes not merely this event [the replacement of the world with the self], but the structure of this event."[71] Wordsworth, paradoxically, is honest about his dishonesty, candid about his own suppressions. He fails to take responsibility for the doubts he partially conceals, but at the same time he represents the structural failure of self-consciousness to distinguish consistently between concealment and revelation. Self-consciousness neither guarantees sincerity, as Rich hopes, nor destroys it, as Wordsworth fears. His poetry offers the knowledge that self-consciousness can only produce honesty by presenting one's distance from the self about which one was supposed to be honest, while leaving the question of in what way the poet himself "knows" this necessarily open.

How, then, are we to compare the moral value of Wordsworth's version of sincerity with that of Rich? Undoubtedly Wordsworth's comparative lack of concern about his own sincerity can be interpreted as a mark of cultural privilege: it is probably easier for him to assume that his personal experiences as a white, middle-class man can be made "universally" intelligible than it is for Rich as a lesbian woman.[72] The ways in which he makes his sincerity undecidable, his lack of availability for questioning, could be interpreted as an exceptionally effective deployment of that privilege. And yet at the same time Wordsworth appears touchingly, and usefully, vulnerable to our criticism. His assumption that his sincerity can be taken for granted is riddled with gaps and discontinuities that invite a compensatory moral pressure from his readers. In contrast, Rich's self-consciousness about speaking with honesty and moral accountability sometimes has the effect of blocking the reader: our critical faculty has already been absorbed and anticipated in the work. Rich is a "sincere" poet not because we can question her sincerity, but because she reveals the processes that an active quest for sincerity entails. Wordsworth, on the other hand, is a "sincere" poet *because* he makes his sincerity questionable. It may be, however, that we need to be trained in a self-consciousness like that of Rich in order to read him in this way.

The Dream of a Common Language

We might expect that a commitment to poetic sincerity would entail a naive belief in the transparency of language. If a poet proposes to express herself honestly in language, then presumably language must be a simple and unresisting tool, so as not to present an obstacle to this self-expression. Wordsworth and Rich defy this expectation entirely. Their commitment to sincerity as first and foremost a condition of (posited or sought-after) moral wholeness means that language becomes a secondary, and therefore fraught, concern. By defining poetry as lived experience, as Wordsworth does when he defines poetry as "the spontaneous overflow of powerful feelings" which correspond to the feelings of all uncorrupted men, and as Rich does when she writes, "if life is uncorrupted / no better poetry is wanted,"[73] these writers separate "poetry" from its embodiment in language. The poetry that the reader confronts, the words on the page, do not necessarily provide access to poetry proper, whose best parts may theoretically be lived outside the realm of language. This belief creates an extraordinary situation in which poetry might be endangered by its very rendition into language. Wordsworth and Rich respond to this situation in two fundamental and similar ways: they consider methods for humanizing a language that is understood as potentially hostile to human self-expression, and they court silence. In the end, their poetry suggests that sincerity in language is not a kind of transparency of language, but a complex operation in which language is metaphorically made to cancel itself out.

Twentieth-century criticism suggests that to understand Wordsworth's poetry, one must come to an understanding of the nature of language itself.[74] In fact, Wordsworth's poetry has provided the battleground for many of the arguments generated by the turn to linguistics in the literary criticism of the past century. Today, two main lines of argument are visible. On the one hand, we have the deconstructive Wordsworth, a category I define broadly to include all studies of Wordsworth that emphasize the gap between consciousness and the experiences it represents to itself, including, to name some indispensable examples, Geoffrey Hartman's reading of the apocalyptic dangers of Wordsworth's representations of nature, Paul de Man's insistence that this gap be named "time," and Thomas Weiskel's and Frances Ferguson's explicit link between the problem of representing consciousness and the equivocal nature of language itself.[75] A different Wordsworth, who might be called the Wittgensteinian Wordsworth, has emerged more recently in response to the perceived excesses of the deconstructive interpretation. A number of critics impatient with examinations of consciousness and representation in isolation (as if conversations take place mainly between human beings and objects, rather than between human beings) are inspired by Wittgenstein's theories to recast Wordsworth's language as a social dialogue.[76] While deconstructive readers of Wordsworth understand the important quality of language to be the gap between the signified and signifier and the failure of language to relate to anything but its own constantly deferring code, Wittgensteinian readers understand the important quality of language to be the way it positions the speaker in a web of social interactions.

Instead of choosing between these two Wordsworths, I want to describe a particular way in which his own theorizing makes such a choice difficult. If deconstruction casts language as in some irreducible way inhuman, an inescapable structure of deferral designed to continually frustrate human desire, and if Wittgenstein insists upon the fundamental humanness of language, its functionality as a social tool, Wordsworth begins his theorizing with a quasi-deconstructive awareness of the alienating possibilities of language (specifically, Augustan poetic diction) and then attempts to humanize this language by reconnecting it to lived human experience. Poetic language that involves "a mechanical adoption of . . . figures of speech"[77] is to be replaced by poetry that produces figures of speech through natural, heartfelt passion. From this perspective, Wordsworth's qualification of his statement that poetry is "the spontaneous overflow of powerful feelings" works as a theory of the poetic mind *and* as a theory of language:

> Poems to which any value can be attached were never produced on any variety of subjects but by a man who . . . has also thought long and deeply. For our continued influxes of feeling are modified and directed by our thoughts, which are indeed the representatives of all our past feelings; and, as by contemplating the relation of these general representatives to each other, we discover what is really important to men, so, by the repetition and continuance of this act, our feelings will be connected with important subjects, till at length . . . such habits of mind will be produced, that, by obeying blindly and mechanically the impulses of these habits, we shall [strengthen the understanding and affections of the reader].[78]

Sincere poetry cannot be achieved by simple spontaneity: "feeling" does not become poetry until it undergoes a dialectic with thoughts, which are "representatives" of past feeling. This dialectic comes as close as possible to being a dialectic between feeling and language (connoted by the word "representatives"), but stops just short of such an admission of language's centrality to the human psyche. What is remarkable is how finely divided Wordsworth's distinctions are. The difference between thought and feeling is only a hair's breadth wide, since thoughts are only "representatives of all our past feelings." Wordsworth's insistence upon time rather than an act of conscious interpretation as the main marker between thought and feeling makes the difference between them seem a matter of contingency, not necessity. (We have seen this more or less neutral use of the concept of time operate in Wordsworth's poetry as a separator of moods that are left uninterpreted, memory as a faculty that permits double-consciousness without self-consciousness.) Finally, this processing of feeling, though not exactly spontaneous, is automatic for a man with good habits, but at the same time Wordsworth's use of the word "mechanical," which usually carries negative connotations in his writing about poetry, renders this automatic (as opposed to natural) process somewhat ambiguous.

The implication for Wordsworth's theory of language is that mental representation has now been humanized. The gap between feeling and the representation of feeling is no longer a potentially abysmal gap between signified and signifier; instead it is a matter of time and the contingencies of human experience. Self-expression involves a certain processing of experience, but this processing can become so reflexive that it is practically spontaneous. In a mode parallel to Wordsworth's simultaneous revelation and concealment of doubt in his poetry, this theory simultaneously preserves and stitches over the gap between language and experience. Representation creates self-difference (the difference between thought and feeling, the difference between the past and the present), but this difference can be reintegrated by the "natural" machinery of language. It is this set of ideas and assumptions about language that produces the linguistic complexity we saw in "Nutting" and "Tintern Abbey."

Wordsworth's "Essay upon Epitaphs" represents the negative pole of his attitude toward language, expressing his fear that the humanization of language may in fact be impossible. In this essay, he addresses the issue of sincerity with a directness found nowhere else in his body of work.[79] Because his investigation of sincerity is explicit here, lacking the useful and protective unself-consciousness about sincerity seen in his poetry and his Preface, Wordsworth's relationship to language becomes much more antagonistic. He writes, for example, "If words be not . . . an incarnation of the thought, but only a clothing for it, then surely will they prove an ill gift; such a one as those poisoned vestments, read of in the stories of superstitious times, which had power to consume and to alienate from his right mind the victim who put them on."[80] But this suspicion of language is expressed most forcefully when the essay argues that sincerity is to be found not in language that has been appropriately fitted to sentiment, but in language that heightens the gap between style and sentiment, or even in silence.

The "criterion of sincerity"[81] that Wordsworth develops in this essay is surprisingly illustrated by examples of what he recognizes as bad taste. He describes, for example, how "the homeliness of some of the inscriptions, the strangeness of the illustrative images, the grotesque spelling, with the equivocal meaning often struck out by it, and the quaint jingle of the rhymes" on some tombstones actually excite his admiration rather than his mirth, since these oddities give evidences of "how deeply the piety of the rude Forefathers of the hamlet is seated in their natures, I mean how habitual and constitutional it is,"[82] that is, how sincere it is. Wordsworth here identifies sincerity as the perceived gap between the supposed feelings of the mourner and the expression of those feelings in language, rather than the coincidence of the two. To give another example, he quotes an epitaph:

> His Honour wonne i' th' field lies here in dust,
> His Honour got by grace shall never rust:
> The former fades, the latter shall fade never
> For why? He was Sir George once but St. George ever,

and he admits that in writing the closing pun the writer's "better affections were less occupied with the several associations belonging to the two ideas than his vanity delighted with that act of ingenuity by which they had been combined."[83] In other words, the writer has disobeyed the stern warning against poetic hubris that Wordsworth makes in each of his essays, but he is forgiven ("I should rather conclude the whole to be a work of honest simplicity")[84] because of rather than in spite of his awkwardness. Wordsworth comments: "Where the internal evidence proves that the Writer was moved, in other words where this charm of sincerity lurks in the language of a Tombstone and secretly pervades it, there are no errors in style or manner for which it will not be, in some degree, a recompence."[85] But it is difficult to imagine what this "internal evidence" or "charm" is, if not the very errors themselves.[86]

At the close of the essay Wordsworth makes a final, quieter statement against language, this time not in favor of bad taste that renounces all claims to appropriate language, but in favor of a silence that could be interpreted as a graphic representation of the gap between sentiment and expression in the incongruous epitaphs that he admires. He describes an epitaph that imparted "more awful thoughts of rights conferred, of hopes awakened, of remembrances stealing away or vanishing . . . [than] any other that it has ever been my lot to meet with upon a Tomb-stone." The epitaph that wins this accolade is simply "the name of the Deceased with the date of birth and death, importing that it was an Infant which had been born one day and died the following."[87] This kind of silence is not an option for the poet, whose work must be undertaken in the accumulation of words. The essay concludes with a more poetically viable example of words wrapped around a silence: an epitaph-poem written by Wordsworth about the life and death of a deaf man. This man's goodness appears to reside in the "introverted spirit" created in him by his disability, and the integrity of this silent core retrospectively gives a new meaning or integrity to sound:

> And yon tall pine-tree, whose composing sound
> Was wasted on the good man's living ear,
> Hath now its own peculiar sanctity
> And at the touch of every wandering breeze
> Murmurs not idly o'er his peaceful grave.[88]

Is it too much to see this passage as an allegory indicating that Wordsworth needs the consciousness of a certain silence, a blank, in order to write the "murmur" of morally sincere verse, his own "composing sounds"?

Wordsworthian sincerity, then, suggests three different versions of poetry undertaken in a language that crosses itself out. In the first version, the careful referral of language to experience, an ongoing (and necessarily incomplete) attempt to humanize language, results in a self-qualifying, self-thwartingly complex blank verse. In the second version, poetic language effaces itself through its awkwardness, as in the epitaphs Wordsworth admires because their awkwardness suggests intense emotion imperfectly expressed. This description might also apply to the more extreme experiments of the *Lyrical Ballads*. Finally, in the third version, language is literally erased as silence. But because actual silence is not useful to the practicing poet, it must be implied in the gap between what can be felt and what can be spoken, or woven into the rich and puzzling interstitching of the poet's blank verse.

Rich's poetry, like Wordsworth's, exhibits a double desire to humanize language and to silence it altogether.[89] But while Wordsworth develops a syntactic flexibility that works both to accommodate language to human experience and to alert us to the intractability of language in the face of experience, Rich elaborates a metaphorical complexity that seeks ways to equate language with human beings, but also, and sometimes contradictorily, to envision the destruction of language. An example of Rich's metaphorical attempts to humanize language can be found in a recent collection of her poetry. In "A Long Conversation," the speaker asks:

> Who out there hoped to change me—
> what out there has tried?
>
> What sways and presses against the pane
> what can't I see beyond or through—
>
> charred, crumpled, ever-changing human language
> is that still you?[90]

Both the implicit question of whether language is a "who" or a "what" and the structuring of these verses as an apostrophe to language anticipate the final naming of language as "human." This attribution also depends upon our ability to imagine language as "charred" and "crumpled," something with an almost mortal vulnerability. A similar imagery can be found in a series of poems from Rich's 1969 volume *Leaflets* and her 1971 volume *The Will to Change* that link the destruction of language to the humanizing of language, producing a figurative logic that simultaneously acknowledges and fights language's stubborn lack of transparency, its inevitable failures. Three poems from this period explore the relationship between suffering and language through the metaphor of burning, suggesting that there is a connection between the burning of the human spirit for self-expression and the burning-up or destruction of language. These poems consider the possibility that the destruction of language is necessary for sincere self-expression, but at the same time they find figurative ways to save language in poetic form.

Rich's clearest vision of the sincerity that might attend the destruction of language is presented in "Our Whole Life" (1969). This poem expresses the hope that the lies that result when we try to translate our individual lives into "the oppressor's language" could be destroyed, "meanings burnt-off like paint / under the blowtorch."[91] It offers an alternative image of burning as authentic speech in the shape of an "Algerian / who walked from his village, burning . . . and there are no words for this / except himself."[92] The poem produces a fantasy of direct speech, but only under the condition of destruction in the most spectacular terms—only self-annihilation can bypass language. This poem's own expression in words, its ability to produce the (perhaps morally questionable, in Rich's terms) simile of the burning Algerian, undercuts its argument against writing, but even the writing itself seems to self-destruct when the poem ends abruptly. Two earlier poems, "Leaflets" and "The Burning of Paper Instead of Children" (both written in 1968), make more extended, circuitous, and metaphorically textured attempts to play with the fire of self-expression without getting burned.

The fifth section of "Leaflets" suggests that poetry is useful because it can be destroyed in order to release new possibilities for communication. Poetry is a leaflet to be crushed, forgotten:

> . . . yours
> in the sense that if you find and read it
>   it will be there in you already
> and the leaflet then merely something
>   to leave behind, a little leaf
> in the drawer of a sublet room.[93]

Of course, this gesture advertises its own failure simply by the fact that we are reading not a disposable leaflet, but a poem in a book: it is only in language that the destruction of language can be imagined. More to the point, the scenario described here is complicated and wasteful—the addressee has to read the poem (both the poem as we find it on the page and the leaflet in the poem) in order to retroactively confirm what, presumably, needs no confirmation—the contents of his or her own heart and mind. Even though the leaflet has been discarded, it retains a persistent kind of life in its drawer, with the implication of future rediscovery. But my point is not that this is a failed poem; it succeeds because of its failures, through the logic of a double negative analogous to the double negatives we witnessed in Wordsworth's "Tintern Abbey." To write against language's mastery in masterful language creates the possibility that poetry might have a life of its own, but only through its own self-cancellation.

Furthermore, the poem does not settle for the destruction of language. It manages at the same time to humanize language by metaphorically transforming the problem of language into the problem of the survival of physical documents and, by extension, human survival. By describing poetry as a fragile piece of paper, the poem conceals language's actual strength as an unavoidable code that outlives any individual human use of it. The poem is not only not a disposable leaflet because it is published in a book, but also because words cannot reduce themselves to an object to be passed back and forth, something with material worth instead of a value that is determined by a complex process of signification and interpretation. But the poem's strategy is to defend poetry as if it were a threatened material object, comparable to

> little figurines or phials
> no stronger than the dry clay they are baked in
>   yet more than dry clay or paper
> because the imagination crouches in them.[94]

Suddenly destruction is no longer a positive strategy under the poet's control but instead a force that attacks culture and human beings from the outside, something that reminds us

> that all true images
>   were scooped out of the mud
> where our bodies curse and flounder

and threatens to devour "much that [we] would have loved . . . as well."[95] The poet claims that language needs rescuing and defense because, as a product of human beings, it is as fragile as human beings themselves are. The fires of destruction restore the poem to a world in which language has been made precious under the false logic of destructibility. Meanwhile, language as an indestructible force has remained untouched—it is the stuff that this poem is made of. Thus the poem is able to contain the contradictory notions that poetry is something we need to abandon and something we must protect because of its dehumanization and repersonification of poetry, its metaphorical flexibility.

As its title suggests, "The Burning of Paper Instead of Children" questions the equation of the body and language set forth in "Leaflets," taking the possibility of the expendability of poetic language still further. The female speaker's neighbor is horrified that his son and her son have burned a textbook, which reminds him of Hitler and a time when it was not always easy to separate the destruction of books from the destruction of bodies. The speaker responds, "The burning of a book arouses no sensation in me."[96] The speaker expresses her skepticism about the value of language in uncompromising terms, first in an epigraph that brings into question Rich's entire project of articulation-as-responsibility: "I was in danger of verbalizing my moral impulses out of existence,"[97] then in a wholesale indictment of all language: "this is the oppressor's language,"[98] and finally in a rejection of the knowledge that language claims to embody:

> there are books that describe all this
> and they are useless . . .
>
> no one knows what may happen
> though the books tell everything.[99]

Of course, these assaults on language cancel themselves out in the same way as do the questionings of language in "Leaflets"—it is only in language that they can be phrased. But it is not only this structural double negative that gives the poem paradoxical life. In attempting to envision a communication that is more sincere than communication in language, the poem's language itself accumulates increasing metaphorical density. Language is to be outwitted not by being made transparent, but by a heightening of its metaphorical complexity.

For example, just as Wordsworth does in the "Essay upon Epitaphs," Rich considers the possibility that silence might be more sincere than words:

> To imagine a time of silence
> or few words
> a time of chemistry and music
>
> the hollows above your buttocks
> traced by my hand
> or, *hair is like flesh,* you said.[100]

This fantasy of sexual communication, a direct and presumably unfakable "intercourse" between two human beings, imagines that representation could happen in the juxtaposition or substitution of parts of the body: "hair is like flesh." But inescapably, this vision is expressed through a function of language—"hair is like flesh" is a simile, an invention of syntax rather than an act of sexual communion. The desire expressed here for nonlinguistic communication undermines itself by the attention it draws to its dependence upon the syntactic flexibility of language, a flexibility that becomes more important than erotic athleticism. The problem of the oppressive inescapability and yet personal necessity of language sketched in the first section of the poem can only be metaphorically transformed, not resolved.

This reading is reinforced by what follows. The speaker states her desire for "relief" from language:

> from this tongue   this slab of limestone
> or reinforced concrete
> fanatics and traders
> dumped on this coast wildgreen clayred
> that breathed once
> in signals of smoke
> sweep of the wind.[101]

Through a logic of association similar to the logic that linked hair and flesh above, the tongue (both physical organ and foreign language) becomes limestone or concrete opposed to the coastal clay which the speaker imagines was once capable of another kind of speech: "signals of smoke." The vision of sexual communion gives way to the vision of an aboriginal body (or "tongue") that can communicate through its natural volatility, not through its translation into an external code of signification. For a moment, it appears possible that the body could smoke with meaning without being consumed. But again, it is only through heightening language's figurative, artificial nature that "language" as the subject of the poem can be subverted.

In a final turn of the metaphorical screw, the poet returns to the physical properties of language encountered in a book, "loneliness" transformed

> so on that page
> the clot and fissure
> of it appears
> words of a man
> in pain
> a naked word
> entering the clot
> a hand grasping
> through bars:
>
> deliverance.[102]

The visible marks on the page are made metaphorically equivalent to experiences of the body: "clot and fissure." But as if leaving this metaphor stable will falsify it, the speaker rapidly shifts it: "a naked word / entering the clot," the word now made separate from the clot, and humanized in a different way by comparison to a naked human being. This shift suggests at least two possible readings of the hand grasping through the bars: if language belongs to the oppressor, then the bar presumably represents language, but the syntax here implies that it is the word that is like a hand, the experience of suffering that is like a bar. This permutation suggests an answer to the poem's greater question—is language a prison or a deliverance?—by transforming its terms. This passage seems to answer that language is what can imagine something as both a prison and a deliverance; language is the terrain of reversibility. Poetic language is the place where you can have it both ways on the condition that you are willing to stay in poetry's element.

But as we might expect, Rich is not finally content to stay within poetry's element; poetry is only meaningful to her to the extent that it can teach her how to live. Against her implicit celebration of poetry's metaphorical flexibility, she closes her poem with a pessimistic, prosaic block of declarative sentences, drawn in part from the compositions written by her semiliterate students in New York's "SEEK" remedial writing program; in part from sentences of "the oppressor's" and "the oppressed's" books; and in part from her own feelings. She introduces this excerpt with the contention that "[a] language is a map of our failures":

> Frederick Douglass wrote an English purer than Milton's. People suffer highly in poverty. There are methods but we do not use them. Joan, who could not read, spoke some peasant form of French. Some of the suffering are: it is hard to tell the truth; this is America; I cannot touch you now. In America we have only the present tense. I am in danger. You are in danger. The burning of a book arouses no sensation in me. I know it hurts to burn. There are flames of napalm in Cantonsville, Maryland. I know it hurts to burn. The typewriter is overheated, my mouth is burning, I cannot touch you and this is the oppressor's language.[103]

Written language may be expendable (Joan did not need it), but it matters that there is a difference between the style of Frederick Douglass and that of Milton; it matters which tenses are available to us, which literacies we possess. The last sentence suggests that the "oppressor's language" has won—it has even destroyed the possibility of a wordless sexual communication. But the statement "this is the oppressor's language" also cancels itself out, for this phrase can be read, "this is an example of the oppressor's language, and you can reject it as such—I reject it, and am indicating that there is another language possible, even if I cannot speak it yet."[104] Finally, for all of its stripped-down urgency, this passage does not

entirely renounce poetic power, producing stylistic effects that run coun-
ter to its own argument. The momentum of Rich's sentences, far from
suggesting that language has struck a dead end, or that language must
provide a false formal closure that cannot be escaped, offers instead a
new sense of language burning itself up, a burning more successfully pre-
servative. As Judith McDaniel puts it, "The poem does not conclude . . .
it ignites."[105] Rich's poetry demonstrates that if language, and more spe-
cifically poetic style, is a map of our failures, it may not be such a useless
thing to have.

Wordsworth's and Rich's casting of sincerity as a seamless integration of
self-expression and language, feeling and moral agency, is powerful not
because this ideal could ever be realized, but because of the shimmering
traces that their attempts to bring this ideal into being leave behind. Their
efforts to be sincere produce, in Wordsworth's case, an unstable and (if
the bulk and quality of criticism dedicated to his work are any measure)
endlessly fascinating syntactic flexibility, capable of containing a mi-
nutely textured variety of seeming honesty and seeming self-deception.
Rich's commitment to sincerity produces a matching metaphorical flexi-
bility, in which she becomes an instrument for picking up signals, a set
of power-glasses, a compass—mimicking, because she cannot overcome
it, the split that self-consciousness produces between observer and ob-
served—and in which language can be both destroyed and preserved. In
these ways, sincerity becomes not a commitment to introducing new au-
tobiographical subject matter into poetry in dialectical opposition to
form, but an act of formal innovation itself.

The highest stake of sincerity in Wordsworth's and Rich's terms is its
claim to truth, its belief that to understand ourselves is to make ourselves
whole, and to make ourselves whole is to mend the larger divisions we
perceive in our world. In the end, both poets must relinquish the equation
of individual and universal truth: the structure of self-consciousness un-
dermines any positivistic claim to personal truth, because it enforces a
separation between the self who tells the truth and the self about whom
the truth is told. But Wordsworth's and Rich's moral ambitions are pre-
served in a more limited sense. Because self-consciousness is a universal
condition of being human, Wordsworth's and Rich's self-consciousness
offers a qualified universality: the universality of loss, the universality of
the negativity or blanks in any human self-understanding. These poets
leave us with a body of truth-claims that could never be verified: it would
be impossible to confirm or deny in any final way Wordsworth's interpre-
tations of his experience in "Tintern Abbey," Rich's experience of the

failure of language in "The Burning of Paper Instead of Children."[106] And yet their claims cannot be reduced to their correspondence to or divergence from either autobiographical fact or generalizable truth. We are left with the stubborn textures of the poems, their untranslatable knowledge, their unverifiable rightness.

CHAPTER TWO

Before and After

*Sincerity as Form in the Poetry of Wordsworth,
Lowell, Rich, and Plath*

S THE SELF TO BE EXPRESSED in a sincere poem a shapeless energy or an inchoate grouping of perceptions and experiences? Or is it something that already possesses an intrinsic form, with its own logic and organization? Does it even make sense to speak of a self that precedes its expression, or do selves only come into being through cultural forms, such as poems? In this chapter I attempt to keep each of these possibilities open while examining the different ideas about the self that are created by different understandings of the nature of poetic form.

From at least M. H. Abrams's *The Mirror and the Lamp* onward, the most striking and influential aspect of Wordsworth's thinking about poetry has been understood to be his reorientation of poetry toward an expressive, as opposed to a mimetic or didactic, goal. Wordsworth, the story goes, is one of the key inventors of our modern concept of the "self," and concurrently our assumption that literature must in some way be true to this self. But this perspective needs to be supplemented by the realization that, at the same time, Wordsworth invented our modern understanding of "form" as something potentially hostile to the self, an idea with importance and influence perhaps equal to his more famous creation. He characteristically describes the difference between artificial form and sincerity as a recovery of past authentic forms of self-expression: "The earliest Poets of all nations generally wrote from passion excited by real events; they wrote naturally, and as men: feeling powerfully as they did, their language was daring, and figurative. In succeeding times, Poets . . . set themselves to a mechanical adoption of these figures of speech . . . A language was thus insensibly produced, differing materially from the real language of men in *any situation*."[1] Wordsworth, then, claims to restore poetry to its original expressive function by eschewing the "gaudiness and inane phraseology" of his predecessors and by regrounding poetry in "language really used by men."[2]

In contrast, rather than believing that conventional form could be hostile to good poetry, Wordsworth's Renaissance and Enlightenment predecessors were apt to assume that formal convention was its very substance. While the idea of a potential gap between poetic form and sincere self-expression was conceivable to some of these earlier poets, it was of comparatively little significance to them. For example, in the early years of the Renaissance, when Sir Philip Sidney advises himself, "look in thy heart and write," this advice is actually attributed to his Muse, and his claim to abandon convention in the name of truth is itself a convention inherited from Petrarch. He is equally sincere, or even more sincere, when in another sonnet from the *Astrophil and Stella* sequence he writes, "I am not I, pity the tale of me." Two hundred years later, Samuel Johnson complains that Milton's "Lycidas" is insincere: "It is not to be considered as the effusion of real passion; for passion runs not after remote allusions and obscure opinions . . . Where there is leisure for fiction there is little grief."[3] While this complaint is much closer to the impatience with artifice that Wordsworth expresses in his Preface and "Essay upon Epitaphs," Johnson's analysis emphasizes generic propriety and decorum as much as personal honesty. This equation of poetic form with personal decorum implies no necessary gap between form and the impulse to expression. Before Wordsworth, poetry is evaluated not by how successfully a separate self is expressed by an unnatural form (more or less successfully naturalized), but by how successfully a poem embodies and elaborates upon a set of particular social and rhetorical codes.

Thus when Wordsworth writes about poetic diction and meter as formal considerations separate from the original impulse to self-expression, aspects of poetry that are unsuccessfully (in the case of poetic diction) or usefully (in the case of meter) fitted to the natural expression of passion, this imagination of the separation between conventionalized form and passion becomes central to his invention of a newly independent kind of self. A disjunction between self and form has to be imagined, after all, before it can exist. Once this disjunction is imagined, we can envision a self that precedes poetic language, precedes culture itself. Once we believe in this self, the Romantic idea that poetry can be renewed through an appeal to personal sincerity becomes possible. This hope of renewal, however, must coexist with its opposite: sincerity needs bad, sclerotic form, a negative image of insincerity starkly defined, in order to retain its elusive, never fully realized promise of self-expression. By becoming self-conscious about a possible gap between the impulse to self-expression and the media available for self-expression, the poet can work toward a solution to this problem—some integration of self-expression with a newly adapted or created form. But this integration can be attempted only at the cost of seeing the problem in a way that prohibits a final solution to the problem, just as self-consciousness both permits and prohibits the imagining of a self undivided by self-consciousness. Imagining a gap between self-expression and certain kinds of known forms allows a new sincerity in poetry to become conceivable, while at the same time ensuring the vulnerability of that sincerity to artificiality, and hence its need to be restaged in continually renovated forms.

Wordsworth's powerful myth of the hostility of certain poetic forms to self-expression has encouraged subsequent poets and critics to think of the self as an intangible entity that precedes or is independent from its expression. For example, when confronted with a poem that appears to make a personal disclosure or explore a personal conflict, many critics and readers first ask: has the poet found a form capable of containing his or her authentic voice, his or her sincerity?[4] This question leads us to imagine a self that has both more and less coherence than the selves we create, encounter, and embody in our daily lives. Though the question is often illuminating in its specific applications, it carries the implicit and misleading assumption that the self is something prior to poetic form, something that form must contain (in the most prevalent metaphor) or to which form must fit itself. This question excludes the possibility that the self may be something that only comes into being *through* cultural forms, including poems. This question also obscures the fact that, in the widest sense, all that we have is form: a self, like anything else, is not conceivable or perceivable except as it takes form. By implying that there is an original yet somehow formless self that precedes self-expression, this question distracts us from the equally pressing problem of the forms the self may take on separately from the forms of verse, and the important issue of the relationship between "form" in this general sense and the specialized language-patterns we encounter in poetry. Finally, in the narrower arena of literary criticism, the idea that self-expression and poetic form stand in some sense in opposition to each other is a major obstacle to taking the premise of sincerity seriously as a determinant of poetic form. And in terms of evaluation, the idea that self-expression and poetic form are potentially in conflict has the unintended consequence of creating a bias against expressive poetry: personal poetry must continually bear the suspicion that it is formally deficient in some way.[5]

The implications of Wordsworth's vision of the hostility of self-expression to certain kinds of forms can be seen nowhere more clearly than in the accounts given of the American "confessional" movement of the 1960s. This movement, exemplified by the poetry of W. D. Snodgrass, Robert Lowell, Anne Sexton, and Sylvia Plath, among others, has been understood as a reaction against the dictates of T. S. Eliot and his New Critical followers. These poets are credited with shedding "such doctrines of objectivity as the mask, the persona, the objective correlative" and replacing them with "a new openness, a willingness to make poetry of experience."[6] We will have reason to question this meta-narrative that puts the so-called confessional poets in opposition to Eliot, but first I want to call attention to the metaphorical richness and consistency of the stories told about these individual writers' graduation from a merely formal proficiency to authentic self-expression.[7] For example, Adrienne Rich writes of her own development, "In [the early] years formalism was part of the strategy—like asbestos gloves, it allowed me to handle materials I couldn't pick up bare-handed."[8] It is not until later in her career that she feels she can use form for the purpose of sincere self-expression. In similar terms, critics again and again tell the story of Robert Lowell's progression from the formally overwrought poems of his first three books to the personally authentic poems of *Life Studies*. Steven Gould Axelrod, for example, notes that Lowell's earlier poetry "seemed to push poetic language and cultural critique in exciting new directions, yet they were directions sanctioned by the ethos of its time . . . the aesthetic and political projects of the New Criticism." In contrast, "breaking the vessel of the formal poetic object, *Life Studies* became a convenient marker of the death of the New Criticism."[9] James Breslin writes another version of this story: "*Life Studies* ultimately renounces tight, external forms and preestablished symbols; it discards rhetorical sublimity and religious myth in a quest to enter a demystified present. Lowell touches what had hurt him most, the prosaic and everyday, and he finds that his fiery creative self can survive the quotidian."[10] In now familiar terms, almost every critic who surveys the career of Sylvia Plath makes a division between the formally complex (in terms of sound, diction, and symbolism) but emotionally reserved early poems of *The Colossus* and the freer, more expressive poems of *Ariel*.[11] To give an extreme example of this contrast: Hugh Kenner suggests that once Plath's "formal defenses are down" in the *Ariel* poems, not only self-expression, but self-destruction is the logical result—"That had been a final use of the intricate formalisms: they detained her mind upon the plane of craft, and so long as it was detained there it did not slip toward what beckoned it."[12] These statements—and I've quoted those that are most metaphorically suggestive, rather than the

more measured versions—certainly contain some truth about the shape
of the careers of the poets they describe, but at the same time they pose an
antagonism between the self and form that must in turn be interrogated.

In these examples, form is imagined as a protective barrier to be dis-
carded, a vessel to be broken, a carapace to be shed—a set of defenses
that, once abandoned, leave an unprecedented vulnerability. The image
of the self that these metaphors underwrite is clear: if certain kinds of
form are restricting vessels, then the authentic poetic self is the self force-
ful enough to break those vessels. If certain kinds of form are a cowardly
sort of self-defense, then the authentic poetic self is the self brave enough
to face life without such defenses. In these terms, the self is imagined as a
more or less formless heroic energy, and is celebrated in its transcendence
or mourned (or idolized) in its annihilation. But this vision of the self's
relationship to form is, of course, only half of the story. Neither the "con-
fessional" poets nor their critics believed that they were abandoning
form altogether, only certain outmoded forms. And particularly because
the so-called confessional poets' celebrated breakthroughs into self-
expression were frequently accompanied by mental breakdowns and
even suicide, critics writing about these poets are often quick to affirm
the positive, healing aspects of finding or giving new forms to personal
experience.[13]

Beginning with Wordsworth, then, poets and critics have attempted to
differentiate between outmoded poetic forms that threaten self-expres-
sion and new, more flexible forms that are conducive to it. To put it an-
other way, Romantic and post-Romantic poets have struggled to discover
how the pre-existing forms of the self (the shape and flow of conscious-
ness, or the undertow of the unconscious, for example) can be coordi-
nated with a true or aesthetically satisfying form in language. This hope
produces a second set of metaphors for poetic form, which represent the
idea that form can develop internally, or "organically," from experience.
As we have seen, in Wordsworth's terms, bad, falsifying poetic form is de-
scribed as mechanical form: when poets "set themselves to a mechanical
adoption of . . . figures of speech," the result is a language "differing ma-
terially from the real language of men in *any situation*."[14] This concept of
mechanical form is implicitly contrasted to organic form. The idea that a
poem should have the same shapeliness, unity, and necessity as a natural
object is an ancient idea, given its most influential formulation for Ro-
mantic and post-Romantic poetry in Coleridge's paraphrase of Schlegel:

The form is mechanic when on any given material we impress a predeter-
mined form, not necessarily arising out of the properties of the material, as
when to a mass of wet clay we give whatever shape we wish it to retain

when hardened. The organic form, on the other hand, is innate; it shapes as it develops itself from within, and the fullness of its development is one and the same with the perfection of its outward form.[15]

The project of renewing poetry through an appeal to personal experience, whether undertaken by the British Romantic poets or the American "confessional" poets, incorporates the belief that an aesthetically sufficient form can be found in the nature of experience itself, and that such a form would be an organic part of experience rather than something imposed externally (mechanically) upon it. To mention only one example, when Rich is asked whether she believes that "experience itself has a shape and that the poet is to reveal that shape," she answers, "The poem is the poetry of things lodged in the innate shape of the experience."[16] It is this kind of shape or form that a newly sincere poetry is designed to reveal.

The organic metaphor, however, is no less troublesome than the metaphors that depict external, "mechanical" form. The idea that self-expression is thwarted by certain kinds of form can be misleading when it fails to consider the possibility of the pre-formed nature of the self, the fact that the self may not be (or not only be) boundless energy made to break a formal vessel, but something with its own potentially rigid forms. But the idea that self-expression can reveal the self's pre-given forms as aesthetically self-sufficient carries its own special problems. Coleridge makes a distinction between form that is impressed externally upon a given material and form that arises naturally from a given material. We then need to ask, what is the material here? If we are to trust the material to reveal its own form from within, does the material then have to include only that which is organic? Can we take for granted that the self, for example, is organic?[17] (Thinkers from Wordsworth to Lacan have wondered if there is not something innately unnatural about the self, or about self-consciousness.) More pragmatically, if it is the poet's job to reveal the organic structures that already inhere in experience, is this revelation wholly passive? If not, how can the poet know that she or he is not imposing an external shape upon experience?[18]

The ideas of form as external control and form as internal, organic shape can only be reconciled if the first, received, kind of form, which is antagonistic to genuine self-expression, can be clearly differentiated from the second kind of discovered form, which seamlessly serves the needs of self-expression. The central argument of this chapter is that it is impossible to fully conceptualize this difference, and that the tension between sincerity as *freedom from* form and sincerity *as* form remains active, productive, and irresoluble. Form cannot simultaneously be a vessel or boundary to be broken and a body to be preserved. Rather, these two understandings are competing, interchanging fictions that determine the shapes of the poems we confront on the page.

One attempt to reconcile these two visions of form that deserves special mention is the idea that achieved poetic form is the objectification of subjective experience. The linking of objectivity to formal realization happens again and again in twentieth-century critical writing about poetry; for example, Alan Williamson writes: "As the poet approaches success in his narcissistic endeavor of self-creation, he begins paradoxically to experience his self as if it were an external object—circumscribed, defined by laws, imbued with its own alien aura or flavor."[19] This insight into the self-objectification of expressive poetry, however, tends to slide (in the writing of critics less careful than Williamson) into a belief that experiencing the self as an object amounts to "objectivity"—an access to truth and to the correct moral perspective on oneself.[20] But the contradictory nature of self-consciousness suggests that experiencing the self as an object is as likely to involve self-loss as self-recuperation. More specifically, there is little reason to believe that an aesthetic objectification of experience, which renders that experience coherent or beautiful or satisfyingly ugly, is the same thing as understanding that experience, or making it in every sense true. One of the aims of this chapter is to chart and resist the metaphorical undertow that would equate the two. As we shall see, it is difficult, and in some cases impossible, to tell the difference between a formal patterning that amounts to an intuition of objective truth and a formal patterning that amounts to a distortion of reality.

The idea that poetic form is a kind of objectivity is given its most influential formulation in T. S. Eliot's concept of the "objective correlative." In the story of the confessional break with New Critical assumptions about poetry, Eliot is cast as the arch anti-Romantic, a critic utterly hostile to the idea that poesis is, at its core, self-expression. But the essay in which he seems to take this position, "Tradition and the Individual Talent," delivers a message similar to that encoded in the idea of "confessional" poetry: that the important question to ask of a poem is whether or not its form serves the purpose of self-expression. The slogans against which confessional poets are supposed to rebel are Eliot's statements that "the more perfect the artist, the more completely separate in him will be the man who suffers and the mind which creates,"[21] and "poetry is not a turning loose of emotion, but an escape from emotion; it is not the expression of personality, but an escape from personality."[22] One immediately notices that the language Eliot uses to dismiss personality and personal emotion is deeply emotional itself.[23] He does not suggest that we control or order or restrain our emotions, but that we engage in "continual self-sacrifice,"[24] that we "escape" (an idea that Eliot explicitly connects to personal desire when he makes reference to "want[ing] to escape"),[25] that we "surrender."[26] But more fundamentally, it becomes clear that Eliot's vision of the antagonism of emotion or personality to form, rather than moving his focus away from emotion and personality and onto more "objective" matters, instead produces a redoubled concentration on the nature of the emotions we encounter in literature. For example, a work of art, Eliot contends, depends upon two elements: not emotion and intellect (as we might expect), but "emotions and feelings."[27] While Eliot argues that the emotions that are important are those unleashed by the artistic process, not merely "personal" emotions, his emphasis remains on literature as primarily a medium of emotional expression. The purpose of art is "to give us a new art emotion" (its newness and value to be evaluated by the criterion of "tradition" that Eliot has set forth). He elaborates: "The emotion in [one's] poetry will be a very complex thing, but not with the complexity of the emotions of people who have very complex or unusual emotions in life."[28] In other words, Eliot is working toward a theory of poetry in which form does not cancel out self-expression, but instead takes on the quality we most insistently associate with this expression—the experience of emotion.[29]

But the concept most often understood to differentiate Eliot's theory of artistic emotions from Romantic expressivism is his concept of the "objective correlative." In the essay "Hamlet and His Problems," he writes: "The only way of expressing emotion in the form of art is by finding an 'objective correlative': in other words, a set of objects, a situation, a chain of events which shall be the formula of that particular emotion; such that when the external facts, which must terminate in sensory experience, are given, the emotion is immediately evoked."[30] Again, imagining the division between an emotion and the object that expresses it only underlines Eliot's assumption of the fundamentally expressive nature of literature.[31] But more devastating to the objective correlative's claim to "objectivity," its correlation of individual feeling to universal truth, is the fact that Eliot finds that he needs the term not because he recognizes its presence, but because he is struggling to describe something which seems to be absent in *Hamlet*. Here Eliot engages in what can only be described as psychological criticism, speculating on the appropriateness of Hamlet's feelings about his mother: "Hamlet (the man) is dominated by an emotion which is inexpressible, because it is in *excess* of the facts as they appear."[32]

Moreover, Eliot is willing, against his own theory of the separation be-
tween the man who suffers and the artist who creates, to equate Hamlet
the character with Shakespeare the poet: "The supposed identity of Ham-
let with his author is genuine to this point: that Hamlet's bafflement at
the absence of objective equivalent to his feelings is a prolongation of the
bafflement of his creator in the face of his artistic problem."[33] True to his
principles, Eliot links Shakespeare and Hamlet less psychologically than
aesthetically—they are both trying to solve the same moral and artistic
problem. But Eliot's argument works to blur the distinction between the
two: if making art involves deciding which formula evokes which emo-
tions, then aesthetic work and psychological work are analogous.

Eventually, Eliot makes a connection that suggests that a kind of "ob-
jective correlative" may be present in *Hamlet* after all:

> It must be noticed that the very nature of the *données* of the problem pre-
> cludes objective equivalence. To have heightened the criminality of Gertrude
> would have been to provide the formula for a totally different emotion in
> Hamlet; it is just because her character is so negative and insignificant that
> she arouses in Hamlet the feeling which she is incapable of representing.[34]

The ambiguity of Gertrude as a character, in other words, perfectly repre-
sents the impossibility of her being the external representation of Ham-
let's feeling that she is criminal. In this sense, though Eliot would not say
so, she is the self-canceling objective correlative to Hamlet's self-cancel-
ing emotions. While Eliot locates this condition in *Hamlet,* we might be
more likely to see it as endemic to all literature, or at least more common
than the recognizable presence of an "objective correlative" as Eliot un-
derstands it. Literature more often approximately expresses an inexpress-
ible emotion than provides the perfect formula for a particular emotion.
Eliot himself seems to suggest as much when he notes that "the intense
feeling, ecstatic or terrible, without an object or exceeding its object, is
something which every person of sensibility has known," especially the
artist, who "keeps [these feelings] alive by his ability to intensify the
world to his emotions."[35] The terms of Eliot's argument permit us to
speculate that an imperfect fit between self-expression and form may be
more expressive of psychological complexity or intensity, even in a sense
more "objective," than the supposedly perfect fit of the objective corre-
lative.

Eliot's acceptance of the Romantic idea of a potential division between
the expression of emotion and its formal realization undermines the be-
fore-and-after story that poets and readers tell about the "confessional"
movement: both Eliot and his successors share the belief that poetry is es-

sentially self-expression. Eliot's example also tells us something more generally about the Romantic artificially formal "before" and sincere or authentic "after": what is important about this story is not whether the emphasis falls on form (in Eliot's case) or on the self (as Wordsworth insists); it is the division between the two that is the fundamental Romantic assumption. From this perspective, Romanticism becomes a way of reading as well as a way of writing, for this division can be read back into any kind of literature (though Sidney does not worry about being sincere in his poetry in the same way that Wordsworth does, we can read his poems for the presence or lack of Wordsworthian sincerity). As we shall see in the readings that follow, Wordsworth is able, from this point of view, to transform Pope into a failed Romantic.

The readings in this chapter have three main purposes. The first is to break the explanatory power of the story of the progression from mere formal accomplishment to authentic self-expression by demonstrating the continuities between poems occurring before and after a poet's putative breakthrough into sincerity. Second, these readings work to uncover sincerity's concealed investment in the kinds of poetic forms that are labeled as hostile to self-expression. Finally, these readings attempt to map out the more contradictory and reversible terrain that is revealed when the distinction between the "before" of oppressive, external form and the "after" of newly freed self-expression is set aside. The self and poetic form are not ultimately separable categories: what becomes strategically important for poets and theorists of poetry alike is where and how the boundary between "self" and "form" is drawn. And as the concluding readings of poems by Adrienne Rich and Sylvia Plath demonstrate, the more self-conscious a poet is about the problem of form, the more unstable and contentious this boundary becomes.

Laborious Discrimination and Rigorous Inquisition: Wordsworth Versus Pope

Wordsworth invents our idea of a gap between self-expression and the forms available for self-expression by contrasting his own, newly sincere poetry with the ossified, imitative poetic forms he identifies in his poetic precursors. His concept of the potential antagonism between poetic form and self-expression depends upon the distance he is able to map between his own poetry and the poetry of the immediate past. But when we examine the terms in which Wordsworth describes this distance, the difference between his procedure and that of his predecessors is not as distinct as we might expect. In particular, the difference between technical virtuosity and emotional complexity, a distinction crucial to Wordsworth's thinking, becomes increasingly difficult to perceive.

Wordsworth criticizes his eighteenth-century precursors in many of his theoretical statements about poetry, but nowhere with such heat and specificity as in his "Essay upon Epitaphs." Toward the end of this long essay, Wordsworth engages in a close analysis of Pope's "Epitaph on Mrs. Corbet." While the placement of this reading may seem to indicate that it is a mere footnote to a meandering discussion of a specialized literary genre, Wordsworth's choice of language suggests that Pope was the implied target from the beginning. Complaints early in his essay against epitaphs that include "detail, minutely and scrupulously pursued, especially if this be done with laborious and antithetic discriminations"[36] and "a balance of opposite qualities or minute distinctions in individual character," which more often than not "resolve themselves into a trick of words,"[37] so literally anticipate his reading of Pope's heroic couplets that the "Essay upon Epitaphs" as a whole can be read just as much as a polemic against Pope as a meditation on a particular genre.

The context of Wordsworth's reading of Pope is his definition of an effective epitaph. The reader will remember that in Wordsworth's opinion a sincere epitaph has two basic components: an appeal to "the common or universal feeling of humanity" and a rendering of "a distinct and clear conception . . . of the individual."[38] As we have seen, these two qualities are not as easily unified as Wordsworth's formulation suggests. The strain of reconciling these claims is exhibited clearly in Wordsworth's reading of Pope. Wordsworth's main complaint against Pope is that he is insincere: "It must be observed, that in the epitaphs of this Writer, the true impulse is wanting, and that his motions must of necessity be feeble . . . The Author forgets that it is a living creature that must interest us and not an intellectual existence, which a mere character is."[39] But it is not obvious from either Pope's language or his tone that he is any less sincere than Wordsworth.

In fact, the epitaph in contention appears to fulfill Wordsworth's precept that human generality and specificity should be kept in balance. Here is the full text:

> Here rests a Woman, good without pretence,
> Blest with plain reason and with sober sense;
> No conquest she but o'er herself desir'd;
> No arts essayed, but not to be admir'd.
> Passion and pride were to her soul unknown,
> Convinc'd that virtue only is our own.

So unaffected, so compos'd a mind,
So firm yet soft, so strong yet so refin'd,
Heaven as it's [*sic*] purest gold by tortures tried
The Saint sustain'd it, but the Woman died.[40]

For Wordsworth, this poem exemplifies false discrimination: "the good qualities are separately abstracted (can it be otherwise than coldly and unfeelingly?)."[41] But one could argue that Pope has done an admirable job of balancing the universal with the individual. He does so by limiting his comments to generalized qualities (goodness, reason, modesty, and so forth), while at the same time giving us a sense of Mrs. Corbet as an individualized (if idealized) person by depicting the finely textured intermixture of these qualities. Wordsworth complains that "plain reason" and "sober sense" are not sufficiently distinguishable,[42] but a more sympathetic reader might take the juxtaposition of these two terms as an occasion for imagining the possible delicate differences between the two, and in turn imagine the kind of woman who would make one aware of these differences. "Plain reason," for example, could suggest a stark architecture of logic, while "sober sense," with its implicit reminder of the five senses and sensibility, could indicate Mrs. Corbet's calm and clear-eyed responsiveness to the separate experiences that make up her daily life. It is certainly possible to believe, with Wordsworth, that Pope means to highlight his own refinement rather than the refinement of his subject. But it is also possible to read Pope's subtlety of language as rendering the psychological subtlety, even psychological depth, of his subject. Similarly, one could agree with Wordsworth that Pope's repetitious insistence that Mrs. Corbet was "good without pretence," that "pride [was] to her soul unknown," and that she was "unaffected" is meaningless,[43] proof that he is merely trying to fill out a line; or one could find in these variations meaningful shadings of character, just as the repetitions characteristic of Wordsworth's own poetry suggest fine variations of meaning. Wordsworth claims that the difference between formal virtuosity and the sincere examination and expression of feelings is easily distinguished, but his reading of Pope fails to make this distinction clear or fully persuasive.

If Wordsworth's criticism of Pope in these instances depends upon his understanding Pope's language as merely ornamental, rather than attempting to take it literally, he reverses this procedure at another point, taking at face value what might be more sympathetically understood in a figurative sense. Against the line, "No conquest she but o'er herself desired," Wordsworth protests, "In the next couplet the word, *conquest,* is applied in a manner that would have been displeasing even from its triteness in a copy of complimentary Verses to a fashionable Beauty; but to talk of making conquests in an Epitaph is not to be endured."[44] Again, another reading is possible. This line contains the poignant surprise that "conquest," in current use as a compliment that depends upon an incongruous connection between conquest on the battlefield and the romantic "conquests" of ladies, here is restored to its original connotation of serious moral action. The idea that one could make a conquest over oneself gives the word an almost religious meaning, as if Mrs. Corbet fights a gallant battle against the power of vice itself. In other words, the inappropriateness of the word "conquest" is an inappropriateness that Pope finds useful: he can use it to dramatize further his point about the moral seriousness of Mrs. Corbet by anticipating and then reversing the reader's expectations. This wordplay may be in deadly earnest, but it is not a maneuver that Wordsworth can accept as sincere. Similarly, Wordsworth finds it impossible to accept the line, "No arts essayed, but not to be admir'd," because he finds it inconceivable that Mrs. Corbet "had recourse to artifices to conceal her amiable and admirable qualities,"[45] inconceivable that modesty (or sincerity) itself is an art. Pope suggests that self-consciousness does not threaten the virtue of modesty but instead increases it, but to Wordsworth this perspective perverts the idea of virtue (sincerity) itself, which by definition is unself-conscious and natural. To make the reader aware of the codes that poet and reader communicate through by the play on "conquest," and to suggest that even modesty (or sincerity) must be negotiated through such codes, is in a sense to render all language as "form," an artificial medium either not inherently adapted to sincere expression, or one that renders irrelevant the question of sincerity outside of a specific social context. The shared insight that all language is external form may paradoxically bring us closer to true communication with each other, just as Pope's play on "conquest" might lead the reader to wonder with some emotion whether any description in words can do justice to someone we have loved or admired. But this is not a possibility that Wordsworth will allow, because it is the distinction between artificial form and the sincere self that permits him to perceive that self in the first place.

One final reason Wordsworth gives for his belief that Pope is not sincere is that Pope addresses his subject in a spirit of admiration (which, according to Wordsworth, becomes disingenuous flattery) rather than in a spirit of genuine love. It is true that Pope does not explicitly address his subject as a beloved, or show himself to be personally injured by her loss (indeed, his wordplay on "conquest" suggests that such a position carries its own perils of cliché), but Wordsworth's criticism depends upon another distinction that does not hold up so firmly as his argument requires. Wordsworth suggests that love envelops the beloved object in "a tender haze or a luminous mist,"[46] but one could imagine that love, rather than idealizing, clarifies the sight (as Wordsworth himself seems to argue when he writes that, in the eyes of love, "parts and proportions are brought into distinct view which before had been only imperfectly or unconsciously seen").[47] If we understand Pope's detailed portrait of his subject as an attempt to render a complex personality rather than an attempt to call attention to his own talents, then the intensity and specificity of his attention could itself be seen as an act of love. Whether or not one fully accepts this more sympathetic reading of Pope's epitaph, it is clear that the distinction Wordsworth means to make between the "living creature" who is the focus of love and the "intellectual existence" which is the object of analysis, between sincere expression and the artificial antitheses that he associates with Pope's heroic couplets, begins to unravel when we confront a specific example of Pope's verse. What Wordsworth reads as mechanical form, we may read as sincere self-expression.

In fact, we could even go so far as to see Wordsworth's own practice as the translation of Augustan form into self-expression by presenting the self as an aesthetic artifact as complex as the poetic artifacts left by his predecessors.[48] In the most general terms, Wordsworth rejects the idea that Mrs. Corbet must employ arts in order to secure her natural modesty, and by extension the idea (represented by Pope) that true nature is "nature methodized," nature ordered by human consciousness. But what is Wordsworth's body of work about, if not the struggle to be "natural" (that is, to reconnect with a benevolent Nature) through exemplary acts of consciousness? Wordsworth must literally employ art to secure his own natural origins. What he has named "form" (the artificial, self-conscious struggle for the effect of naturalness) in Pope has become the content of his own work, which maps the distance between a youthful, unrecoverable oneness with nature and his adult memories and "intimations" of this oneness. The blindness that Wordsworth exhibits toward the meaning and nature of his own accomplishment when, for example, he suggests (in reference to epitaphs) that "intricacies of human nature . . . [can] be interesting only to a few"[49] appears only to reinforce his commitment to tracing those intricacies in other terms.

To give a specific example, Wordsworth's inventory of himself as a poet in *The Prelude* has the feeling of an anticipatory epitaph:

> . . . [As] I through myself
> Make rigorous inquisition, the report

Is often chearing, for I neither seem
To lack that first great gift, the vital Soul,
Nor general Truths, which are themselves a sort
Of Elements and Agents, Under-powers,
Subordinate helpers of the living Mind:
Nor am I naked of external things,
Forms, images, nor numerous other aids
Of less regard, though won perhaps with toil,
And needful to build up a Poet's praise.[50]

This description has some of the qualities that Wordsworth deplores in Pope: a dependence on finely made and potentially imprecise distinctions (how different are "elements," "agents," and "under-powers"? how do we distinguish between "forms" and "images"?); the consideration of self-conscious effort as a proper help to virtue ("won perhaps with toil"); and most of all a willingness to pay intellectual attention to the intricacies of the human virtues and their relations to one another. What Wordsworth has denigrated as mere form in Pope has been fully assimilated into his most "sincere" of self-expressions. Wordsworth has not so much rejected the "laborious discrimination" he finds in Pope, as given it a new, personal value: formal complexity is rewritten as emotional, experiential complexity. Following Wordsworth's lead, we can look back and discover a proto-Romantic Pope, a Pope whose formal complexity may denote psychological subtlety, though this is not a Pope whom Wordsworth himself would ever claim.

The Musical, Difficult Poem and the Breakthrough Back into Life: Early Lowell and Later Lowell

In the before-and-after story told about the career of Robert Lowell, we discover a translation of formal virtuosity into psychological complexity analogous to the process Wordsworth undergoes. Lowell's immediate predecessors, the American High Modernists, had made it clear that difficulty was a necessary feature of modern literature. Eliot, for example, writes: "We can only say that it appears likely that poets in our civilization, as it exists at present, must be *difficult.*"[51] But at mid-career, Lowell begins to feel that Modernist difficulty is in danger of becoming a mere mannerism:

Poets of my generation and particularly younger ones have gotten terribly proficient at these forms. They write a very musical, difficult poem with tremendous skill, perhaps there's never been such skill. Yet the writing seems divorced from the culture. It's become too much something specialized that can't handle much experience. It's become a craft, purely a craft, and there must be some breakthrough back into life.[52]

As in the case of Wordsworth, Lowell comes to believe that an appeal to personal experience is needed to renew lyric poetry; as he later puts it, "Why not say what really happened?"[53] But also as in Wordsworth's poetry, the formalist complexity against which Lowell understands himself to be reacting becomes difficult to distinguish from the psychological complexity that is meant to replace it. The readings that follow show how Lowell's poetry troubles the distinction between the difficult, well-crafted poem and "what happened."

While it is Lowell's later poetry (*Life Studies* and after) that is understood to release the authentic self that was constrained by the formal elaborateness of his earlier poetry, the story of the progression from formal constraint to expressive freedom is complicated from the beginning. Critics assessing Lowell's earlier work suggest that these poems make it difficult to distinguish between the presence of formal control and its absence. R. P. Blackmur serves as an elegant representative of this response:

> Robert Lowell's *Land of Unlikeness* . . . shows, not examples of high formal organization achieved, but poems that are deliberately moving in that direction and that have things put in to give the appearance of the movement of form when the movement itself was not secured. In fact, Lowell's verse is a beautiful case of citation in any argument in support of the belief in the formal inextricability of the various elements of poetry: meter is not meter by itself, any more than attitude or anecdote or perception, though any one of them can be practiced by itself at the expense of others, when the tensions become mere fanaticism of spirit and of form . . . It is as if he demanded to *know* (to judge, to master) both the substance apart from the form with which he handles it and the form apart from the substance handled in order to set them fighting.[54]

Blackmur indicates that Lowell takes control of form and control of content separately to an extreme that amounts to a "fanaticism of form"— control that has become its opposite. His suggestive comments do not detail how one tells the difference between "things put in to give the appearance of the movement of form" and "the movement itself," or how one tells the difference between mastery of form and mastery of substance, but he manages to suggest that questions of control could be multiplied endlessly, and that an overbalance of control can actually threaten the poise of a poem. In similar terms, Randall Jarrell praises Lowell for having written poems in which "the degree of intensity . . . is equaled by their degree of organization." He elaborates: "The things in Mr. Lowell's poems have, necessarily, been wrenched into formal shape, organized under terrific pressure, but they keep to an extraordinary degree their stubborn, unmoved toughness, their senseless originality and contingency."[55] Jarrell's language suggests a conflict between intensity and organization, but what he comes to speak of is the intensity *of* organization, an intensity that is meant not to organize objects but to showcase their resistance to such organization. Again, extreme formal control becomes difficult to distinguish from an extreme resistance to control.

Under these circumstances, it is no longer clear that we can think of Lowell's earlier poems as personally inhibited; or, if they are inhibited by their formal virtuosity, this inhibition is so explicit and tortured, so much on the surface of the poems, that it is powerfully expressive in its own right. There are real differences between the early and late phases of Lowell's career that can be generalized, but, like the real differences between the poetry of Pope and the poetry of Wordsworth, these differences are not adequately explained in terms of the abandonment of certain kinds of formal control in preference for liberated self-expression. Instead, form (the intentional arrangement of structure, imagery, and sound) takes on different meanings in each phase. In the early phase of Lowell's career, form (here, highly organized patterns of meter and rhyme) suggests an ordering intelligence that seems to operate independently from the ambiguous emotions that the speaker actually claims to experience. In the later phase of Lowell's writing, form becomes looser (line lengths appear to be more arbitrary, structure more desultory, sound and rhythm less obviously patterned) and seems to mimic more closely the emotional disarray that the speaker experiences—but in some ways form also becomes more "mechanical," rather than being organically integrated with those experiences. From this perspective, Lowell's supposedly "confessional" verse appears less expressive than his earlier, more formal verse.

Multiplying lines of formal continuity and discontinuity can be observed in two of Lowell's poems about his paternal grandfather: the first part of his early elegy "In Memory of Arthur Winslow" in *Lord Weary's Castle* (1946) and the later elegiac "Dunbarton" in *Life Studies* (1959). Lowell's earlier poem is marked by a mixture of high-level formal organization and apparent tonal and emotional disorganization. In formal terms, the poem moves in a remarkably regular iambic pentameter, interrupted, in both of the stanzas that make up the poem, only by shortened sixth lines and closing alexandrines. The poem opens:

> This Easter, Arthur Winslow, less than dead,
> Your people set you up in Phillips' House
> To settle off your wrestling with the crab—
> The claws drop flesh upon your yachting blouse
> Until longshoreman Charon come and stab
> Through your adjusted bed.[56]

The poem's metrical regularity creates a system in which exceptions can be seen to prove the rule: the surprises in the shortened lines—in stanza 1, the shortened line contains the paradox that the "crab" of cancer will only be destroyed when Winslow himself is destroyed; in stanza 2, the shortened line announces the resurrection of Jesus in the unexpected setting of the Boston Public Garden—are therefore prepared for by a metrical signal. Regularity of meter is matched by regularity of rhyme: each stanza follows an intertwined, symmetrically self-completing *abcbcadeed* rhyme scheme. This macro-organization of meter and rhyme is accompanied by a micro-organization of sound—virtually every line of the poem is knit together with a complex ordering of alliteration and assonance.[57] These structures assure us that there is an ordering intelligence behind the poem. The presence of this intelligence prompts us to suspect that other, less quantifiable aspects of the poem—tone, emotional valence—are ordered by an omnipresent intention as well.

But this assumption of organization is brought up short by the poem's obscurities. First, the speaker's relationship to his subject shifts from line to line, blurring the emotional clarity we might expect from a grandson's elegy about his grandfather. The subject of the elegy is first named "Arthur Winslow," which suggests a distanced and formalized relationship, but in the following stanza he is addressed directly as "Grandfather Winslow"; then the speaker changes attitudes again by calling his subject "Arthur."[58] The relationship between speaker and subject is further destabilized by the mixed temporality of the poem: even though the title of the poem declares it to be in memory of Arthur Winslow, the poem itself is undertaken in the present tense, as if Winslow is still alive. And although in the first stanza, Winslow is addressed only to be told what presumably he already knows ("Your people set you up in Phillips' House"), at the stanza's end the speaker takes on Winslow's own point of view: "You ponder why the coxes' squeakings dwarf / The *resurrexit dominus* of all the bells." In the second stanza, the poet finally addresses Winslow directly ("Grandfather Winslow, look, the swanboats coast"), but not to say anything that a grandson might say to a grandfather; instead the speaker directs Winslow's attention to his own vision of Winslow's death.[59] Though each of these types of address has precedents in the flexible tradition of the elegy, the inclusion of so many in such a condensed poem creates a constant sense of dislocation.

Our difficulty in determining the spatial, temporal, and psychological position of the speaker in the poem is increased by the poem's indeterminate tone. "In Memory of Arthur Winslow" constantly juxtaposes Christianity and classical mythology with the mundane, slightly shabby world of nursing homes, boat clubs, and public gardens of mid-twentieth-century Boston. The poem's guiding trope might be described as the trope of incommensurability, figured by the incompatibility of these two realms. But it is unclear what emotion this incommensurability provokes in the speaker and is meant to yield to us. For example, Lowell literalizes the etymological connection between cancer and the image of the crab by describing Grandfather Winslow's cancer as a crab that pulls off bits of his flesh. This image, while rendering his disease uniquely horrible, also dehumanizes it—we are invited not to sympathize with Winslow's human pains and limitations, but instead to witness a surreal battle. Just as the image of the crab works simultaneously to magnify and to diminish Winslow's illness, it is difficult to determine whether the implicit connection drawn between Charon, the coxswains, and (in stanza 2) the swan boats is meant to imbue the ordinary world with mythic dignity or to mock mythic pretension.

It is not impossible to develop an interpretation of these disparate elements; from a point of view sympathetic to Lowell's achievement, one could argue that his poem makes an impact because of its ability to communicate various tonal possibilities simultaneously. But this indeterminacy also carries the danger that the poem may leak affect, leaving the reader to respond tentatively and equivocally to each individual line and strongly to none. One function of the formal tightness of a poem like "In Memory of Arthur Winslow" may be to plug up these affective leaks, making the poem's emotion feel deliberate and motivated even when the precise nature of the emotion or its motivation remains unclear. At each turn, the presence of formal rules (the rhythmic and sonic patterns that organize the poem) helps us believe that the poem's unruliness has a yardstick against which it can be measured; that the incommensurability of sacred and profane images can be resolved into a symmetry like the symmetry of rhyme; that undecidability itself can be a decisive stance. This is the kind of reading that a New Critical approach might encourage. But, as we have seen, prominent New Critics recognized various forms of excess in these earlier poems, even without the benefit of hindsight provided by *Life Studies*. The gap—which Lowell widens here—between formal organization and ambiguous content could be understood paradoxically to release the self that is not supposed to be freed until the later volume. We can see its outline against the fierce order of the early poetry.

Lowell's later elegy for his grandfather, "Dunbarton," enacts a partial reversal of this distribution of certainty and uncertainty. As one might expect from the before-and-after story told about Lowell's career, tone in this poem is somewhat more clearly marked, and form (in terms of structure, rhythm, rhyme, and sound) much less so. Here Winslow is always referred to as "Grandfather," most often "my Grandfather," and the speaker is clearly identified as an "I" of a specific time and place.[60] This stability increases the number of assertions we can make with confidence about the poem's tone: though still marked by Lowell's characteristic reticence, it is tender, nostalgic (his satirical bent given limited play in the phrase "suave Venetian Christ"), conspiratorial, and self-deprecating. In comparison with "In Memory of Arthur Winslow," which is stripped of true adjectives, the majority of them participles ("yachting blouse," "adjusted bed," bread-stuffed ducks"), the tone of "Dunbarton" is established by vividly descriptive language: "virgin," "wine-dark," "dank," "sugary," "umber yellow."[61] Meanwhile, the inevitability of meter and rhyme that characterized the progression of "In Memory of Arthur Winslow" is absent. Lines, usually short, but ranging from two to eight beats, end abruptly and for no obvious reason. Our hunger for form, for beauty, and for inevitability is thrown back upon the relationship between grandfather and grandson itself.

It would seem, then, that the progression of Lowell's career can be read in terms similar to those we developed in reference to Wordsworth: the formal complexity exhibited in his earlier work is rewritten as an emotional complexity in his later work. "Dunbarton" does appear to psychologically absorb form in certain ways; form appears to take on some of the qualities of experience. For example, the poem includes a number of half-rhymes and sound patterns: proper/farmer, Grandmother/Grandfather, son/Boston/Dunbarton, and so forth.[62] But these patterns no longer form a reliable architecture independent of the movements of tone; they no longer suggest the presence of an ordering intelligence separate from the personal moods and motivations of the poem's speaker. Instead, sonic symmetries appear to arise almost at random from the poem's content. More often than not, half-rhymes operate as puns do, the aural connection between "son" and "Boston" and "Dunbarton" (the site of graves) suggesting the deathly import of what feels to Lowell like a premature inheritance, but not making us feel that Lowell-the-poet has predetermined this suggestion, that it is merely a matter of the craftsman's intention. Instead, the almost random quality of this rhyme suggests that it has surprised the person making the poem, so that the mere coincidence of the similar sounds in "Boston" and "Dunbarton" makes both us and the poet ask, is this symmetry a mere coincidence? Or has some sinister, external intelligence determined it? Instead of wondering whether or not a particular image (like the bread-stuffed ducks in the earlier poem) is meant to impart a feeling of menace, we no longer imagine that artistic intention could answer that question, and instead feel ourselves on the same level of uncertainty as the poet. The ordering intelligence—perhaps God, or the unconscious, or a terrifying destiny—has apparently been cast outside the control of the poet.

But if we accept that the gap between formal organization and tonal disorganization in the earlier poem may actually permit, rather than hold back, the emergence of a self that transcends conventional formal constraints, the question arises of what happens when this gap collapses. It is possible that this collapsing of the gap between form and content, this absorption of the ordering intelligence into an experiencing consciousness, disperses the force of the self that the new style, according to the conventions of the before-and-after story, was meant to express more powerfully. As Laurence Lerner observes in a slightly different context, "If [the plot of the poem] were an invented fiction, we should be astonished at how incompetent the invention was, especially from a poet of such obvious competence."[63] The relationship between grandfather and grandson does not take on a dramatic shape; the moment of death never arrives in this elegiac poem as it does in "In Memory of Arthur Winslow"—everyone in this portrait is and remains "less than dead." The relationship between Lowell and his grandfather is mainly described by other people, the members of the household who call Lowell's grandfather his "father," and though the two move through the world next to each other, riding in the car, stopping for a snack, raking leaves, even urinating together, there is no moment of mutual recognition; the child Lowell recognizes himself in a newt only when he has wandered off from his grandfather, and even the final, almost overblown statement of intimacy, "In the mornings I cuddled like a paramour / in my Grandfather's bed" happens in the grandfather's absence—the speaker embraces the bedclothes, not the grandfather himself.[64] Perhaps the direct address in the earlier elegy is possible because of its formal indirection; perhaps a voice half-strangled by the formalities of language can be more emotionally direct than a voice speaking in an undertone. But I do not wish to follow certain of Lowell's critics by accusing his later verse of losing the formal elegance of the earlier poetry.[65] Instead, I want to argue that in the later poem, "form" takes on a different meaning and function.

At the same time that rhyme and rhythm fail to mark "Dunbarton" as a poem, its line breaks, made emphatic by the comparative shortness of its lines (many have three or fewer beats), set it firmly apart from prose. While the compression of "In Memory of Arthur Winslow" puts pressure on each individual detail, and both the presence of formal ordering and the lack of information we are given about the speaker's feelings make us want to read each detail as symbolic, the frequently broken lines of "Dunbarton" put a different kind of pressure on detail. Marjorie Perloff makes the useful observation that the dominant trope in Lowell's poetry is metonymy rather than the Romantic trope of metaphor,[66] and we can see that the comparative dispersal of "Dunbarton" means there is less pressure toward the symbolic meaning of each detail than in the earlier elegy. Instead, the details build toward a novelistic realism, but in a halting fashion—in Alan Williamson's terms, "the effect is a little like watching a film slowly enough to see the lines between frames; harsh and irritating, but with distinct advantages for self-scrutiny, particularly when contrasted with those surrealist styles whose fluidity tends to make of the unconscious, whatever its contents, a Peaceable Kingdom."[67] To put it another way, there is a click as each detail is briefly frozen before being let go, as in a still photograph. The obscurity that clings to "Dunbarton," despite its clearer tone, has to do with the unexplained eeriness of this click, the moment of suspension that leaves many things about the speaker's relationship to his family intimated but unsaid. If you accept this reading, then form has been reduced to the most mechanical aspect imaginable: it is a machine punching out blank space. And yet, at its most mechanical, it becomes (if the response many readers have had to *Life Studies* is any indication) a prime indicator of emotional mystery or depth. "In Memory of Arthur Winslow," which, according to Lowell, precedes the "breakthrough back into life," releases a potent self nonetheless by the sense it gives of that form's psychological inadequacy. Conversely, even though the form of "Dunbarton" seems to be more organically integrated with the psychology of the speaker, that form ironically becomes a cipher of silence instead of the presence of an authentic voice. In these terms, there is no clear before-and-after story to tell about the formal progression of Lowell's poetry—only the possibility that such storylines may multiply endlessly.

Incisions in the Ice and Radiation Sickness: Early Rich and Later Rich

We have seen that some of Adrienne Rich's poems that are supposed to integrate poet and speaker actually bear the marks of an extreme dis-integration. This paradox also plays out in the drama of form that Rich's and Sylvia Plath's poems enact, as the poems that are supposed to unite form and sincerity into a unified whole, far from healing the split between the two, read more like a reopened wound. Perhaps even more self-conscious about the problem of form than their male counterparts, both Rich and Plath have written a number of poems that examine thematically what it means to give poetic form to experience. This self-consciousness, rather than working to resolve the question of the relationship between authentic self-expression and form, only makes this question more acute.

In the essay "The Muralist," Rich considers whether the formal control she has learned as a poet can be translated into a moral self-control that will help her to work toward a better world. She envisions the ideal conditions of poetic creation in the following terms:

> When I'm writing poetry . . . the old integrative powers rush together: it's as if the process of poetry itself temporarily releases me into that realm of human power which Marx said is its own end . . . New questions, new problems—of shape, of strategy, of materials, and, yes, of purpose—unfold even as you unlock present difficulties. There is a happiness in finding *what will work* simultaneously with the discovery of *what it works for*, which has often been reduced to separate issues of "form" and "content."[68]

In Rich's vision, means and end, form and content, are experienced as indistinguishable during the moment of creation, suggesting that aesthetic and moral questions have successfully been united. But we know from statements that Rich makes elsewhere, and from the sense of strain in her poetry, that she often finds it difficult to marry these two realms of concern. She is consistently, as she describes herself, "the poet who knows that beautiful language can lie, that the oppressor's language sometimes sounds beautiful."[69] Finding what will work does not always guarantee that what it works for will be acceptable to the poet's moral purposes.

Later in the same essay, Rich makes an analogy between moral and aesthetic responsibility in somewhat different terms. After discussing statements by the sculptor Elizabeth Catlett about the importance of social awareness in the creation of sculptural form, Rich goes on to consider Catlett's remarks as if they also applied to poetic form:

> When Catlett says *You must, as an artist, consciously determine where your own level is*, I believe she is speaking on behalf of art [as well as social responsibility]. Just as if she had said *You must, as a sculptor, consciously become aware of the properties and difficulties of many kinds of wood, of metals, of kinds of stone, clay*. You must become responsive, responsible, to the materials.[70]

Catlett's insistence on social awareness is "just as if" she has insisted on a formal awareness, and this analogy permits Rich to imagine that responsibility to a community and responsibility to the techniques of one's art could be the same kind of responsibility. This analogy depends, however, on the fact that the sculptor experiences a separation between herself and her medium, whereas the poet does not. Wood, metals, kinds of stone, and clay are materials the artist must learn as alien to herself. The discipline of that learning then makes a good analogy to the moral discipline that Rich envisions as necessary for the proper level of responsiveness to one's social environment. The problem is that the poet experiences no such separation between herself and her medium; she is awash in language continually, just as she is awash in her social environment: it is impossible *not* to work in language, *not* to reflect her environment. This situation means that technique (moral or artistic) is not a matter of mastering a specialized craft; it is a matter of attempting to position oneself meaningfully amidst all the ongoing paraphernalia of ordinary life. The connection that Rich makes between her own work and that of the sculptor, seemingly an integration of "what works" and "what it works for," is actually a vision of dis-integration made possible by the sculptor's separation from her materials.

The image of the sculptor, or the woman who is detached from the materials of her creative work, appears again and again in Rich's poetry, notably in "The Diamond Cutters" (1955) and "Power" (1974). The former poem was supposedly written before Rich began to integrate her impulses toward self-expression and social responsibility with her formal choices, but I believe that its form and content, and its poet and speaker, are actually more unified than in her later poem "Power." In "Power," according to the story Rich tells about her career, the woman in the poem and the woman writing the poem are closer to being the same person. But "Power" actually exhibits a more fractured, equivocal relationship between poetic form and content, and between poet and speaker, than the earlier poem does. Our expectations are reversed, and again it appears that self-expression is as likely to be achieved by perceivable gaps between form and content as it is by their integration.

Although Rich's early poem "The Diamond Cutters" insists upon a separation between the poet's mind and her materials and maintains a grammatical separation between the poet and the speaker through its use of the second person, at the same time it achieves a striking unity between form and content, and between the diamond cutter's and the poet's task. The poem opens with a description of the raw diamond that will be cut into a gem. Emphasis falls upon its hardness and coldness: "it had once resisted / The weight of Africa, / The hammer-blows of time," "this coldest one."[71] It would be difficult to imagine a substance less humanly friendly, less analogous to a human life. Nevertheless, the following stanza describes the intelligence that will cut this stone as sharing the qualities of the diamond. This intelligence is separate and intractable, an instrument of mastery: the speaker instructs it to "Delineate at will / Incisions in the ice."[72] This will has been "dredged up from dark" through the process of evolution, just as the diamond is dredged up from the earth. The analogy between diamond and intelligence achieves two opposite gestures at once: it unifies the diamond cutter's or poet's mind with her materials by attributing the same qualities to them, but these shared qualities are also precisely what keeps the diamond and the shaping intelligence apart: their implacable self-containment. The language of the poem in the concluding three stanzas continues to insist upon the separation of the two, warning, "The stone may have contempt / For too-familiar hands," explaining that the stone is "the adversary," and advising, "Be hard of heart, because / the stone must leave your hand / . . . Keep your desire apart."[73] The heart and the intelligence of the poet should be hard like the stone, even inhuman as the stone is inhuman, but this similarity does not bring them together—it is an analogy made for the purpose of separation.

We have, then, a peculiar mixture of the integration of mind and matter (because they share similar qualities) and their dis-integration (because those qualities dictate that they remain separate). The stylistic consequence of this mixture appears to be a fierce integration of form and content. The intelligence that has ordered the poem's sound and movement has obviously taken the advice of the speaker in the poem. Each line is separate and chiseled as a diamond, falling reliably into a conventional, Yeatsian three-beat line (which here feels foreshortened, constrained, as if the poet is practicing a carefully calculated restraint), usually iambic (the exceptions also feel calculated, such as the fumbling of the meter on the word "fumbling"). The stanzas of the poem are consistently in eight lines, each building up short clauses to form a complete sentence. The language is shorn of ornament, holding back adjectives, avoiding enjambment. The lack of reliable rhymes in each stanza could be interpreted as a slackening of this formal self-control, but to my mind it has the effect of emphasizing, even exaggerating, the sense of control by imposing organization on smaller units: our attention is drawn not to the symmetry of stanzas, but more minutely and precisely to each individual line (often internally structured by sound patterns, such as those in "Delineate at will / Incisions in the ice"). In a superficial but undeniable way, form and content are completely integrated; "what will work" matches "what it works for."

However, when Rich reprints this poem in a later selection of her poetry, she is singularly dissatisfied with it, adding (as we saw in the previous chapter) an endnote that disowns the metaphorical equivalence of the poet's work with that of the diamond cutter and deplores her past ignorance of "the long tradition of domination, according to which the precious resource is yielded up into the hands of the dominator as if by a natural event."[74] Whatever integration of form and content is achieved by "The Diamond Cutters" does not, for Rich, count as the right kind of moral integration. Her later work (from *Leaflets* onward) can be seen as an attempt to achieve a higher level of integration, to include in her poems the gesture that here is relegated to an endnote. But even though, according to the poet, these later poems do a better job of melding the speaker and the poet into one authentic voice, more often than not the stylistic consequence of this putative unification is a widened gap between form and content, as well as between the speaker of a poem and its subject.

An example is the poem "Power," which like "The Diamond Cutters" interests itself in deposits in the earth, and in the human activity required for the purification of these deposits. But if "The Diamond Cutters" denies the human costs of the excavation and purification of the elements of the earth, "Power" insists upon them, recording the sickness that Marie Curie suffered because of her work as a chemist. Rich writes of how Curie "denied to the end" the knowledge that

> . . . she suffered   from radiation sickness
> her body bombarded for years   by the element
> she had purified.[75]

But at the same time, "Power" clouds the relationships that "The Diamond Cutters" makes clear. While it is obvious that the speaker of "The Diamond Cutters" believes that she can learn lessons as a poet from the work of the diamond cutters, it remains ambiguous what lesson the poet in "Power" learns from the example of Marie Curie. On the one hand, Rich seems to wish to separate herself from Curie, chastising the scientist (somewhat as she chastises herself in the endnote to "The Diamond Cutters") for not recognizing the link between her work and her suffering: "She died . . . denying / her wounds."[76] The poem evidently has, at least in part, the purpose of undoing Curie's denial. But at the same time, the poem opens the possibility that the speaker is implicated in Curie's denial, that like Curie she too has spent her life, as the final lines of the poem put it, "denying / her wounds came from the same source as her power"[77]—and, what is more, that it may not be possible to do otherwise and continue working. Rich's endnote to "The Diamond Cutters" expresses hope that the brutalizing lack of human sympathy which that poem imagines to be necessary to the artistic process is not necessary after all, and that sympathy with the actual miners who retrieve diamonds from the earth is a more responsible method of poetic production. But "Power" raises the question of whether, after all, there is not something inhuman, and necessarily so, in any work of purification, whether it involves scientific knowledge or poetic effect. This later poem holds two contradictory positions simultaneously: Rich separates herself from Curie in order to critique her, in which case she fails to unify her own voice with that of her subject; and Rich identifies with Curie, in which case she unifies herself with the woman she describes, but only as a paradoxically open statement of her own self-deceptions, a statement that makes no promise to end the condition of denial.

Although it comes from the period in which the woman in the poem and the woman making the poems supposedly begin to be the same woman, this poem fails to unite the two, or unites them only equivocally. At the same time, "Power" is written during the period in the poet's career in which poetic form and content supposedly begin to work for, rather than against, each other. At first glance, it does appear that the form of "Power" follows the contours of the poet's consciousness more faithfully than that of "The Diamond Cutters": syntax and line-lengths are more flexible and associative, and the workings of the poet's mind are no longer constrained by predetermined stanza forms. But this new looseness can be seen to contradict rather than reinforce the poet's subject matter. In "The Diamond Cutters," the formal control of sound and rhythm mimics the poem's contention that making poems involves a rigorous self-control. "Power" considers a similar association of poetry with purification, but its own form denies this analogy through its looseness, its lack of "purity" of sound or structure.

We could take this apparent commitment to a more open form as a decisive repudiation of Curie's self-damaging procedure. And yet in a less obvious way, "Power" shares some of the basic formal inclinations of "The Diamond Cutters." The short, abrupt lines of "The Diamond Cutters" (with their intimations of polish and care) are retained by "Power" in the form of clauses set off by spaces within an individual line. For example, in the opening line of the poem, "Living   in the earth-deposit   of our history,"[78] the phrases "in the earth deposits" and "of our history" read like the short lines of "The Diamond Cutters," even retaining the characteristic three beats. From this perspective, the basic unit of Rich's later poem is the same as its earlier one—brief clauses set apart visually on the page. The freedom with which she now combines these units—their length is more variable, and multiple units are placed together on a single line to mark out larger sets of associations—does not necessarily denote the presence of a flowing, unifying consciousness that sutures the separations that had broken the lines of "The Diamond Cutters." Instead, the reader is more likely to have the impression that "Power" retains the abruptness, the lack of connective tissue, that we experienced in "The Diamond Cutters" as a halting emphasis that interrupts normal syntax, a similar lack of a fluent "I" holding the perceptions of the poem together. In "The Diamond Cutters" this abruptness was patterned, and therefore we could read it as evidence of the poet's ordering intelligence, but in "Power" the isolation of the lines reads like a suspension of reference, a marker of our uncertainty of where the "I," despite being present in the poem, actually stands. The breaks and gaps that used to ensure the presence of the shaping poet now mark her absence. The integration of poet and speaker, of form and content that Rich describes in her essays as the heart of her poetic project seems here to be enacted as the suspension of an earlier form of integration, leaving the mark but not the presence of a complex consciousness. "Power" does not so much body forth a newly authentic speaking presence through a newly "free" verse as demolish and reassemble older connections, older forms. These suggestive ruins do release a new kind of self, and perhaps even a new kind of sincerity, but only on the condition of its elusiveness.

The Earthenware Head and the Illusion of Greek Necessity: Early Plath and Later Plath

Rich's considerations of the problem of form gain their unique force from her attention to the possible links between formal self-control and moral self-control. Rather than unreflectively associating the making of aesthetic objects with objectivity and a morally appropriate sense of perspective, Rich poses but then interrogates analogies between making poetic forms and living a moral life. In parallel terms, and with a similar seriousness of purpose, Sylvia Plath explores possible analogies between formal self-control on the one hand, and death and survival on the other. She asks: is making a formally perfect poem like committing suicide or like living? The answer is more complicated than some of her critics would suggest. As in the case of Rich, the poetry of Plath's early period demonstrates a formidable unification of form and content, poet and speaker, contradicting the before-and-after story often told about her career. Her later poetry, rather than consolidating this unification in an integrated act of self-expression, actually fractures what was previously united, in particular the unification of poet and speaker. It is this fracture, the opening of the gap between form and content rather than its suturing, that releases a new kind of voice.

Plath's suicide at age thirty, which brought an abrupt halt to a creative outpouring that had produced some of the most arresting poems in American literature, gives her before-and-after story a special sense of urgency. To many of those left to absorb the shock of her death, her suicide seemed in a stroke to fuse the poet with the often self-annihilating speakers in her later poetry, and to conflate the metaphorical realm of poetry with the literal actions of the poet's life. Examples of this response include Lowell's Foreword to the American edition of *Ariel*—"In her lines, I often hear the serpent whisper, 'Come, if only you had the courage, you too could have my rightness, audacity, and ease of inspiration.' But most of us will turn back. These poems are playing Russian roulette with six cartridges in the cylinder"[79]—and an early review by A. Alvarez: "The achievement of her final style is to make poetry and death inseparable. The one could not exist without the other . . . Poetry of this order is a murderous art."[80] Alicia Ostriker no doubt speaks for many when she describes her first response to *Ariel* as "a thought compounded of something like *Good God, it's real* and *Damn, she did it* . . . and a physical sensation like that of being slapped hard: rush of adrenalin, stunned amazement."[81] This initial response has been tempered with second thoughts and has received well-deserved criticism ever since.[82] I intend to contribute to the dismantling of the before-and-after story told about Plath's career—in which the crafter of formally accomplished but timid verses is transformed into a powerfully expressive but suicidal poet—not by sidestepping the frequent appearance of suicide as a theme in her work, but by emphasizing that, for her, suicide is as much a trope as a lived possibility. She self-consciously deploys this trope in order to explore the boundaries between metaphor and reality, form and content.[83]

Even more so than the early poetry of Robert Lowell, Plath's poetry has been described as a realm in which the presence of extreme control and its absolute absence occupy the same space. Her own description of her poetic practice blurs these two realms: she states, "I believe that one should be able to control and manipulate experiences, even the most terrifying—like madness, being tortured, this kind of experience—and one should be able to manipulate these experiences with an informed and intelligent mind."[84] Plath chooses the most negative synonym for control— "manipulate"—and claims it as an artistic positive. But her vision of this control involves the most extreme states of being out of control: madness, being tortured. The difficulty of telling the difference between controlling and being controlled is underlined by another of Plath's statements: "I feel like a very efficient tool or weapon, used and in demand from moment to moment."[85] Being a very efficient tool or weapon suggests the ability to use or control experience, but here it is the poet, not the experience, that is being "used." Critics echo this idea by proposing that control and wildness are indistinguishable in Plath's work.[86] Kenner provides the most telling formulation, writing of Plath's regular stanzas that "there's more of compulsion neurosis than mathematics in those forms; the breaks between stanzas are like cracks in the sidewalk, on which she is careful never to step. The resulting control, sometimes *look* of control . . . in fact enacts its own inability to govern."[87] Whether or not we agree with Kenner's assessment, he poses an important question: if madness is not the absence of form, but instead imposes its own rigid form, then how can we differentiate between form-as-sanity and form-as-madness? The trope of suicide complicates matters still further. The act of suicide can be viewed as a violent fusion of self-control and utter lack of control. In one sense, by taking her own life, the suicidal person takes control of that life in an unprecedented and unanswerable way. But at the same time, the act of suicide tells us that the suicidal person has completely lost control of his psychological health and survival. I suspect that Plath is attracted to the trope of suicide at least in part because it unites the idea of formal self-control as self-expression and the idea of formal self-control as the death of self-expression.

And yet distinguishing between the two is a constant concern of Plath's, a concern perhaps all the more urgent given her sharp sense of how easily the self-control of a sane intelligence and the compulsive self-control of madness can become confused. M. L. Rosenthal writes of the poems in *Ariel,* "We shall never be able to sort out clearly the unresolved, unbearably exposed suggestibility and agitation of these poems from the purely aesthetic energy that shaped the best of them."[88] But it is the difference between psychic vulnerability and aesthetic energy in which Plath herself is interested. The "sorting out" that Rosenthal deems impossible is a central theme of her work. Plath's later poetry, rather than abandoning her earlier formal control, self-consciously thematizes it. As this form of control comes to be associated with a kind of death, the living, expressive woman builds ever more cunning methods of escaping it.

Plath's early poem "The Lady and the Earthenware Head" (1957) is ultimately rejected by the poet as "too fancy, glassy, patchy, and rigid—it embarrasses me now—with its ten elaborate epithets for head in five verses."[89] But when examined closely, the poem exhibits two of the achievements associated with Plath's later work: the mutual implication of poet and speaker, and the exquisite fit between form and content. At the same time, the poem offers an allegory about artistic imperfection, suggesting that imperfection cannot be eliminated or "killed"—somehow, the poet must find a way to live with it. Like "The Diamond Cutters," "The Lady and the Earthenware Head" unifies the poet and speaker through its consideration of the discipline of writing poetry, except that in this instance, the work of art (an ugly model head—again, we are in the medium of sculpture) has already been completed, and the speaker of the poem is left with the problem of disposing of it. She has difficulty ridding herself of the head not because she made it (a partial gap is left between speaker and poet, in the sense that we are never explicitly told whether or not the speaker is the sculptor),[90] but because it resembles her; it is the "[a]pe of her look." She considers throwing the head away, but is afraid that subjecting the head to abuse might "waken the sly nerve up // That knits each original to its coarse copy."[91] Her sense of the uncanny link between herself and her copy is reinforced in the next stanza, when her attempt to dispose of the head in a river makes her feel as if she is drowning. She then decides to balance the head in a willow tree, hoping to provide it with a more "natural" death in which the "uncouth shape" is worn down to "simple sod again," but this solution is also rejected, and at the end of the poem the offensive head remains upon her shelf.[92]

How are we to read this allegory? In the first place, it contradicts those readers of Plath who believe that she was willing to sacrifice anything, including her own life, for the achievement of poetic perfection. Instead, the poem suggests that artistic imperfection must be in some way accommodated, rather than destroyed.[93] In another sense, the poem offers an inconclusive meditation about the relationship between metaphorical violence done to (or within) a work of art and violence done to a human being. If we read the "head" as "poem" and the woman whom the head resembles as the poet, then its message hovers between two possibilities. The first is that the poem and its poet are truly connected by a "sly nerve," so that any violence done to the poem (or metaphorically within the poem) amounts to real violence done to the poet. The second possibility is that this connection is merely a superstition of the speaker's, a possibility suggested both by her determination to free herself from the head and the ironic tone of the poem. The first possibility reads almost as a parody of the critics who connect the violence in Plath's poetry with the violence of her death, and who take her suicide as proof of the "sly nerve" that links the destinies of Plath's life and art. The second perspective views this possibility as foolish even while recognizing its power. The poem's refusal to decide between the two perspectives suggests that Plath would hold back her endorsement both from readers who insist upon and readers who deny the "sly nerve" connecting even an imperfect form and its subject. Instead, she demands that the reader keep her attention focused on the choices available to someone who believes simultaneously in an uncanny link between an artistic object and what it represents and also in their fundamental separateness. She works to keep both possibilities alive, as if having to choose between them would itself be a kind of death.

Just as this early poem maintains an explicit, though complicated, connection between poet and speaker, it maintains, in its very formal imperfections, a kind of perfected unity of form and content. Here is a sample stanza, the first:

> Fired in sanguine clay, the model head
> Fit nowhere: brickdust-complected, eye under a dense lid,
> On the long bookshelf it stood
> Stolidly propping thick volumes of prose: spite-set
> Ape of her look. Best rid
> Hearthstone at once of the outrageous head;
> Still, she felt loath to junk it.[94]

The formal virtuosity of the poem is immediately obvious: the evidence of subsequent stanzas reveals a regular *abacbbc* rhyme (though many of these rhymes are half-rhymes, and the meter is irregular, varying longer and shorter lines), and (as Plath herself points out) the poem wears its lexical inventiveness on its sleeve: the head is "effigy," "pate," "coarse copy," "simulacrum," "mimic head," "rendering," "uncouth shape," "grisly visage," and "hag-head," and the poem's adjectives ("sanguine," "brickdust-complected," "spite-set," "thick-silted," "laurelled," "green-vaulted," "bell-tongued," "drear and dulcet," "evil-starred") also advertise their ingenuity.[95] Sound is ordered and effective, with Plath's mastery of alliteration insistently evident in lines such as "Stolidly propping thick volumes of prose: spite-set" and "Let bell-tongued birds descant in blackest feather."[96] We can wholeheartedly agree with the poet that these effects are ineffectively elaborate, showy and stilted. But what is remarkable about this poem—and accounts for a large part of its wry humor—is the way in which these formal "mistakes" successfully mimic the problem the poem puts forth. This modern version of the stilted poetic diction that Wordsworth railed against "waken[s] the sly nerve up" that links poetic form and content. For the head itself behaves like the poem: its ruddiness ("sanguine clay," "brickdust-complected") is like the poem's adjectival over-coloration; if the poem is heavy, the head is heavy enough to be "[s]tolidly propping thick volumes of prose"; and like the poem itself, the head is "outrageous" and "pompous." In this way, the poem exhibits a unity between form and content, as well as between poet and speaker, that was not supposed to come until the poet's later, formally uninhibited work.

If this example of Plath's earlier poetry, contrary to what we are usually told to expect, unifies form and content, and poet and speaker, her later poetry works—at least in part—to drive a wedge between the two. Her most famous and to some readers most "confessional" poem, "Daddy," offers a speaker who talks in nursery-rhyme cadences, and it gains its effect from the *inappropriateness* of this form to its disturbing content, not from their proper fit. In a different way, the poem that seems to link poetic perfection and suicide most explicitly, "Edge," also works to separate form and content, and most fundamentally to separate poet and speaker.[97] The poem opens:

> The woman is perfected.
> Her dead
>
> Body wears the smile of accomplishment,
> The illusion of a Greek necessity
>
> Flows in the scrolls of her toga.[98]

The implications seem clear: the only sure way to achieve aesthetic "perfection," a classical sense of "necessity," is through self-murder. The speaker's children, needy, willful, ordinary extensions of the self, are folded into this perfection: "Each dead child coiled, a white serpent."[99] The speaker has folded the children "back into her body as petals / Of a rose close,"[100] a rose which does not even bleed odor, as the night flower does. The one witness to the scene, the moon, holds in "her hood of bone" the same white, indifferent perfection as the dead woman's body, even as "[h]er blacks crackle and drag."[101] The simplification of shapes and colors creates a perfection in aesthetic design that suggests the sacrifice has served its purpose.

Here, according to the before-and-after story told about Plath's work, formal constraint has given way to authentic self-expression. The form of the poem powerfully mimics its content; both form and content move toward an austerity that all but erases the mess of everyday living. But this poem breaks the unification between poet and speaker that we witnessed in "The Lady and the Earthenware Head." As in the earlier poem, we remain in the realm of the third person, but here the action of the woman in the poem and the actions of the poet have been radically disaligned. Qualifications ripple across the surface of the poem: the "[b]ody wears the smile of accomplishment," but the woman has accomplished her purpose only on the condition that she lose all purpose: her body wears a smile, but she can no longer make her face express her will. The classical necessity the dead body has achieved is "[t]he *illusion* of a Greek necessity," not its actuality. But more fundamentally, unlike the woman who has killed herself, the poet undertakes the work of animation, not the work of death: the body wears a smile; the bare feet seem to speak; the body folds like a flower; the moon, hard and indifferent, is still personified, imagined as a witch with a hood and a cloak of "blacks [that] crackle and drag."[102] This closing image disrupts the formal perfection of the poem—it is an image of ambiguous motion and sound that ruins the stillness of the portrait. As surely as the earthenware head does, "Edge" possesses living imperfections. Poetic diction has been abandoned, and the protagonist of the poem has been in a sense depersonified, but the personifying activity of poetry carries on its life.

The way in which the words unfold on the page also suggests that the poem is rallying strategic "imperfections" to hold off the killing perfection imaged in the poem. Rather than using meter and rhyme to create a classical whole, Plath has composed ragged couplets that make it feel as if the poem is unraveling. The only end rhyme in the poem, linking "perfected" and "dead," is a half-rhyme that works like a joke—the live poet winking at us from behind her immobile creation. The one perfect rhyme of the poem, "rose close," is internal, and works like a flaw in the middle of the line, a place where the reader stumbles. Instead of enjambing the first line of each couplet into the second, the poem enjambs lines across stanza breaks, so that we have to step over a void on the page between "Her dead // Body," "a Greek necessity // flows," "Her bare // feet," "little // Pitcher," "She has folded // them back," and "the garden // stiffens." This arrangement does not suggest classical logic or beauty, but produces an abrupt, halting effect, one that suggests uncertainty about whether the poem will be able to make each leap and continue building a bridge of living language over the blank of death. In the end, death is an available metaphor for perfection, but it is in no way a sufficient metaphor, a metaphor that can literally become the end of the need for metaphor. "Form," as an obstacle, as a saving imperfection, is a necessary obstacle, one that will continually regenerate itself in different terms.

Sincere self-expression does not become "poetry" when it finds a viable poetic form. This formulation assumes that the self precedes form, which is only one of the productive myths of Romanticism. But neither can we say that the self already possesses an aesthetically satisfying form. Poets need to imagine that the self and form are in some sense in opposition to each other in the same way that they need to imagine that a true unself-conscious self and a false self-conscious self are in opposition to each other (or vice versa—either can be the founding move of a struggle for "sincerity"). But of course, once the possibility of a false self is intuited, it can never be fully set aside, and similarly the fear of falsifying form haunts post-Romantic poets. Poetry (and the reading of poetry) involves the provisional and shifting positing of a boundary between form and content, a continual attempt to appropriate "good" forms for self-expression and to cast "bad" forms out. Fortunately, the obstacle of bad form turns out to be a productive obstacle, just as the obstacle of the false self makes a new push toward personal sincerity conceivable if not fully achievable. When the self appears to find an aesthetically satisfying form, we cannot say that that self has been objectified, that it has in any final way become morally good or true. We can only say that it is temporarily at rest, until the falseness of its form is in turn discovered, in turn becomes a mere convention, which again must be dissolved.

CHAPTER THREE

Sincerity and the Staged Confession

The Monologues of Browning, Eliot,
Berryman, and Plath

A T THIS POINT we would be justified in wondering, was it a mistake ever to try to identify the speaker of a poem with the poet in the first place? Could we avoid the innumerable difficulties we have encountered thus far, the poet by relinquishing the goal of personal sincerity and setting herself apart from the speakers of individual poems, and the reader by assuming that the poet never speaks directly in a poem, but only as a more or less fictionalized speaker? This method of reading has been recommended from at least the 1930s, when critics began to resist the assumption that their interpretations must be limited by what they could reconstruct of the poet's intentions.[1] E. R. Harty offers a useful summary of this reading strategy. Because the "situational context" that a poem creates is always in some sense fictional,

> a poem is always, in principle, impersonal, inasmuch as the voice which utters it is a fictional construct, a literary creation distinct from the poet. Even poems which seem intensely personal expressions are subject to this interpretive convention . . . It follows that even in those cases where the poet *intends* to speak in his own voice, to express his own thoughts and feelings, by employing a poetic genre he automatically abdicates his right to be so construed.[2]

In other words, if we agree to this interpretive convention, we are to read all poems as if they were dramatic monologues, defined here not in the strict sense as a poem spoken by a character separate from the poet to an auditor sharing the same space on a particular occasion, but rather in the loosest possible sense as poems that explicitly mark the speaker of the poem as separate from the poet. The genre of the dramatic monologue recognizes and codifies the gap between poet and speaker that we have observed in even the most putatively sincere poetry. If self-consciousness produces a gap between the self observed and the self observing, which is fatal to the coherence of identity that is the goal of poetic sincerity, the dramatic monologue, in contrast, takes this gap as its initial premise. One might conclude that the poet who writes (or the reader who reads) as if she already knows that poetry alienates the poet from her authentic voice stabilizes the gap inherent in self-consciousness, and perhaps is even able to discipline self-consciousness into controllable irony or self-knowledge. But, as we would by now expect, self-consciousness is not so easily stabilized. Just as poems that attempt to unify the poet and the speaker in a poem are haunted by the separation of the two, poems that claim to separate the poet and the speaker are threatened by the propensity of these two individuals to collapse into each other.

If all poems can or should be read as dramatic monologues, we would expect poems that present themselves as dramatic monologues to represent the simple case of poetic voice. But even before we encounter the complications that individual examples introduce, there is evidence in the amount of debate surrounding the genre that dramatic monologues create their own problems rather than providing a solution to the problem of lyric voice. The term "dramatic monologue" did not exist when the prototypical monologues were being written: although Browning labeled certain of his poems "dramatic," critics invented the concept of the dramatic monologue only in retrospect, and the term has always been a provisional and unstable one.[3] Most readers, following those who formulated the term in the early twentieth century, agree that a dramatic monologue in the strict sense requires three things: a speaker who is distinctly marked as separate from the poet (for example, through a title that signals to us that the poem is in the voice of "Fra Lippo Lippi" or "Ulysses" instead of Browning or Tennyson); a specific auditor or auditors (for example, the watchmen in "Fra Lippo Lippi" or the mariners in "Ulysses"); and a specific occasion for speech (Fra Lippo's illicit escape from his monastery, Ulysses' imminent departure). But disagreements soon set in. For example, if Fra Lippo Lippi is simply a mouthpiece through which Browning conveys his own beliefs about art, rather than a character whose point of view (as well as historical situation) is different from that of his creator, is this poem still a dramatic monologue, or would it be more accurate to describe it as a masked lyric? Are the auditors and occasion in "Ulysses" specific enough to qualify the poem as a dramatic monologue?[4] Attempts to account for all of the variation among poems labeled as dramatic monologues have produced complicated systems like that of Harty, who creates a spectrum from the "impersonal lyric" to the "dramatic lyric" to the "dramatic monologue."[5] The controversies that mark the critical literature on the dramatic monologue suggest that the question of whether the dramatic monologue ever exists in pure form is as open as the question of whether the sincere lyric ever exists in pure form.

While the genre of the dramatic monologue permits us to imagine that the feelings and motives of the speaker of a poem and the poet can be clearly distinguished, I believe that the genre achieves at most a partial separation. But to contend that dramatic monologues have difficulty in maintaining the separations they pose between poet and speaker is not to argue that all dramatic monologues are sincere lyrics in disguise. The idea of the dramatic monologue is useful because it offers the seductive promise that we may distinguish between the poet's intention and the stated desires of the speaker in the poem, even though this promise can never be fully realized. The experience of reading a dramatic monologue, in which we have a double awareness of a speaker who is revealing him- or herself and a poet controlling and offering implicit judgments upon what is being revealed, is different from the double awareness we experience in reading a putatively sincere lyric, in which our sense of the truthfulness of the presence speaking to us is countered by our knowledge that that presence is in some sense an illusion. For example, Wordsworth's "Tintern Abbey" exhibits some of the conventions of the dramatic monologue: it is spoken by a specifically located speaker (who, the title tells us, is "Revisiting the Banks of the Wye during a Tour, July 13, 1798"), who begins *in medias res,* and who addresses a specific silent auditor (though we are not aware of her presence until the end of the poem).[6] But insisting that this dramatic particularity creates a meaningful distance between the speaker and the poet is of little help in reading lines such as these:

> . . . Nor less, I trust,
> To [these images] I may have owed another gift,
> Of aspect more sublime; that blessed mood,
> In which the burthen of the mystery,
> In which the heavy and the weary weight
> Of all this unintelligible world,
> Is lightened:—[7]

The significance of these lines depends upon our belief in a speaker-poet who is trying to fathom and describe an experience so mysterious that it

forces him to press syntax to its limits, struggle with abstractions, and ex-
press himself in negative constructions. We could make partial sense of
these lines by imagining that they are meant to indicate a character sepa-
rate from the poet, but then we must ask: what judgment does Words-
worth make on this speaker? For example, does the imprecision of the
speaker's language suggest that the poet means for us to condemn his
character's mysticism? If we understand the speaker of these lines to
be separate from the poet, they risk becoming mere parody, their high
seriousness only laughable. It is truer to the poem, and to everything
we know of Wordsworth, to believe that we are supposed to share the
speaker-poet's sense of awe in the face of things that he cannot explain.
We can ask whether the poet is being fully honest with himself, and more
broadly whether the insight into himself he claims here is actually possi-
ble, but these questions require linking the poet with the speaker, not
imagining them as separate identities.

One reason it feels false to read the speaker in "Tintern Abbey" as the
speaker in a dramatic monologue is because its "I" lacks clear social or
historical markers, which the speaker of a dramatic monologue generally
exhibits. According to Herbert Tucker, the dramatic monologue critiques
the dehistoricized, supposedly sincere speaker in Romantic lyrics through
the strategy of "show[ing] subjectivity up by betraying its situation in
a history."[8] To apply Tucker's argument to the case at hand, whereas
Wordsworth fails to explicitly recognize the limits and potential absurdi-
ties of the speaker he presents, writers of the dramatic monologue (such
as Browning) make those limits visible to us by locating the lyric speaker
in a web of social relationships. But before we join Tucker in congratulat-
ing the writers of dramatic monologues for demystifying the pretensions
of their Romantic precursors, we must notice that this view replaces
the insistent (though self-defeating) presence of the sincere "I" with the
equally illusionary presence of a recoverable, stably ironic authorial in-
tention.[9] The dramatic monologue genre (for the poet) or model (for the
reader) of the lyric produces a fantasy no less misleading, while at the
same time no less attractive, than that of the "sincere" lyric. If a "sin-
cere" poem, at its best, makes us feel as if we have direct access to the
poet's truest, most profound feelings, then a dramatic monologue, at its
most compelling, makes us feel as if we have direct access to the poet's
true, though ironically coded, intentions. For example, in a poem like
Robert Browning's "My Last Duchess," the repulsiveness of the speaker,
the Duke of Ferrara, is clearly marked by his apparent murder of an inno-
cent woman. The starkness of the separation between Browning and the
Duke lets us draw sharp outlines around each individual: we can locate

"Browning" in the poem by charting the standard of his deviation from the Duke. Browning may not be present in the poem as a speaker, but his intention is clearer to us than the intention of the poet in a sincere lyric. We cannot, for example, locate "Wordsworth" in the same way that we can locate "Browning," because Wordsworth seems to be simultaneously everywhere (in his insistence on his own "I," his own perspective) and nowhere (if we try to pin him down he is likely to evade us). Abandoning the lyric's insistence on the sincere "I," the dramatic monologue can insist even more dogmatically upon the authorial "I."

But while the sincere "I" is compromised by the self-thwarting movements of self-consciousness, the clarity of the poet's intention in a dramatic monologue is undermined in at least three ways. In the first three sections of this chapter I describe how the characters in dramatic monologues themselves become increasingly self-conscious and thus compromise their separation from their poet-creator. In the last section I show how, from the reader's point of view, what we know of a poet's biography—as well as the potential discordances between his assumptions about moral value, those of the monologue's speaker, and our own—can destabilize the separation between poet and speaker. The dramatic monologue cannot give us selves more authentic than the sincere lyric can either in the person of the ironic, masterful poet or in the distilled personalities of the characters who confess their secrets to us. We can only witness the effects of these various beings contending with one another.

Browning, His Duke, and the Problems of Portraiture

Robert Browning's "My Last Duchess" is often cited as the quintessential dramatic monologue.[10] The poem produces a vivid double awareness of the audacity of the character presented and the judgments that the poet expects us to make about him. We know that Browning and his speaker are separate beings because the character of the Duke is located in the past and staged in conversation with a similarly specified character, the envoy, as an auditor; and most of all because the Duke behaves in a way that we and the poet can agree is repellent: he has ordered the murder of his first wife. Under these circumstances, it is fairly easy and, in a limited way, satisfying to decode the ironic authorial meaning behind the Duke's statements to the envoy with whom he negotiates terms for his next marriage. For example, when the Duke declares, "That's my last Duchess painted on the wall, / Looking as if she were alive,"[11] we can hear the ominousness of that "as if," and with hindsight note the irony that the

Duke apparently prefers his former wife "as if alive" rather than actually alive. In the central section of the poem, in which the Duke explains what it was about his former wife that irritated him, we can contrast his interpretation of her behavior with our own and with the one we can ascribe to Browning. Toward the end of the poem, when the Duke assures his listener that the Count's "fair daughter's self," not her dowry, is "his object,"[12] we understand that Browning means for us to notice that the Duke is telling a more literal truth than he realizes: he wants his new wife, like his former one, to be his "object" or possession. But despite these clear contrasts between the Duke's attitude and what we can reconstruct of Browning's, the separation between Browning and his Duke is not so complete or untroubled as it first appears. The moments in which we can identify Browning's intentions in the implicitly ironic reverberations of the Duke's statements are countered by the moments when the Duke's self-consciousness creates unexpected resemblances between himself and his author.

First of all, the Duke and Browning undertake a similar project in the poem: both are working to present a singularly imperious personality to what they hope will be an impressionable audience. We know that the Duke is going to some effort to present an arrogant personality to his listener, rather than simply acting as or being this personality, because of the self-consciousness of his speech. In a sense, there are two Dukes within the poem: one Duke is the unself-conscious character whose will-to-power is so great that he is capable both of murdering his last wife and of revealing that murder in casual conversation; the second Duke is the self-conscious character who speaks with a continual eye to the effect his revelations will have upon his listener, and who exhibits an openness and vulnerability that would be implausible in the first Duke. In the following passage, in which the Duke comments on the painting of his former wife, both Dukes can be seen in action:

> . . . I call
> That piece a wonder, now: Frà Pandolf's hands
> Worked busily a day, and there she stands.
> Will it please you sit and look at her? I said
> "Frà Pandolf" by design, for never read
> Strangers like you that pictured countenance,
> The depth and passion of its earnest glance,
> But to myself they turned (since none puts by
> The curtain I have drawn for you, but I)

And seemed as they would ask me, if they durst,
How such a glance came there; so, not the first
Are you to turn and ask thus.[13]

Ferrara's aggressiveness in anticipating and guiding his listener's reaction (imagining what his listeners would ask, "if they durst," placing this particular listener's question in the context of an experience he has had before and over which he possesses full control) suggests his command of the situation, but at the same time, the Duke undermines the effect of his manipulation by calling attention to it. Would a man determined to use his knowledge of his listener's probable responses in order to manipulate those responses reveal his hand so readily?

As the poem unfolds, the fissure between the violent Duke capable of the decisive action of ordering a murder and the self-conscious Duke susceptible to analyzing his own situation grows. He begins to interrupt himself, asking "how shall I say?" and he drops his imperious demeanor to declare intimately, "Sir, 'twas all one! My favors at her breast, / The dropping of the daylight in the West."[14] Building to the climax of the poem, in which he will reveal that he has had his wife killed, he explains his motivations:

> . . . She thanked men,—good! but thanked
> Somehow—I know not how—as if she ranked
> My gift of a nine-hundred-year-old name
> With anybody's gift. Who'd stoop to blame
> This sort of trifling? Even had you skill
> In speech—(which I have not)—to make your will
> Quite clear to such an one, and say, "Just this
> Or that in you disgusts me; here you miss,
> Or there exceed the mark"—and if she let
> Herself be lessoned so, nor plainly set
> Her wits to yours, forsooth, and made excuse,
> —E'en then would be some stooping; and I choose
> Never to stoop.[15]

The Duke's claim to have difficulty expressing himself could be read as strategic self-deprecation designed to make his hold over his listener all the stronger, but such indirection is out of keeping with the directness of murder. The Duke himself draws attention to this incongruity by indicating the potential chasm between self-conscious speech and the assertion of power. According to him, having to make one's will explicit in words is a kind of "stooping," a self-defeating assertion of a power which is only power if it is taken for granted. By this logic, the Duke's desire to remind his wife, and, in the present scenario, the envoy, of his "nine-hundred-year-old-name" blunts the impact of that name, which should be its own force and require no special pleading. It is as if by entering into language (or poetry) in the first place, the Duke becomes something other than what he says he is, and in a sense something different from what Browning tells us he is. As a creature of words, he is compelled to explain himself, to describe what might otherwise have been taken for granted if we inhabited his world ourselves. Rather than Browning's intentions and those of the Duke being at odds, Browning's problem—using language to present a forceful character who, if we believe what he says, has little use for words—and the Duke's problem—impressing his own superiority and ruthlessness upon his listener by speaking, even though he believes that advertising one's own power is a kind of "stooping"—are aligned.

No doubt we could imagine a personality for the Duke complex enough to account for both his violent assertions of will and his strange openness and even vulnerability, and it would be inaccurate in any case to insist that insecurity and a propensity to violence are necessarily in opposition to each other; but the fact that the Duke's contradictions are specifically cast as a problem of language ("how shall I say?") indicates an unexpected congruence between his concerns and those that we can attribute to the poet. This link between speaker and poet can be seen from a number of angles. For example, one way to account for the Duke's self-conscious and verbally explicit anticipation of his auditor's reactions is to understand it as a function of the dramatic monologue genre itself, which requires that the poet invent ways to inform us of the listener's response to the speaker without shifting into dialogue. The Duke then verbally anticipates the listener's responses not because this action is strategically advantageous within the context of the scene, but because Browning has to find some way to let us know how the Duke's listener is responding to him. The Duke's mixture of strength and weakness could at least in part be understood as a contradiction inherent to the genre itself, which depends upon a speaker who is both insistent and susceptible to inadvertent self-revelation. (A quick survey will confirm that dramatic monologues in general tend to favor assertive, unstable personalities.) From this point of view, the Duke's character is a direct result of the technical decisions faced by the poet. Rather than representing an independent character that the poet presents from an objective, often ironic distance, the Duke's volubility and instability become a projection of the poet's own generic needs.

One might object that the parallels between the Duke's contradictions and the practical problems facing the poet who constructs a dramatic monologue are merely circumstantial, and are not strong enough to seriously undermine the ironic distance that Browning places between himself and his creation. But there is a final piece of evidence in the poem that suggests that Browning and his Duke are aligned in a more important sense. One of the poem's central themes is the relationship between real human beings and their simulacra. The Duke's relationship to his former Duchess is now a relationship to her portrait (both the one hanging on the wall and the verbal one that he produces for the benefit of the envoy). The poem is concerned with the two, implicitly related ways in which the Duke has made her "his object": by authorizing her representations, and by ensuring that she exists only in the form of these representations by having her killed. This theme bears directly upon Browning's own relationship to his portrait of the Duke. If we can fully separate Browning from the Duke, because the Duke's character has been rendered delimited and fully describable, then the Duke himself becomes a lifeless object, one amenable only to the interpretation of its "owner," the authorial intention and judgment that lurk behind his words. But the poem at least subconsciously diagnoses such a relationship as a kind of murder. We are left with two possibilities: either Browning in a sense does to the Duke what the Duke has done to his first Duchess, in which case the irony of the poem is destabilized and the poem becomes an ironic commentary on Browning's own position; or the Duke becomes larger and more ambiguous than the labels we are able to attach to him, more dimensionally human, like the speaker of a "sincere" lyric or Browning himself. In either case, the poet's problems of representation return uncannily in the personality and situation of the Duke himself, as if a certain kind of irrepressible personal self-consciousness, which cannot be delimited to the speaker's individual self-consciousness, cannot be kept out of even the most distanced, objectified portraits. The separation between speaker and poet cannot fully withstand the subterranean connections between the two.

Such connections, which exceed the natural investment we would expect any poet to have in a character he or she creates, are the norm rather than the exception in Browning's dramatic monologues. A number of his monologues are directly concerned with the nature of art, including "The Bishop Orders his Tomb," "Andrea del Sarto," and "How it Strikes a Contemporary," making a connection between the poet's speakers as artistic creations and his own role as creator. One of the most famous of these, "Fra Lippo Lippi," extends the meditation begun in "My Last

Duchess" on the effect of aesthetic distancing upon human relationships. As in "My Last Duchess," the ability to view another with aesthetic detachment is a source of power, although here power takes a more benign form. Fra Lippo Lippi, caught by night watchmen outside his monastery after hours, interrupts his defense of himself to declare of one of his captors, "He's Judas to a tittle, that man is! / Just such a face."[16] While the monk-as-human-being is in danger, the monk-as-painter can escape his situation by appreciating the suitability of his oppressor as a model for a religious portrait. By the end of the poem, the boundaries between the monk's imagined painting and the scene in which he finds himself have blurred, and the creator enters into his own creation:

> . . . up shall come
> Out of a corner when you least expect,
> As one by a dark stair into a great light,
> Music and talking, who but Lippo! I!—[17]

By drawing our attention to the power and social purposes of Lippo's storytelling (here, it saves him from being arrested by the police), Browning invites us to consider his own choices, investments, and purposes in creating his characters. And just as Lippo's imagined painting opens up to include him, the self-consciousness exhibited by Browning's characters opens up, unexpectedly, to include "who[m] but Browning," the suppressed personal "I."

Eliot and the Breakdown of the Ironic Smile

It is this aspect of the Victorian dramatic monologue—the opportunity it provides for poets to invent characters who then transgress the pre-established boundaries of their created personalities—that is further intensified in modern American poetry.[18] In this section and the next I will consider American poems that, while they are not dramatic monologues in the strictest sense, engage (in order to break) the genre's promise of a full separation between poet and speaker. Perhaps the most famous modernist dramatic monologue is T. S. Eliot's "Love Song of J. Alfred Prufrock." Given Eliot's dictum that "the more perfect the artist, the more completely separate in him will be the man who suffers and the mind which creates,"[19] we might expect that he would be attracted to the dramatic monologue genre, with the promise that it holds of separating the speaker from the poet. But when Eliot discusses Browning's dramatic monologues, he does not emphasize this separation; instead, contrasting the dramatic monologue with drama proper, he expresses skepticism about the poet's ability to separate himself from the character through whom he speaks:

> The fact that a number of characters in a play have claims upon the author, for their allotment of poetic speech, compels him to try to extract the poetry from the character, rather than impose his poetry upon it. Now, in the dramatic monologue we have no such check . . . What we normally hear, in fact, in the dramatic monologue, is the voice of the poet, who has put on the costume and make-up either of some historical character, or of one out of fiction . . . The poet speaking, as Browning does, in his own voice, cannot bring a character to life: he can only mimic a character otherwise known to us. And does not the point of mimicry lie in the recognition of the person mimicked, and in the incompleteness of the illusion? We have to be aware that the mimic and the person mimicked are different people: if we are actually deceived, mimicry becomes impersonation.[20]

This passage suggests that Eliot believes that, rather than maintaining the distinction between speaker and poet, the dramatic monologue deliberately makes this distinction "incomplete," as we discovered in somewhat different terms in Browning's "My Last Duchess." While this passage more obviously applies to Eliot's turn from poetic to theatrical writing than to his early poetry, "The Love Song of J. Alfred Prufrock" offers an especially memorable spectacle of an incomplete separation between speaker and poet, between dramatic personality and self-conscious human being.

"Prufrock" exhibits a number of the conventions of a strict dramatic monologue: the title of the poem marks its speaker as separate from the poet; the speaker addresses an explicit "you"; and the poem includes a momentous exchange with a specific auditor (a lady who appears to be a potential love interest), which, although we are to imagine it as a dialogue, is narrated in monologue form. The poem in turn deliberately distorts each of these conventions: it is difficult to distinguish the "you" that the poem addresses from ourselves, the readers of the poem; and instead of staging a single scene of revelation, the poem moves between the everyday, the mythical, and the surreal, sometimes in a single sentence.[21] But most important, the poem radically expands each of the kinds of blurring between poet and speaker that we witnessed in "My Last Duchess."

First of all, Prufrock's self-consciousness makes it nearly impossible to distinguish his own perspective on himself from that which we can attribute to Eliot. We can see the difficulty of maintaining this distinction through the example of a critic who expends great analytical energy in doing so. Robert McNamara argues that "Prufrock" is a parody of what he understands as the paralyzing Victorian self-consciousness that beset Eliot's predecessors:

> ["The Love Song of J. Alfred Prufrock"] offers a critique of the fantasies of coherent selfhood and the representational forms that support it, and . . . shows Prufrock's paralysis as the result, in large part, of his desire for a totalizing image of himself. Eliot is aware of the problem [of the bourgeois narcissism of modern literature that] Lukács identifies, but unlike Lukács, Eliot recognizes that the ideology of the unified, coherent self is part of the problem, not part of the solution.[22]

According to McNamara, Prufrock's problem (the difficulty of formulating a coherent self) is emphatically not Eliot's problem. Working from this assumption, McNamara contrasts Prufrock's "Voice" with what he identifies as the authorial intention (or "acts") that implicitly criticize this voice. As McNamara sees it, Prufrock's "inadvertent self-disclosures" can be measured against "the authorial acts that reveal the contradictions the Voice would conceal."[23] In other words, McNamara reads Prufrock's fragmentation as the symptom of a problem that Eliot has diagnosed. But how can we be sure that Eliot does not share Prufrock's disease?

Because Prufrock exhibits an almost overwhelming amount of self-consciousness (it is the most marked trait of his personality), it becomes difficult, if not impossible, to separate what Prufrock knows about himself from what we can imagine that Eliot knows about Prufrock. For example, Prufrock declares:

> . . . I am not Prince Hamlet, nor was meant to be;
> Am an attendant lord, one that will do
> To swell a progress, start a scene or two,
> Advise the prince; no doubt, an easy tool,
> Deferential, glad to be of use,
> Politic, cautious, and meticulous;
> Full of high sentence, but a bit obtuse;
> At times, indeed, almost ridiculous—
> Almost, at times, the Fool.[24]

Can Eliot believe anything worse of Prufrock than Prufrock believes of himself? Passages such as this one would seem to present a problem for the distinction that McNamara attempts to make between Prufrock's attitude and Eliot's criticism of Prufrock's attitude. McNamara contains this problem by positing authorial intention at one more remove:

> The voice of self-analysis . . . produces only one more identification with an established, conventional, and hence falsifying pose, and repeatedly proves, despite its implicit claims to disinterest, to be fully self-interested. Authorial action takes place in a space not falsified by rhetorical masks and the demands of personality, and as such can make and sustain greater claims than can be sustained by such a voice.[25]

McNamara insists that Prufrock's attempts at self-analysis are "falsifying," while Eliot's implicit analysis of Prufrock is authentic. But at this point we must ask, how can he tell the difference? The only figure that could guarantee such a complete separation between poet and speaker is a poet who appears to be barely human, independent as he must be from the claims of rhetoric and of personality. This idea of authorship is surely as much a fantasy of unified and effective selfhood as the fantasy that McNamara understands Eliot to be attacking.[26] The proximity of "The Love Song of J. Alfred Prufrock" to the dramatic monologue form makes it possible to imagine that a complete separation between speaker and poet has been achieved, but this fantasy (we cannot locate an "Eliot" who definitively shares or renounces it) remains vulnerable to the poem's own procedures.

"Prufrock" just as dramatically expands the connection we found in "My Last Duchess" between the artistic problems that must be resolved by the poet and the problems of identity and destiny that must be resolved by the speaker. For example, Prufrock refers to the necessity of "prepar[ing] a face to meet the faces that you meet,"[27] and in a parallel sense, Eliot prepares in Prufrock a face to meet the reader. When Prufrock asserts, "I have known the eyes already . . . / The eyes that fix you in a formulated phrase,"[28] it is almost as if Prufrock says to us, "You, reader, may wish to fix me as a character separate from Eliot, but my very consciousness of this possibility suggests that such a fixing would be incomplete." And in a fundamental way, Prufrock himself questions whether the genre of the dramatic monologue, as well as the genre of the "sincere" lyric, is possible. When Prufrock asks: "And should I then presume? / And how should I begin?"[29] it is as if he asks: In what voice can I speak, and to whom can I speak? How is it possible for any of us to speak, in or out of character, and who will know how to hear us?

At this point, a basic question arises: why does the poem need an explicit distinction between Eliot and his speaker in the first place? What function does the character of Prufrock serve? The poem offers one answer in the form of its epigraph, which attempts to establish the conditions in which a confession can be made that, because of its special circumstances, remains off the record. In this epigraph, one of the damned souls trapped in Dante's *Inferno* prefaces his story with these words: "If I thought that my reply would be to someone who would ever return to earth, this flame would remain without further movement; but as no one has ever returned alive from this gulf, if what I hear is true, I can answer you with no fear of infamy."[30] The soul who speaks here is willing to speak openly only on the condition that his listener remains trapped with him in his own element. This entrapment is in an important sense illusionary: Dante will carry the stories he learns in hell back to the world of the living. But the temporary illusion is an enabling one—it suggests that the privilege of fiction is to allow a confession that is not a confession, an honesty that would be impossible under other conditions. Eliot's fiction of the character Prufrock, we are given to understand, allows him a freer mode of expression than would be possible in his own voice. At the end of the poem, the artificial yet imaginable space marked out by the vestiges of the dramatic monologue genre collapses: "human voices wake us, and we drown."[31] Once the poem awakens from the conditions of its own being, and we hear actual "human voices," not just the voice of a persona, disclosure is no longer possible.

But the function of Prufrock as a character is more incendiary than this otherworldly epigraph and closing would suggest. Prufrock's defining personality trait is his self-consciousness, and at the same time this self-consciousness destroys personality in the sense of an individual destiny, or in the sense of a collection of meaningful experiences that add up to a distinct identity. The specter of self-revelation, the central drama of the dramatic monologue, is continually conjured up only to be dismissed. At the opening of the poem, Prufrock acknowledges the possible existence of "an overwhelming question" that the poem might answer, but just as quickly swerves away from it: "Oh, do not ask, 'What is it?' / Let us go and make our visit."[32] Toward the ending of the poem, the pattern is repeated: "Would it have been worth while, / . . . To have squeezed the universe into a ball / To roll it toward some overwhelming question?"[33] The implicit answer that the poem gives is "no." One reason why the "overwhelming question" of the poem is deemed unanswerable or meaningless is that the speaker's anticipation of the auditor's responses, another convention of the dramatic monologue given demonic force in this poem, completely destroys the possibility of transformative exchange. Prufrock asks:

> Would it have been worthwhile . . .
> To say: "I am Lazarus, come from the dead,
> Come back to tell you all, I shall tell you all"—

> If one, settling a pillow by her head,
> Should say: "That is not what I meant at all.
> That is not it, at all."[34]

Others cannot save Prufrock from his own self-consciousness and give his life shape and meaning because this self-consciousness has too completely anticipated them. Instead, the poem replaces the linear time of dramatic revelation with the circular time of self-consciousness, "time yet for a hundred indecisions, / And for a hundred visions and revisions / Before the taking of a toast and tea."[35] Prufrock's fluctuations of self-consciousness prohibit a definitive revelation of character, a character that would imply a dramatic scenario, or that could become a destiny beyond the fate of paralysis.

In "Prufrock" we find a human being beset by post-Romantic self-consciousness and struggling to live with sincerity pitted implicitly against the idea of a dramatic character who maintains an unbreachable core of individuality and rises heroically to meet his destiny. Ultimately, the poem's impact remains intact, despite familiarity and generations of imitators, because it manages to keep both creatures alive, and with them a poet who both is and is not Prufrock, who can stage Prufrock as a somewhat pathetic character, but who lends Prufrock a self-consciousness that, while implicitly criticized, cannot be condescended to, for the poet himself cannot escape its fate. Prufrock, the hesitant creature, unable to take any decisive action, is met by the Prufrock who suffers from a terrible fluency, a conflagration of the mixture of coldness and expansiveness we encountered in Browning's Duke. The poem systematically brings "My Last Duchess" to its logical conclusion—the spectacle of a personality destroying itself.

Eliot's "Portrait of a Lady" stages a quieter battle between the conventions of the sincere, self-expressive lyric and the dramatic monologue. It narrows its focus to a more specialized form of self-consciousness, examining the usefulness of maintaining the distance that "Prufrock" discards—the ironic distance between poet and character that the dramatic monologue form is supposed to entail. The poem is not a dramatic monologue in any strict sense of the term. We are given two speakers rather than one: the "lady" of the title, who speaks as a monologuist would, revealing her particular personality to us through her style of speech and through what she leaves unsaid; and the "I" of the poem, who is not explicitly marked as separate from the poet, and who offers his reaction—not aloud, but only mentally—to what the lady says. The poem, then, is designed to make audible what the strict dramatic monologue leaves silent: the inner reaction of the auditor to the speaker. The poem holds to the conventions of the dramatic monologue, however, in the sense that the "I" never answers the lady directly in the poem, but speaks *sotto voce* to himself (and to us). What we have here, then, is a monologue with silent interior commentary, rather than a dialogue.

This commentary addresses the tension implicit in the strict dramatic monologue, in which we can imagine a rebellious listener being forcibly held in place by unrelenting speech. For example, the lady comments:

> "So intimate, this Chopin, that I think his soul
> Should be resurrected only among friends
> Some two or three, who will not touch the bloom
> That is rubbed and questioned in the concert room."
> —And so the conversation slips
> Among velleities and carefully caught regrets
> Through attenuated tones of violins
> Mingled with remote cornets
> And begins.[36]

With the phrase "carefully caught," the speaker of the poem draws our attention to the deliberateness of the lady's speech, and thus encouraged to read between the lines we notice the tentative but at the same time aggressive assumption of intimacy on her part. This aggression can be understood not only to represent the lady's particular personality, but also as an aggression latent in the Romantic belief that sympathy is at the center of aesthetic experience—the sincere Romantic poet's assumption of and demand upon the reader's imaginative involvement. Further evidence for this reading comes in the poem's later reference to Matthew Arnold's "The Buried Life," which depicts the Romantic desire for a fully honest communion between souls. As B. C. Southam sees it, "Portrait of a Lady" is "a re-writing of ["The Buried Life"] as a *conversation galante,* a complex statement, with shifting tones of irony, quite different from the relative simplicity of Arnold's singleness of tone and feeling."[37] From this perspective, "Portrait of a Lady" is not only about a battle of wills between the lady and her auditor; it is about a tension between the sincere lyric (represented by the lady's open, intimate speech) and the dramatic monologue (which puts the lady's speech in quotation marks and indicates that it may be as much manipulative as sincere). In its consideration of the social roles that undergird any act of communication, the poem raises the questions: to what extent are we doomed to or saved by sincere speech? to what extent are we doomed to play social roles, or saved by them?

Given the placement of the lady's "sincere" confessions to her auditor in quotation marks, and given what we know of Eliot's distrust of sincerity as an aesthetic criterion more generally, we might expect this poem to unambiguously stake its allegiance with the dramatic monologue rather than the sincere lyric, to choose the freedom of ironic distance over the claustrophobia of sincere speech. But this preference is exactly what the poem comes to question. We receive a hint of the instability of the ironic distance that the "I" in the poem struggles to maintain in the second section of the poem:

> You will see me any morning in the park
> Reading the comics and the sporting page.
> Particularly I remark
> An English countess goes upon the stage.
> A Greek was murdered at a Polish dance,
> Another bank defaulter has confessed.
> I keep my countenance,
> I remain self-possessed
> Except when a street piano, mechanical and tired
> Reiterates some worn-out common song
> With the smell of hyacinths across the garden
> Recalling things that other people have desired.
> Are these ideas right or wrong?[38]

This passage presents a reductive version of the transformation of human beings into characters. Just as the English countess, murdered Greek, and bank defaulter are distant and faintly ridiculous, the lady whose portrait Eliot gives us can herself be summed up as "the *précieuse ridicule* to end all preciosity, serving tea so exquisitely among her bric-a-brac,"[39] the complete removal of sympathy sufficient to render her harmless. But the fact that the "I" bothers to "remark" the human foibles recorded in the tabloids suggests that, despite their tawdriness, they hold some interest for him, and his apparent detachment is given the lie when he is undone by the music of the street piano.[40] Though the performance is poor, and the song a cliché, it has the power to move the speaker, and by extension we suspect that the worn-out, common clichés of the tabloids also have the unexpected power to move, if the combination of elements is suggestive enough. The speaker here indicates the difficulty of maintaining an ironic pose that separates himself from the lady, and himself from Eliot. People in this poem threaten to become mere characters but at the same time keep insisting upon their own uncategorizable life, and the speaker cannot decide which perspective is more valuable.

That what is at stake is not only the speaker's relationship to the lady but also his relationship to himself becomes clear in another exchange. When the speaker returns to tell the lady he will be going abroad, she replies:

> "Perhaps you can write to me."
> My self-possession flares up for a second;
> *This* is as I had reckoned.
> "I have been wondering frequently of late
> (But our beginnings never know our ends!)
> Why we have not developed into friends."
> I feel like one who smiles, and turning shall remark
> Suddenly, his expression in a glass.
> My self-possession gutters; we are really in the dark.[41]

Here the boundary that has been drawn between the detached, observing self and the vulnerable, participating self is undone. When the lady says something predictable, the speaker's self-possession flares up because she is behaving like a stereotype, someone he has already classified and whose limits he understands. But then the lady drops part of her mask in the social exchange. She ceases to presume upon the friendship between herself and the speaker and instead admits that the friendship never really existed (while at the same time alluding perhaps to a more intimate relationship that they have shared). This admission still happens in an atmosphere of manipulation: when the lady claims that "our beginnings never know our ends," the first person plural again demands acquiescence, and we have reason to doubt whether she says anything without some sense of the "end" effect it will have on her listener. But this new mixture of direct honesty and indirect manipulation is enough to unsettle the speaker. Suddenly, he recognizes himself in what he thought was mere role-playing: his attitude may be ironic, but he cannot escape the nonironic implications of the scene in which he takes part. He sees himself as separate from himself (in the mirror), but in a way that imposes an unwanted recognition, not in a way that reinforces detachment. We might imagine that in an analogous way, Eliot both recognizes himself and fails to recognize himself in the poem. His self-possession permits him to see both the lady and his own stand-in as distantly regarded and therefore harmless characters, but the possibility of suddenly recognizing himself in either character holds this self-possession under perpetual threat.

Throughout the poem, as in this passage, the speaker's ability to smile at the circumstances in which he finds himself has been the measure of his detachment. Early in the poem the lady charges: "[Y]outh is cruel, and has no remorse / And smiles at situations which it cannot see." The speaker tells us, "I smile, of course."[42] At the poem's close, the speaker imagines that the lady has died while he is still trying to compose a letter to her and describes himself as:

> Doubtful, for a while
> Not knowing what to feel or if I understand
> Or whether wise or foolish, tardy or too soon . . .
> Would she not have the advantage, after all?
> This music is successful with a "dying fall"
> Now that we talk of dying—
> And should I have the right to smile?[43]

The speaker addresses us directly, and it seems at this point as if Eliot speaks, not his persona. The question of the right of detachment, the "right to smile," remains radically open in this poem, which heightens the tension latent in all dramatic monologues—the tension between people as recognizable types or characters playing a particular social role, and people as unpredictable, multi-dimensional beings; the tension between the identification of the poet with his speaker and his separation from this speaker. The question of the right to smile is also opened up by Arnold's "Buried Life," which laments:

> Yes, yes, we know that we can jest,
> We know, we know that we can smile!
> But there's a something in this breast,
> To which thy light words bring no rest.[44]

Though Eliot resists Arnold's conclusion that, after all, moments occur when "the heart lies plain,"[45] his poem, like Arnold's, circles around that "something" in the breast that seems eternally on the brink of expressibility. Eliot's perspective is surprisingly close to that of Arnold when he makes explicit the way in which every dramatic monologue questions the circumstances under which we have the right to the ironic smile of detachment.

Berryman's Nonfunctional Speaker

Like innovative poets before and since, Robert Browning has been credited with bringing colloquial speech into English poetry in a new way. One measure of the distance between the sincere lyric and the dramatic monologue is the difference between the colloquial impulse in Words-worth's poetry and in Browning's. In Wordsworth's imagining, poetic language is to be made suitable for sincere speech by becoming less marked as a specialized discourse. In Browning's imagining, poetic language is to be made suitable for individualistic speech by becoming as specialized as possible, so that we believe in the authenticity of Fra Lippo Lippi's speech because it sounds completely different from the speech of the Duke. Eliot's quasi–dramatic monologues represent to some degree a movement away from this reorientation toward the vernacular. These poems are no longer written in conversational blank verse, and their uneven line lengths, rhyme, and allusion characterize them as specialized poetic speech as well as the speech of a unique personality. (Along this line of development, we might view the highly particularized styles of poets such as Hopkins or Roethke as constituting, in disparate ways, a different kind of "dramatic monologue," one in which the life of the speaker is set apart from the daily life of the poet by the distance of his language from ordinary speech.) Representing a different line of development, John Berryman's *Dream Songs* attempt in a sense to re-naturalize the dramatic monologue. By incorporating slang, by appearing to unselectively represent the more or less random movements of human consciousness, and most of all by restaging the gap between poet and speaker as a natural function of self-consciousness, Berryman presses the dramatic monologue back in the direction of personally direct, sincere speech.

Berryman's *Dream Songs* are dramatic monologues in the inclusive sense in which I have been using the term: the speaker, named Henry, is explicitly set apart from the poet. Henry's speech, while incorporating colloquial elements, is difficult, shifting, and fragmented. Here, for example, is the opening of Dream Song 57:

> In a state of chortle sin—once he reflected,
> swilling tomato juice—live I, and did
> more than my thirstier years.
> To Hell then will it maul me? for good talk,
> and gripe of retail loss? I dare say not.
> I don't think there's that place
>
> save sullen here, wherefrom she flies tonight
> retrieving her whole body, which I need.[46]

This passage has a number of colloquial features: slang ("swilling," "gripe"), syntax that seems to conform more to the temporal flow of speech than to any particular logic, and phrases that we would be more likely to find in ordinary conversation than in poetry ("I don't think there's that place," "which I need"). But at the same time, the colloquial flow is broken up (and the poem made difficult to read out loud) by nouns or verbs made to do the work of adjectives ("chortle sin"), adjectives put in the "wrong" context ("sullen here"), and syntax that is mock-poetic or simply peculiar ("live I," "To Hell then will it maul me," "wherefrom she flies tonight"). In fact, Berryman's practice makes it difficult to distinguish between language that is broken or "wrong" for the purpose of imitating ordinary speech, and language that is broken or dislocated for the purpose of defamiliarization and poetic effect. The acute accent on "think" is a good example of this ambiguity: it makes it necessary to read the phrase out loud in order to get its meaning ("I don't *think* there's that place" sounds more equivocal than without the emphasis), which gives it a conversational impact; but the accent also looks like the marks put in to show how a poem's meter is to be read, setting the phrase apart from conversational speech. Berryman takes to an extreme a tension found in Browning's poetry: while Browning is admired for contributing to the colloquial flexibility of English poetry, his readers have sometimes found that his use of specialized speech makes his poems more difficult to read.[47] Berryman's poems do not flow like natural speech (and they include such poetic markers as use of the sonnet form, consistent stanza breaks, and frequent rhyme), but he extends the colloquial in the sense that he creates the kind of speech that might result if we were to say out loud everything that we thought or felt.

Berryman naturalizes the dramatic monologue in another sense by differentiating the poet and speaker without placing them in conflict with each other. Although Henry and the poet are set apart from each other, they appear to work as counterparts, speaking in one consistently inconsistent voice that veers from self-parody to pathos and back again. The preface that Berryman appends to the *Dream Songs,* meant to underline the separation between speaker and poet, also shows the ways in which such a separation is, in a sense, unimportant:

> The poem then, whatever its wide cast of characters, is essentially about an imaginary character (not the poet, not me) named Henry, a white American in early middle age sometimes in blackface, who has suffered an irreversible loss and talks about himself sometimes in the first person, sometimes in the third, sometimes even in the second; he has a friend, never named, who addresses him as Mr. Bones and variants thereof.[48]

This passage indicates some indifference toward speaking masked ("in blackface") or not, toward whether one speaks in the first, second, or third person, toward what one is named (if "Henry" and "Mr. Bones," why not "John Berryman"?), and toward the identity of the person who addresses one. The *Dream Songs* indeed offer a dizzying array of modes of address, sometimes within individual poems: as we have been warned, Henry sometimes speaks in the first person and is sometimes described by a more or less omniscient third-person narrator (also, according to the preface, to be identified as "Henry"). At times, Henry speaks in a black dialect that sets him apart from Berryman, and at other times he seems to act as a mouthpiece for Berryman's opinions (see, for example, "Rilke was a *jerk*" in Dream Song 3). The final effect of all these fluctuations, paradoxically, is not to multiply or fragment the personality expressed in these poems, but to consolidate it, because whether it is in first or third person, whether masked or direct, the characteristics that come through are consistent.

Although this effect can only be appreciated through a wider sampling of the 385 Dream Songs than is possible here, some of its features can be seen in poems in which there is an apparent split between Henry and an unnamed "I," for example, in Dream Song 14. The "I" who speaks this song complains that life bores him; even "Henry bores [him]."[49] While this statement suggests that the "I" and "Henry" cannot be identical, the "I" voice speaks in Henry's idiom. If the "I" of a lyric poem tends to be associated with the poet, here Henry, to whom is attributed a love of "valiant art," seems to be more of a poet than the "I," who claims to be bored by great literature. But in the end, the point of the poem appears to be that the "I" is bored with himself, and that "Henry" is just another name for himself. The problem with admitting boredom, according to the speaker's mother, is that "'Ever to confess you're bored / means you have no / Inner Resources.'"[50] If anything is "confessed" here, it is that there is nothing to confess, that one has no "inner resources," perhaps no interiority at all. Under the circumstances, the "I" is thrown back on external resources, such as the fictional character "Henry" who can reflect the "I" without claiming to represent the poet's inner depths.

Perhaps even more important than the indifference the *Dream Songs* show to the distinction between the "I" and "Henry" is the indifference the sequence shows to the distinction between monologue and dialogue. Berryman creates a world in which talking to oneself becomes indistinguishable from talking to others. Here, for example, is "Henry's Confession" (Dream Song 76):

Nothin very bad happen to me lately.
How you explain that?—I explain that, Mr Bones,

terms o' your baffling odd sobriety.
Sober as man can get, no girls, no telephones,
what could happen bad to Mr Bones?
—If life is a handkerchief sandwich

in a modesty of death I join my father
who dared so long agone leave me.
A bullet on a concrete stoop
close by a smothering southern sea
spreadeagled on an island, by my knee.
—You is from hunger, Mr Bones,

I offers you this handkerchief, now set
your left foot by my right foot,
shoulder to shoulder, all that jazz,
arm in arm, by the beautiful sea,
hum a little, Mr Bones.
—I saw nobody coming, so I went instead.[51]

It takes some concentration to separate these two voices into dialogue be-
cause they both use discontinuous tones and logic, which suggests they
are part of a larger fabric of discontinuity instead of representing a simple
binary division. The speaker of the poem, presumably Henry (and called
"Mr Bones" by his interlocutor), says that nothing bad has happened to
him lately, speculates that "life is a handkerchief sandwich," alludes to
the suicide of his father, and speaks the final line. Henry's addressee, who
remains unnamed (though one is tempted to call him "Mr Bones," a con-
fusion that seems to be built into the poem, as if it resists our separation
of the dialogue into two voices), explains Henry's relative good luck
(though in terms that do not seem to belong to Henry, who has never
been known for his sobriety or sexual continence), says "You is from
hunger," and proposes a minstrel-show song and dance as comfort.[52] The
two speakers are distinct in the sense that one alludes to sadness and the
other acts as comforter, but the poem makes more sense when under-
stood as Berryman-Henry comforting himself (among other things, with
the "jazz" of his own song) than as a recognizable "other" comforting
him. By breaking down the distinction between speaker and poet, and be-
tween talking to oneself and talking to another, Berryman refuses the re-
sources that the dramatic monologue originally offered: the opportunity
to speak in a voice other than one's own and the opportunity to imagine a
listener for that voice.

At this point, we may well wonder why Berryman chooses to write under the name of "Henry" in the first place. William Martz, for example, concludes:

> Henry, in sum, is a brilliant but insufficient unifying device. The question of how imaginary he is, and of how much the real-life John Berryman he is, is important only insofar as the poem creates a nonfunctional tension between the two. Who would object if Henry were wholly imaginary and one were hardly able to see or to care about a reference to the real-life John Berryman in the poem? Who would object if Berryman deliberately wrote an autobiographical and perhaps even a confessional poem? What we care about is only that the poem exists beautifully as a poem, and yet in the final analysis the device *is* the poem, and so it is unsettling to lose our sense of the fictional Henry in favor of the quasi-fictional Berryman.[53]

Martz implies that, unless the separation between Berryman and Henry serves a particular function (for example, the function that we have seen in other dramatic monologues of opening the possibility of ironic distance between poet and speaker), it becomes a mere distraction, and straightforward autobiography would be more effective. His term "nonfunctional" in one sense describes Berryman's strategy perfectly in relation to other kinds of dramatic monologue: Berryman dismantles the distancing function of the dramatic monologue as it is used by the poets who preceded him. But rather than serving as a distracting obstacle to what might have been a more straightforwardly autobiographical poetry, Henry is the method by which Berryman is able to write autobiographical poetry. The poems convince us that Berryman himself habitually thinks of himself in the third person, and that he calls himself Henry. The name "Henry" is simply Berryman's device for describing his personal self-consciousness (the way in which all of us to some extent think of ourselves in the third person), rather than the marking of a separate consciousness.[54] That Henry is necessary to Berryman's autobiographical project, rather than an avoidance of it, is suggested by "Henry's Confession," quoted above. The circumstances of Henry's father's suicide (also the circumstances of Berryman's father's suicide) are stated in the middle stanza and framed by the need for comfort, but the pressure to make them mean something is resisted. They are not interpreted through a lyrical meditation; they are simply juxtaposed with a song and dance. Berryman's invention of Henry creates a space in which the events and tragedies of a life can be presented without the potentially falsifying pressure to make them meaningful. Here we see the use of the "nonfunctional" separation between speaker and poet in his poetry.

Of course, this resistance to meaning, this casting of self-consciousness as a multiplication of surface styles instead of a path to emotional depth, carries risks together with its fragile promise of authenticity; and Berryman's refusal of the resources of the dramatic monologue has implications beyond the relative success or failure of his own verse. The achievement and limitations of his poetry can be summed up in the observation that self-consciousness is no longer a difficulty for the poet. As in would-be sincere lyrics, the *Dream Songs* revolve around tentative, difficult acts of introspection, but they lack the accompanying pressure toward unity and integration. In Wordsworth's poetry, for example, we discovered a tantalizing contradiction between revelation and concealment. But because Henry-Berryman feels no moral urgency to present himself as a coherent, consistently responsible individual, he has no motive to conceal autobiographical facts, and the reader is not involved in a dramatic tension between what the speaker is willing to reveal and what the poet is compelled to conceal. The *Dream Songs* often make reference to Henry's sense of exposure: "I don't see how Henry, pried / open for all the world to see, survived" (Dream Song 1); "We are using our own skins for wallpaper and we cannot win" (Dream Song 53); "I am obliged to perform in complete darkness / operations of great delicacy / on my self" (Dream Song 67).[55] But these claims for the life-and-death significance of self-exposure remain mere claims—they have no dramatic life in the poem. As an audience, we are not addressed as an "other" expected to judge what we are told, but are simply included as an extension of Berryman's self-consciousness.

Just as the *Dream Songs* escape the strain but also lose the focus and drive of the putatively sincere lyric, they avoid the dissonance of ambiguous conflict between the speaker of a poem and its creator, but also lose the friction generated when we are forced to consider to what degree speaker and poet are morally at odds. From the most sympathetic standpoint, Berryman is credited with greater moral awareness than Henry. Martz, for example, writes that although the poems sometimes express "great insecurity and immaturity of personality," Berryman "recognize[s], simultaneously, the grief of it all and seek[s], as always, a mature understanding of it. Put another way, there is a strong element of defensiveness in his personality, but since this is coupled with piercing honesty he emerges as a poet who delves into life and takes us with him."[56] But it is fair to ask whether we can equate the nonconfrontational self-consciousness that allows Berryman, Henry, and their interlocutors to function interchangeably with moral awareness on Berryman's part. Under these conditions, Berryman's ability to think of himself in the third person through the figure of Henry is not proof that he knows or understands more than Henry himself does.

In Eliot's "Prufrock" and "Portrait of a Lady," the conventions of the sincere lyric and the conventions of the dramatic monologue are juxtaposed and put into battle against each other. The charm of Berryman's poetry is the way in which the character Henry, self-deprecating but also capable of humiliation and genuine hurt, makes it seem as if the dust on the battlefield has cleared and these competing models have been fully reconciled. The *Dream Songs* intimate some of the energies that thinking of oneself in the third person allow one to release, and give us the psychological process of creating and voicing a persona instead of the finished, relatively impenetrable product of a completed personality. They render self-consciousness as an impetus to fluent speech rather than a limit on the poet's freedom. But because they lose both the centripetal pressure of sincerity and the centrifugal pressure of the dramatic monologue, they remind us what we gain when these two genres are practiced in more absolute and contentious forms. American poetry cannot finally resolve the conflict between Romantic sincerity and the Victorian and modern reactions against sincerity; it must continue to restage it.

Biography, Moral Value, and the Boundaries of the Dramatic Monologue

In Browning's dramatic monologue "Bishop Blougram's Apology," the speaker tells us that

> Our interest's on the dangerous edge of things.
> The honest thief, the tender murderer,
> The superstitious atheist, demirep
> That loves and saves her soul in new French books—
> We watch while these in equilibrium keep
> The giddy line midway: one step aside,
> They're classed and done with.[57]

The dramatic monologue, in other words, must maintain a tension between two-dimensional stereotypes, whose moral condition we can evaluate with confidence, and three-dimensional beings, who are defined in part by their unpredictable ability to contradict themselves. This tension not only shapes the characters we encounter in such poems; it also has implications for our understanding of the relationship between these characters and their creator. We have just seen how the self-consciousness of a character within a dramatic monologue destabilizes the genre internally, compromising the distinction between the speaker and the poet. But this distinction is also threatened by the external contingencies of moral valuation and the availability of biographical information. One of the reasons we are certain that Browning does not mean for us to identify him with the Duke is that the Duke is a murderer, and it is safe to assume that Browning disapproves of murder. It is also easy to keep the Duke and Browning separate because there are no tantalizing biographical correspondences between the speaker's and the poet's lives that link the two. The task of reading would become more complicated if, for example, we were told that Browning himself was an Italian Duke whose wife had died under mysterious circumstances. But what happens when the values represented by a speaker in a poem cannot be judged according to a general consensus, or when biographical information relates the speaker and the poet while the poem marks their difference?

In the example of "My Last Duchess," the dramatic monologue works as a conservative genre in the sense that it expresses values that have already been determined (in this case, the value of the worth of human life) rather than opening up the question of value. But critics have long maintained that the dramatic monologue is, or at least can be, a radically open-ended form. Most influentially, Robert Langbaum argues that this genre serves the needs of a society that is questioning and testing new values.[58] He believes that the dramatic monologue is defined by a tension between sympathy and judgment, and that this tension provides a method by which Romantic and Victorian writers "find and justify new values" in the wake of the Enlightenment.[59] In his reading of "My Last Duchess," then, Langbaum argues that we sympathize with the Duke more strongly than we judge him: "What interests us more than the duke's wickedness is his immense attractiveness . . . We suspend moral judgment because we prefer to participate in the duke's power and freedom, in his hard core of character fiercely loyal to itself."[60] Langbaum's reading, whether we ratify it or not, points to a source of instability within the dramatic monologue form—an instability that is multiplied when we cannot be certain whether the poet believes his or her speaker's statements are condemnable.

This question of moral value is one of the central factors that distinguishes the would-be sincere lyric from the dramatic monologue. When faced with a poem spoken in an "I" voice that may or may not be separate from the voice of the poet, one way for the reader to determine the genre of the poem is to measure the distance of the speaker's implied values from what can be assumed about the poet's values. This measurement is not always easily taken; in fact, it is not always clear when such a distance exists. For example, Robert Lowell says of Anne Sexton: "Many of her most embarrassing poems would have been fascinating if someone had put them in quotes, as the presentation of some character, not the author."[61] In other words, according to Lowell, stances that are unacceptable in putatively sincere lyrics may be made acceptable by the distancing implied by a separation of speaker and poet, a distancing that assures us that the poet knows that the speaker's attitudes are in some way inadequate. But where and how do we see these saving quotation marks? If Lowell can see clearly that the speakers in some of Sexton's poems are "embarrassing," could not this observation be evidence enough that their statements are in implicit quotation marks, just as our assumption that Browning does not share the Duke of Ferrara's attitudes helps prevent us from confusing the poet and the speaker? E. R. Harty summarizes this dilemma even-handedly:

> In those dramatic poems with an individualized speaker to whom pathological, unwholesome, limited, or unbalanced states of mind or opinions must be attributed, there is a natural reluctance on the part of the reader of normal sensibility to identify the speaker as the poet, even when none of the situational parameters serve to alienate the speaker's voice and the poem is otherwise ostensibly a personal statement. In those cases the poems will be read as dramatic monologues as a preferred interpretative strategy, unless biographical evidence from the cultural code shows a clear correspondence between the author and his persona. Some poems seem to contend with themselves in this respect, manifesting an irreconcilable clash of opposing forces of attraction and repulsion between speaker and poet.[62]

In the absence of clear markers of a distinction between poet and speaker, the extent to which we separate the poet from the speaker will depend in part upon the assumptions we can make about the values they do or do not share, the confidence with which we can agree upon what counts as a "pathological, unwholesome, limited, or unbalanced state of mind" that must necessarily be understood at a slant to the plumb line of the author's intention.[63] The example of Anne Sexton serves as an index of how contentious such an attempt at agreement might be—what may appear pathological or unwholesome in her poetry from a traditional standpoint (such as her treatment of themes like masturbation and menstruation) may seem natural or salutary from a feminist standpoint. But I want to suggest that the questions of value at stake in measuring the possible distance between speaker and poet are not new to recent canonical debates (though these debates put new pressure on them); rather, these questions represent an inherent instability in the dramatic monologue model of poetry itself.

Two poems, one Victorian and one modern, illustrate the persistent functioning of this instability. In Tennyson's "Ulysses" and Sylvia Plath's

"Lady Lazarus," the question of the relationship between the speaker of the poem and the poet is complicated by our uncertainty about the extent to which the poet shares the speaker's values. And this question is complicated further still by biographical continuities that link the poet with the speaker even as they are being marked as separate. In the first case, "Ulysses" exhibits the minimal requirements of a dramatic monologue—the speaker of the poem (Ulysses) is distanced historically and mythologically from the poet, and the occasion of his speech is provided by a preexisting story, not by the life of the poet. But this clarity has not guaranteed a consistent interpretation of the poem. Instead, critical opinion has been sharply divided: are we to understand Ulysses as a simple mouthpiece through which Tennyson can express his own feelings, or does Tennyson set himself at an ironic distance from his speaker? In the first reading, importance is given to Tennyson's own comment that the poem "was written soon after Hallam's death, and gave my feeling about the need for going forward, and braving the struggle of life."[64] The following famous and stirring lines are then understood as bracing Tennyson for this struggle:

> I am a part of all that I have met;
> Yet all experience is an arch wherethro'
> Gleams that untravell'd world, whose margin fades
> For ever and for ever when I move . . .
> And this gray spirit [is] yearning in desire
> To follow knowledge like a sinking star,
> Beyond the utmost bound of human thought . . .
> [Although w]e are not now that strength which in old days
> Moved earth and heaven, that which we are, we are,—
> One equal temper of heroic hearts,
> Made weak by time and fate, but strong in will
> To strive, to seek, to find, and not to yield.[65]

In the second reading, Tennyson's own statement about the meaning of the poem is set aside (or reinterpreted to suggest that Ulysses' example of "braving the struggle of life" is to be shunned rather than embraced),[66] and the parts of the poem in which Ulysses seems to treat his family and his people unfairly are highlighted:

> It little profits that an idle king,
> By this still hearth, among these barren crags,
> Match'd with an aged wife, I mete and dole

> Unequal laws unto a savage race,
> That hoard, and sleep, and feed, and know not me.[67]

This reading suggests that we are to join Tennyson in condemning Ulysses not only for condescending to his son, Telemachus, with lukewarm praise and the dismissive, "He works his work, I mine," but also for undertaking a journey that amounts to suicide.[68] Under these circumstances, we must understand Tennyson to be placing an ironic distance between himself and his speaker.

There is no final way to choose between these two readings. When we examine lines such as those describing the desire "[t]o follow knowledge like a sinking star / Beyond the utmost bound of human thought,"[69] we might object that knowledge and movement are being falsely conflated here, because the poem is notably vague about the content or value of the knowledge that Ulysses will gain. But it is impossible to say for certain how harshly we should judge this conflation, or whether we should attribute it to Ulysses or to Tennyson himself. External evidence multiplies the problems rather than solving them. For example, the possibility that Tennyson based his Ulysses on Dante's Ulysses[70] suggests that overstepping the bounds of human thought is morally wrong and spiritually perilous, while Tennyson's own statement about the poem's personal motive identifies him with Ulysses. To choose between the ironic and sincere readings of the poem, we would need a stable model of authorship, a model that could tell us precisely the extent to which Tennyson does and does not share his speaker's values, the extent to which Tennyson does and does not separate himself from his speaker. But the dramatic monologue form is designed to make such a certainty particularly difficult—the separation between Ulysses and Tennyson is obvious and on the surface (in a way that the separation between the poet Wordsworth and the speaker "Wordsworth" is not obvious, though we know that in some sense such a distinction must exist), but at the same time there is no stable position from which we can say definitively what such a separation means. We are made aware that the poet may have different opinions and feelings from those of the speaker, but we are unable to say exactly what these feelings and opinions are, even though the meaning of the poem remains in an important sense undeterminable without them. As one critic puts it, our sense of a particularized but ambiguous authorial presence is what renders the dramatic monologue "both persuasive and somehow unreliable."[71] The dramatic monologue seems to hold the promise of our being able to map the ironic distance between speaker and poet, but the example of "Ulysses" suggests that this promise is illusory.[72]

Sylvia Plath's "Lady Lazarus" provides a more recent version of the kind of debate surrounding "Ulysses," and serves as another example of how modern American poetry heightens the tensions that mark the Victorian dramatic monologue. The title of Plath's poem, like the title of Tennyson's, marks the speaker as separate from the poet: it is Lady Lazarus, not the poet, who speaks. The dramatic occasion of the poem further demarcates the speaker from poet: Lady Lazarus exhibits her newly resurrected body to an audience, which views her as part of a freak show. But as in our experience of "Ulysses," our ability to keep poet and speaker separate in our minds is undermined by what we know of the biographical circumstances surrounding the poem.[73] Lady Lazarus's suicides and resurrections bear an uncanny resemblance to the poet's own: Lady Lazarus kills herself "[o]ne year in every ten"[74] and tells us that she is now resurrecting herself from her suicide at age thirty, while we know that the poet lost her father when she was eight years old (leading perhaps to her first suicidal feelings), attempted suicide for the first time at the age of twenty, and successfully committed suicide at the age of thirty (rendering the poem not only historically accurate in a sense, but also startlingly prescient). Although this information can be used as a key for decoding the poem, I want to suggest that, as with Tennyson's statement about his motive for writing "Ulysses," the availability of biographical information makes the poem more, not less, difficult to interpret. For again, we are faced with two irreconcilable possibilities: first, that Lady Lazarus is a mere mask through which Plath confesses her suicidal impulses to us, and second, that Lady Lazarus is a character from whom Plath distances herself.[75]

M. D. Uroff effectively summarizes the evidence for the latter point of view:

> To associate the poet with the speaker directly, as many critics have done, does not account for the fact that Plath employs here as before the techniques of caricature, hyperbole, and parody that serve . . . to distance the speaker from the poet . . . In "Lady Lazarus," the nature of the speaker is peculiar and defies our ordinary notions of someone prone to attempt suicide . . . The person who speaks here does so not to explore her situation but to control it. She is first of all a performer, and, although she adopts many different roles, she is chiefly remarkable for her control not only of herself but of the effects she wishes to work on those who surround her.[76]

It would be difficult indeed to imagine a more performative poem than "Lady Lazarus," with its dizzying array of audience-directed speech acts. Lady Lazarus brags ("One year in every ten / I manage it— // A sort of walking miracle"), challenges ("Peel off the napkin / O my enemy. / Do I terrify?"), displays ("These are my hands / My knees"), confides ("The first time it happened I was ten. / It was an accident"), threatens ("There is a charge // For the eyeing of my scars"), and defies ("Out of the ash / I rise with my red hair"). The poem explicitly places the speaker on a stage in front of a "peanut-crunching crowd" whose reactions are anticipated and manipulated. This staging suggests that there is a playwright behind this character, and that Lady Lazarus's irrationality, her wild veering between extremes of aggression and self-abasement, and the suicidal defeatism that undercuts her final, pseudo-triumphant resurrection, are known to the playwright (the poet behind the speaker) just as they are visible to us. And yet, while it would be difficult to imagine a more self-consciously staged poem than "Lady Lazarus," it is also difficult to imagine a poem where the stakes of self-expression are higher, since the biographical coordinates of the poem are nothing less than the life and death of the poet herself. The tension we observed in "Ulysses" has been intensified to an almost unbearable degree.

Because there is less consensus about the nature and quality of Plath's achievement than about that of Tennyson, critical reaction to her work more starkly illustrates the evaluative implications of deciding whether a poem is a sincere lyric or a dramatic monologue. First, the sheer number of critics who are willing to ignore the ways in which the speaker of the poem is formally set apart from the poet suggests that a poet must have accrued a certain amount of critical respect before she is given the benefit of the doubt involved in imagining a separation between speaker and poet.[77] In other words, the reluctance to identify speaker and poet that Harty tells us attends "those dramatic poems with an individualized speaker to whom pathological, unwholesome, limited, or unbalanced states of mind or opinions must be attributed"[78] varies according to the poet's reputation and the critic's sympathies. Irving Howe's comments on Plath demonstrate the injurious effects of denying the possibility of an ironic division between speaker and poet: he describes "Lady Lazarus" as a confessional poem "about [Plath's] recurrent suicide attempts" and then dismisses the irony that he perceives in the poem as "an archness . . . that is shocking in a way she could not have intended."[79] This arbitrary limit on the poet's intention permits Howe to read the speaker's awareness of her audience not as a sign of Plath's ironic separation from her speaker, but as further evidence that the poem is "confessional": "This is a kind of badness that seems a constant temptation in confessional poetry, the temptation to reveal all with one eye nervously measuring the effect of revelation."[80] Phillip Hobsbaum's insistence upon a biographical reading of Plath's poem similarly leads him to assert that "at no point does it appear that [Plath] clearly understood what she was saying. Therefore the writing is fraught with unresolved ambiguities."[81] Like Howe, Hobsbaum resists the possibility that these ambiguities might be intended to present a contradictory character rather than to express the poet's own confusion, and therefore he cannot make sense of the poem.

The alternative—giving Plath credit for seeing Lady Lazarus's limitations and carefully mapping out the distance between Lady Lazarus's point of view and what we can reconstruct of Plath's judgments about this point of view—seems truer to the poem's accomplishment, but as we have seen, this alternative is complicated by the biographical coordinates of the poem. What is left for critics, and for us as readers, to do is to try to find a way to formulate the coexistence of the poem as a potential confession and the poem as a dramatic monologue. One attempt at such a formulation is made by Uroff, who, as we have seen, recognizes "Lady Lazarus" as a "parody," but then argues that the aesthetic distancing and control that make this parody possible are "intimately entwined with [Plath's] suicidal tendencies. The suicide is her own victim, can control her own fate."[82] Uroff reaches the conclusion that "the poet behind the poem is not caricaturing Lady Lazarus . . . she is rather allowing Lady Lazarus to caricature herself and thus demonstrating the way in which the mind turns ritualistic against horror."[83] In a similarly complex but somewhat unsatisfactory judgment, Joyce Carol Oates praises Plath's "tragedy"[84] but cannot decide whether Plath should be credited as an artist who has created the tragedy of "Lady Lazarus" or Plath's own life is tragic. On the one hand, Oates argues that "the 'I' of the poems is an artful construction, a tragic figure whose tragedy is classical, the result of a limited vision that believed itself the mirror held up to nature,"[85] but then she ascribes this "limited vision" rather than the "artistic construction" to Plath: "Plath acted out in her poetry and in her private life the deathliness of an old consciousness, the old corrupting hell of the Renaissance ideal and its 'I'-ness, separate and distinct from all other fields of consciousness."[86] Oates's difficulty in deciding whether Plath is a master tragedian or the victim in a pathetic cautionary tale demonstrates one more way in which the proximity of "Lady Lazarus" to the dramatic monologue genre makes it seem possible, and yet impossible to confirm, that there is an ironic distance between the speaker and the poet.[87]

It would be tempting to give Plath full credit for intending the contradictory responses she produces in her critics, if for no other reason than to offset the lack of sympathy with which some critics have approached her work. But I would argue instead that our uncertainty about how much Plath "knew" about what she was doing is part of the uncanny power of poems such as "Lady Lazarus." The way in which the poem hovers on the threshold between dramatic monologue and sincere confession is what makes it enduringly fascinating. This ambiguity is raised to yet another power by the poem's deployment of a kind of self-consciousness that we found in the poetry of Browning and Eliot. It is difficult to distinguish Plath from Lady Lazarus not only because of the biographical coordinates of the poem, but because Lady Lazarus apparently describes what it is like to be a poet,[88] a poet who is doomed both to tell the truth and to reveal "the truth" as fiction by the staginess of her performance:

> Dying
> Is an art, like everything else.
> I do it exceptionally well.
>
> I do it so it feels like hell.
> I do it so it feels real.
> I guess you could say I've a call.[89]

This poem imagines a condition in which it is equally impossible to write a sincere lyric, innocent of the power one holds over one's audience and the socio-historical implications of the role one plays, and to write a dramatic monologue, in which the performance can be depended upon to remain a mere performance, in the full control of the poet who pulls the strings. In the following chapter I consider two poets who spent the better part of their careers in this limbo: Lord Byron and Anne Sexton.

CHAPTER FOUR

The Drama of Breakdown and the Breakdown of Drama

The Charismatic Poetry of Byron and Sexton

HE POETRY that most influences us often does so in part because of our sense of the personality and lived experiences of the poet writing. We may be drawn to poets whose life stories or temperaments exhibit similarities to our own, or alternatively to poets whose lives are foreign to us, whose personalities appear utterly original. Moreover, the experience of reading certain poets (and poems) seems to depend more upon these biographical and temperamental factors than is the case with other poets. It may matter deeply to us that Keats died young when we read "Bright Star," but very little that Wyatt died young when we read "My Galley." This kind of discrepancy can be traced to a number of external factors: the inclinations of the reader, the availability and packaging of biographical information about a given poet, and the historical situations of both poet and reader. But is it possible to analyze the uniquely personal appeal that certain poets make within the formal boundaries of their poems themselves? In this chapter, I address this question in two related ways: by defining a charismatic version of sincerity, in opposition to the universalizing sincerity exemplified by Wordsworth and Rich, as an attempt to explain one way in which this personal appeal works; and by analyzing the work of two poets whose literary achievements are widely believed to depend upon their lived personalities: Lord Byron and Anne Sexton.[1]

In our examination of poetic sincerity thus far, we have witnessed one way in which poetry makes a personal appeal. When a poet, such as Wordsworth or Rich, claims to be writing sincerely, we must assess this claim in part on the basis of our own experiences. Only by consulting our feelings can we judge whether the emotional responses that Wordsworth depicts are proportionate to their occasion, or whether the "I" we encounter in one of Rich's poems is psychologically plausible. Wordsworth and Rich, then, make their appeal along an axis of similarity to the reader: the truth of their writing depends upon the reader's ability to recognize him- or herself in the poems. If this appeal is to be successful, the sincere poem must find ways to mitigate what is "merely personal" in the poet's makeup. Now we must ask: what happens when we are confronted with a poet who apparently depicts his or her lived experiences but refuses this pressure toward impersonality? It is this type of poetry I propose to label the poetry of charisma, and it can be defined as the negative image of the poetry of universalizing sincerity: whereas sincere poetry in the Wordsworthian sense addresses the reader as a fellow self, charismatic poetry addresses the reader as an other. If morally sincere poetry blurs the line between life and art by committing the poet to similar responsibilities in each, charismatic poetry does so by deploying a similar personality in each. While a sincere poetics implies that poetry is the natural expression of a life in which all of one's faculties have been integrated, a charismatic poetics implies that poetry is the irrepressible expression of an unusually intense life. For a poet who professes sincerity in Wordsworth's or Rich's vein, art is a work of life, but for the charismatic poet, life is a work of art.[2] If a sincere poet is concerned with "the expression of a voice or an anxiety about voice," a charismatic poet elaborates "a personal, highly volatile style."[3] Finally, while sincere poetry implies that there is a self that precedes language, or a private code that the self can create by talking to itself without imagining an external audience, charismatic poetry implies that there are only public styles, and that language is always a strategic and performative negotiation with an audience.[4]

Charismatic poetry follows a Rousseauvian model of sincerity rather than a Wordsworthian one. In the Wordsworthian model, the sincere person is recognizable because he or she speaks a truth that lacks sensationalism and appeals to common experience. Opposed to this sincerity is the sincerity associated with originality, exemplified by the opening of Rousseau's *Confessions,* in which he claims: "I am made unlike any one I have ever met; I will even venture to say that I am like no one in the whole world" and "I have bared my secret soul," as if these claims are synonymous.[5] But any claim, such as Rousseau's, to radical originality moves self-expression from the essentially anti-dramatic or discursive nature of Wordsworthian sincerity to the dramatic nature of what I am calling charisma, because this originality must be staged both in relationship to an audience and in opposition to the norm. For example, Rousseau makes his claim of originality in relation to two kinds of spectators, his readers and his God:

> I shall come forward with this work in my hand, to present myself before my Sovereign Judge, and proclaim aloud: "Here is what I have done . . . I have bared my secret soul as Thou thyself hast seen it, Eternal Being! So let the numberless legion of my fellow men gather round me, and hear my confessions. Let them groan at my depravities, and blush for my misdeeds. But let each one of them reveal his heart at the foot of Thy throne with equal sincerity, and may any man who dares, say 'I was a better man than he.'"[6]

The meaning of Rousseau's sincerity is entirely dependent upon the response of his audience, underlined by his own admission of the gratuity of his confession (the Eternal Being already has seen his secret soul, rendering Rousseau's confession in a sense beside the point) and the double staging of his challenge to his readers as an address to God. Unlike Wordsworthian sincerity, which suggests that truth comes from introspection, and requires that one discover in introspection a commonality that will then serve as a public guarantor of that truth, charisma claims truth as the dramatic effect of a transaction between a unique personality and the expectations and desires of an audience.[7]

"Charisma," originally implying divine inspiration, and in particular inspired speech, takes on its modern meaning in the writings of Max Weber. According to Weber's definition, charismatic leaders are those who "have been neither officeholders nor incumbents of an 'occupation' in the present sense of the word, that is, men who have acquired expert knowledge and who serve for remuneration. The natural leaders in distress have been holders of specific gifts of the body and spirit; and these gifts have been believed to be supernatural, not accessible to everybody."[8] While this charisma is soon "routinized" into a bureaucratic government, Weber asserts that "genuine charisma is absolutely opposed to this objectified form. It does not appeal to an enacted or traditional order, nor does it base its claim upon acquired rights. Genuine charisma rests upon the legitimation of personal heroism or personal revelation."[9] For the present study, Weber's definition of charisma serves as both a methodological indicator and a warning. First, his definition suggests that an ahistorical approach may be as or more effective in describing charisma than a historical one. If charisma is by definition resistant to historical determinism, then it is likely that reference to socioeconomic factors, for example the current explanation of Byron's celebrity as the embodiment of "the residual affective charge that still clung to the paraphernalia of aristocracy," which "could be vended to a reading public avid for glamour," will have limited explanatory efficacy.[10] Or, to give another example, the fact that Sexton offered the spectacle of madness to a society obsessed with normalcy, and articulated the experience of men's domination of women (sometimes critiquing it, sometimes embracing it) in a society on the cusp of feminism, may account in part but not wholly for her appeal. Following Weber's intuition that charisma cannot be fully explained by its circumstances, I attempt in this chapter to theorize it in formal rather than historical terms. But Weber's definition also offers a warning to the would-be theorist of charisma that it may resist theorization (or "routinization") altogether.

With this warning in mind, here is a provisional definition of charisma as a specifically poetic effect: a charismatic figure is a poet-speaker who addresses us with the dramatic specificity of a literary character, but who at the same time makes us believe that this character is continuous with his or her own lived personality. We are permitted to know (examine, judge) this figure in the way we are able to know fictional characters as opposed to people in everyday life, but at the same time we are under the impression that we do not merely know a character; we know the living poet.[11] It is likely that all poetry emits a charismatic charge to some degree by offering a speaking presence that simultaneously is and is not "real." But what I am labeling charismatic poetry is a special case, in that it presents bounded characters, and then transgresses the boundaries of those characters by associating them with the poet. In the previous chapter, we encountered a particular logic by which the dramatic monologue form breaks down: sometimes even though a poem alerts us in various ways that the speaker is separate from the poet, what we know about the poet's life violates this boundary.[12] What I am calling the charismatic effect arises from this kind of ambiguity. As one critic has said of Sexton, a charismatic poetics works towards

> a dramatic monologue in which the *persona* is not treated dramatically, as a mask, that is, in the manner of Browning's *Dramatis Personae*, but is projected lyrically ... In other words, although the poem's style and method is unmistakably dramatic, the *persona* is the naked ego involved in a very personal world and with particular, private experiences.[13]

But charismatic poetry cannot achieve a seamless union of the dramatic and the personal any more than a sincerity based on a claim of originality can be fully reconciled with a sincerity based on a universalizing belief in human nature. Instead, charismatic poetry exhibits an uneasily coexisting attraction and repulsion between poets and the surrogates who speak in their poems. It is the ambiguity of the relationship between poet and persona that unites the disparate poetic achievements of Lord Byron and Anne Sexton.

Defining Poetic Charisma

No other poets in British or American literature have quite the notoriety of Lord Byron and Anne Sexton, who generate force fields of personal magnetism that exist in an uneasy relationship with poetic accomplishment. In 1821 *London Magazine* declared: "The personal interest, we believe, has always been above the poetical in Lord Byron's compositions; and, what is much worse, they seem to have been . . . studiously calculated to produce this effect."[14] More sympathetically, Northrop Frye writes, "The main appeal of Byron's poetry is in the fact that it is Byron's . . . He proves what many critics claim to be impossible, that a poem can make its primary impact as a historical and biographical document."[15] In similar terms, William Pritchard writes of Anne Sexton, "one wasn't sure just what one was responding to—the poems? Or something else—the life that was all tied up with them?"[16] Robert Lowell suggests that it is impossible to choose between these two possibilities when he writes that Sexton's "gift was to grip, to give words to the drama of her personality. She did what few did, cut a figure."[17]

Despite obvious differences of historical period, geography, social class, gender, and temperament, Byron's and Sexton's lives exhibit an unexpected number of similarities. Both were good-looking, sexually adventurous human beings of questionable emotional and psychological stability, whose glamorous reputations during their lifetimes were further burnished by their premature deaths. There is reason to believe that both poets suffered from childhood sexual abuse, Sexton allegedly by her father, and Byron allegedly by his nurse.[18] Both poets demonstrate a gift for storytelling and possess a dark, unpredictable humor. And both have undergone wild fluctuations in critical reputation. Byron's first book of poetry, *Hours of Idleness,* was detested by his "Scottish reviewers," but he went on to become the most widely read poet in Europe. Victorian and modernist readers often dismissed him as a negligible poet;[19] postmodern critics have found him an indispensable one. Sexton, for her part, enjoyed almost unheard-of early success, which slowly declined over her lifetime. While her reputation is too recent to show the fluctuations visible in Byron's, the sharp divisions in critical response to her work (some critics finding her poems indispensable, others speculating that they belong more "to the history of publicity than of poetry")[20] suggest that assessments of her contribution to literature will continue to be notable for their inconsistency. There is critical consensus (even among Byron's and Sexton's admirers) that both produced a quantity of careless work.

Because the charismatic version of sincerity is staged in provocative relationship with an audience, and the reader is much more directly implicated in judging the sincerity of these poets than in judging poets who anticipate their readers by attempting to take responsibility for themselves, the term "sincerity" appears more often in criticism addressing the work of Byron and Sexton than it does in criticism treating poets such as Wordsworth and Rich.[21] Judged according to the standards we used in assessing poetry working toward a universalizing sincerity, both Byron and Sexton are found wanting: we miss the complexly theorized appeal to common humanity that we find in Wordsworth, and the determination to take rigorous and ever-expanding moral responsibility for herself that we find in Rich. But in its place, we are given the opportunity to participate more directly and intimately in the questions of guilt and innocence that the protagonists of Byron's and Sexton's poems face. The issue of guilt serves two purposes in their work: first, the insistence of their speakers on having committed extraordinary sins is central to their claims of charismatic originality. Byron's heroes have undergone "a moment" in which they "plunge [their] years / In fatal penitence,"[22] and this special guilt ensures their uniqueness among men: one hero "deem'd his spirit now so firmly fix'd / And sheath'd with an invulnerable mind, / That . . . he, as one, might 'midst the many stand."[23] Moreover, the question of guilt assigns dramatic roles to both poet—the accused—and audience— the judge. The demands that Byron's and Sexton's poetry make upon our sympathy and judgment define the very identities of their speakers.[24]

Sexton is a "confessional" poet not in the sense of being dependably concerned about her own sincerity, but in the sense that, like Rousseau, she stages her self-expression as an appeal to an audience that may grant punishment or absolution. At the beginning of her career she writes, "I was born / doing reference work in sin, and born / confessing it. This is what poems are,"[25] and at its close, she confirms her vocation:

My life
has appeared unclothed in court,
detail by detail,
death-bone witness by death-bone witness,
and I was shamed at the verdict
and given a cut penny
and the entrails of a cat.

But nevertheless I went on
to the invisible priests,
confessing, confessing.[26]

By Sexton's own admission, writing poetry is the compulsive search for
an audience who can hear her, who can register her nakedness, and
whose verdict she can accept.[27] Byron too indicates that sincerity is some-
thing at stake in a relationship with a given audience, rather than some-
thing made and guaranteed by private life. For this reason, he continually
thrusts the question of sincerity into the foreground of his poetry. While
Wordsworth's Romantic epic, *The Prelude,* uses the word "sincerity"
rarely, Byron's Romantic epic, *Don Juan,* uses the word obsessively, at
one point claiming its Muse as "the most sincere that ever dealt in fic-
tion."[28] The joke that this line makes—the supposedly sincere Muse deals
in fiction, not in truth—provides one clue to Byron's investment in the
term: he wants to explore the paradoxical possibility that (as he puts it
elsewhere in the poem) a lie is "the truth in masquerade."[29] But to make
this point, Byron finds it necessary to contrast the truth in masquerade
with false pretensions of sincerity, and to retain sincerity as a term that
can paradoxically live in fiction. The closest we come to a Byronic defini-
tion of sincerity in the positive sense comes not as a result of introspec-
tion but as a declaration of independence:

> . . . being of no party,
> I shall offend all parties:—never mind!
> My words, at least, are more sincere and hearty
> Than if I sought to sail before the wind.
> He who has nought to gain can have small art: he
> Who neither wishes to be bound nor bind,
> May still expatiate freely, as will I,
> Nor give my voice to Slavery's Jackal cry.[30]

While Wordsworth tries to create freedom from convention by elaborat-
ing an inner life, Byron stages it externally as something that necessarily
happens in opposition to others. For the plain truth to mean something,
it has to be spoken to hypocrisy. Because, according to Byron, sincerity is
relational, even confrontational, it is to be determined by a poet's rela-
tionship to his audience, rather than his relationship to himself.

The poet-speakers we find in Byron's and Sexton's poetry are recogniz-
able as "characters" not only because they make direct demands upon
our moral judgment (rejecting the privacy we would normally extend to

fellow human beings), but also because they are specified in terms of their sexuality. They appeal to us as "others" not only to mark their individuality but also to offer themselves as potential objects of our desire. This aspect of their poetry can be seen in the responses their poems elicit: *Childe Harold's Pilgrimage* inspired dozens of women to make Byron's personal acquaintance, and it has been argued that, unlike Wordsworth, Byron is "a man writing to women."[31] Thomas McDonnell represents the impact Sexton makes on some of her readers: "Not so incidentally, by the way, Anne Sexton is a strikingly beautiful woman, as anyone can see from the photo on the back dust jacket of her latest volume, *Live or Die*. The fact is that press agents and movie makers do not know what authentic glamour is, chiefly because they don't know what a woman is; and Anne Sexton is one of the few women writing poetry in the United States today of whom it is possible to say that her womanness is totally at one with her poems."[32] But this quality is also legible in the poems themselves. Eroticism can be read in Byron's stormy relationship with the readers of *Don Juan*—at the end, Byron declines to write further, "Unless some Beauty with a kiss should bribe"[33]—and in Sexton's constant offering of her vulnerable body and its needs—for example, "My loves are oiling their bones / and then delivering them with unspeakable sounds";[34] "Before today my body was useless. / Now it's tearing at its square corners."[35]

The sexual postures of these poet-speakers are made still more provocative by the power relationships they create with the reader. To put it bluntly, Byron has the reputation of a sadist while Sexton has a reputation as a masochist. Historical records suggest that a large part of Byron's personal sexual appeal was attributable to this reputation: Lady Caroline Lamb famously described him as "mad, bad, and dangerous to know" and then set about becoming his lover. This stance can be witnessed in his poetry in the imperiousness of Harold, Manfred, and the narrator of *Don Juan*. In the case of Sexton, her "masochistic preoccupation with her own hurt"[36] has long titillated and troubled readers. Alicia Ostriker expresses in clear terms the discomfort raised by Sexton's self-abasement: "The absence of protest, it must be said, is a defining characteristic of Sexton's . . . In the lyrics that hint at incestuous desire and exploitation by Anne Sexton's father and grandfather, Sexton withholds the anger we may wish her to feel . . . The story Sexton tells about love says, in part, that normative femaleness means falling in love with the father, being seduced by him, being complicit in that seduction, and proceeding to resurrect his deified image in other men. This is a plain enough pattern in Sexton."[37] If both Byron and Sexton appeal to their readers in part by trying to seduce them, then the question of the reader's consent becomes a complicated one. As Ostriker puts it, "Forced to respond personally to the poetic fiction of a direct address expressing need, hope, pain, joy, anger, and despair, calling on our love and sympathy, or attacking us for our indifference and neglect, we may be delighted, we may be repelled. Either way, we have been, to some undetermined degree, seduced."[38] Even disapproval becomes a form of consent: we are still inhabiting the fantasy the poet has created. By simultaneously acting as characters—beings with bounded personalities and with recognizable powers and vulnerabilities, amenable to our judgments—and as living human beings—more complex than any characterization, rendering judgment difficult—Byron and Sexton transgress both the contract between the reader and the literary characters he or she encounters, and the contract between the reader and the poet. These transgressions, rather than Byron's and Sexton's personal transgressions against societal convention, create the scandalous charisma of their poetry.

Because Byron and Sexton make in their poetry an intimate and aggressive or vulnerable appeal to the reader, it becomes difficult to apply our normal categories of critical evaluation to them. For example, Neil Myers writes, "One thinks of Sexton . . . not in terms of verbal facility, ironic texture, and other technical sports, but in terms of sheer affective power, and of [her] inward pain."[39] He goes on to claim, "in such poetry, we do not 'read' so much as experience."[40] James Dickey makes the implications for the critic explicit: "Anne Sexton's poems so obviously come out of deep, painful sections of the author's life that one's literary opinions scarcely seem to matter; one feels tempted to drop them furtively into the nearest ashcan, rather than be caught with them in the presence of so much naked suffering."[41] A number of critics have taken this difficulty as proof that Byron or Sexton is an inferior artist—surely a true poet would not need to depend upon the vicissitudes of personal magnetism for success. But I want to suggest that, whatever our assessment of individual poems written by these poets may be, the way in which their poetry insists that we consider the role of the poet's life and personality in their aesthetic impact is an achievement in itself. Byron and Sexton force us to confront the difficulty of separating a poem's formal appeal from its personal appeal and hint that such separations may never be absolute. And it appears that the controversy surrounding Byron's and Sexton's literary reputations contributes to, rather than detracts from, the fascination they exert over their readers.

In the readings that follow, I argue that rather than creating personae distinct from themselves, Byron and Sexton make use of multiple personae that are both themselves and others. As Byron writes of Harold in

Childe Harold's Pilgrimage, he "makes / A thousand images of one that was, / The same, and still the more, the more [the mirror] breaks."[42] We feel the closeness of Byron and Sexton to their characters not only because of our awareness that the qualities of the speakers and characters in Byron's and Sexton's poems usually correspond to the reputations of Byron and Sexton in real life, but because of the fragility of the dramatic fictions that they create. Along with protagonists who live in uneasy proximity to the poets themselves, they invent plots that give way to the repetitions of a personality that has become unalterable and antagonists that are absorbed back into monologue. This failure to maintain the conventions of drama itself becomes a central drama of their work, and helps account for their charismatic power.

Unrecognized Doubles, Unassimilated Voices

Childe Harold's Pilgrimage provides a paradigmatic example of a character whose personality has become so fixed that it forbids any true narrative development; in fact it threatens narrative structure altogether. What Byron depicts and to a degree analyzes in this poem are the uses and problems of perceiving oneself as a delimited character with unchangeable traits. His digressive anti-narrative is made possible by Childe Harold's failure to recognize himself definitively in the fallen heroes, desolate landscapes, and ruined buildings that he encounters on his travels, a failure that parallels Byron's own refusal to identify himself completely with Harold. Byron produces a double of himself in Harold, and Harold encounters potential doubles of himself in the figures of Napoleon and Rousseau, but the lack of recognition that separates each man from his double means that the poem's hero must seek ever new dramatic counterparts rather than moving into sustained introspection. This predicament is both a resource for the poem and a limitation.

The nature of Harold's individuality, the originality that simultaneously isolates him from every other human being and makes him believe that he has a claim to superiority over them, requires both an extreme claim of interiority and a refusal to explore that interiority, which in part account for the peculiar narrative structure (or lack thereof) of the poem. His identity centers around an unnamed sin, which, he says, has made his life "a place of agony and strife, / Where, for some sin, to Sorrow I was cast, / To act and suffer."[43] At times, this sin seems to be nothing less than interiority itself:

> . . . I *have* thought
> Too long and darkly, till my brain became,

In its own eddy boiling and o'erwrought,
A whirling gulf of phantasy and flame:
And thus, untaught in youth my heart to tame,
My springs of life were poison'd.[44]

This passage presents an apocalyptic vision of self-consciousness, in which the brain's attention to itself multiplies into uncontrolled destruction and poisons its own roots. If we accept for a moment the premise that it is Harold's consciousness of himself that is his original sin, then Byron suggests that the punishment for this sin is "phantasy," the mise-en-scène of one's inner drives and demons. As Harold himself puts it in the following canto, "Of its own beauty is the mind diseased, / And fevers into false creation."[45] But the poem cannot decide which is more dangerous: solitude or other people. Thinking too much on one's own can cause the mind to boil over, but Harold also claims that he must be alone in order "to keep the mind / Deep in its fountain, lest it overboil / In the hot throng, where we become the spoil / Of our infection."[46] Connected by the language of boiling, the fantasies that people the mind and the human beings that people the world threaten to become indistinguishable dangers. If self-consciousness cannot or will not be made the motor of lyric introspection, and thus attempt to contain the multiplications of consciousness within a unified self, then (Byron suggests) it becomes a demonic dramaturge.

This demonic drama is exactly what Byron gives us, though it is unlikely that he would accept the idea that his character's sin is merely ordinary self-consciousness. (At a minimum, Byron would insist that Harold suffers the paradoxes of self-consciousness with an acuteness that sets him apart from his fellow man and ensures his uniqueness.) But whatever Harold's sin, the unusual and deeply secret nature of his transgression means that forgetfulness, rather than memory, will be the guiding impetus for his wanderings and for Byron's writing. In this way, his insistence on his own interiority comes to coexist with a desire to escape that interiority:

> . . . though a dreary strain, to this I cling,
> So that it wean me from the weary dream
> Of selfish grief or gladness—so it fling
> Forgetfulness around me.[47]

Because Wordsworth's fall from the state of nature is unwilled and therefore essentially innocent, he is free to try to access this earlier state, and to map the distance between it and the condition of experience in the hope that his postlapsarian work of interpretation may somehow be redemptive. In contrast, because the Byronic fall is a guilty one, subsequent acts of interpretation carry the danger of repeating the original crime. For this reason, poetry must battle with the self instead of affirming it, conceal the self instead of expressing it. The purpose of poetry is

> . . . to feel
> We are not what we have been, and to deem
> We are not what we should be,—and to steel
> The heart against itself; and to conceal,
> With a proud caution, love, or hate, or aught,—
> Passion or feeling, purpose, grief, or zeal.[48]

Childe Harold's Pilgrimage, then, is both sharply inward-turning and sharply outward-turning: inward-turning in the sense that Harold broods continually on his sin, the deep secret that defines his individual uniqueness; and outward-turning in the sense that his horror at his sin means that he must flee himself in continual wandering. The forgetfulness that Harold's sin imposes will be refigured as his failure to recognize heroic figures that he might profitably have understood as counterparts.

A correlate of Harold's quest for forgetfulness is his world-weariness. While he wishes to know less of himself and his world, he suggests that it would be impossible for him to know more. At times, Harold commits himself to the Romantic task of feeling as ferociously as possible, as if lyric suffering could thereby be transformed into heroic action: for example, man becomes a caged bird who "will beat / His breast against his wiry dome / Till blood tinge his plumage, so the heat / Of his impeded soul would through his bosom eat."[49] But this commitment to intense feeling easily lapses into an overheated malaise. Harold warns: "they who war / With their own hopes and have been vanquish'd, bear / Silence, but not submission: In his lair / Fix'd Passion holds his breath."[50] The stalemate of this silence and fixity transforms experience into attitude, a worldly ennui meant to suggest but incapable of reenacting previous emotional intensity. Eliot's Prufrock similarly concludes that experience has nothing left to teach him—he "has known [it] all"—but his ability to see himself in a number of different lights and guises keeps his world-weariness from hardening into a self-defining attitude. In contrast, Harold's sense of having already experienced everything means that the poet's narrative is left with the task not of reexamining past experiences in hopes of discovering an element that has been overlooked, but following the "sterile track" of emotional resources used up long ago.[51] World-liness leads to narrative encounters that fail to transform, merely holding out the promise of a passivity that may protect the speaker from guilt. By suggesting that all that is important can be experienced once and for all by a single character, Byron in a sense delimits all narrative possibilities into a single attitude, a character who is so experienced that he represents the end of all need for stories. Plot is annihilated by character, and then the character is bereft without a plot.

It is under these conditions that Harold continually, with the compul-siveness of an obsession, encounters figures who are clearly counterparts of him but from whom he can learn and understand nothing. Harold's lack of recognition is structurally necessary for several reasons: to recog-nize himself in another would be to relinquish his claim to originality (he would have to begin to understand himself as one of a type), and at the same time would force a new kind of introspection that would threaten his aim of forgetfulness. In structural terms, if Byron (or his surrogate Harold) were to explicitly recognize himself in one of the figures he in-vokes, the sequential finding of new counterparts—the substance of his narrative—would be arrested. Nevertheless, as if to haunt Harold with the knowledge that he could be a mere type, or to suggest that he could acknowledge his own temperament without being smitten down by guilt, these figures keep appearing. One such figure is Napoleon, whose spirit, according to Byron, is "antithetically mixt / One moment of the mighti-est, and again / On little objects with like firmness fixt, / Extreme in all things!"[52] This description would apply equally well to Harold or to the reputation that Byron has made for himself, but he goes on to criticize Napoleon, without in any way implying that he applies these criticisms to himself:

> An empire thou couldst crush, command, rebuild
> But govern not thy pettiest passion, nor,
> However deeply in men's spirits skill'd
> Look through thine own.[53]

Harold also wields (or wants to wield) decisive power, to "crush, com-mand, rebuild," and also seems unable to overcome the self-destructive impulses within himself. But he willfully refuses to recognize this paral-lel—a refusal stranger than mere hypocrisy, and one that is all the more obvious to the reader when Harold notes the irony that Napoleon can see others clearly, but not himself. Harold exhibits similarities with Napo-leon down to the failure of perspective that self-knowledge might bring, but this similarity blinds him to the similarities he records. The insistence on nonrecognition is underlined when Harold concludes, "One breast laid open were a school / Which would unteach mankind the lust to shine or rule."[54] This statement begs the question, why does not Byron lay a breast (his own?) open in order to provide this decisive lesson? He can see the power of an individual human example, but he cannot fully draw a lesson from this example because he refuses to draw the necessary connection between the contents of Napoleon's breast and the contents of his own. Interiority must remain secret and full of portent beneath the play of dramatic personalities.

This pattern is repeated when Byron invokes Rousseau, a figure even closer to himself in their shared vocations as writers. He presents us with

> . . . the self-torturing sophist, wild Rousseau
> The apostle of affliction, he who threw
> Enchantment over passion, and from woe
> Wrung overwhelming eloquence.[55]

Again, this description could easily apply to Harold and Byron, particularly when Byron goes on to state that Rousseau's own "breath . . . made him wretched,"[56] just as Harold has claimed that his own being poisons itself. Like Rousseau, Byron wrings, or would like to wring, overpowering eloquence from his own suffering. The second part of the stanza reinforces this connection:

> . . . he knew
> How to make madness beautiful, and cast
> O'er erring deeds and thoughts a heavenly hue
> Of words, like sunbeams, dazzling as they past
> The eyes, which o'er them shed tears feelingly and fast.[57]

Here, Byron seems to recognize the possibility that writing can be transformative, setting madness and error in a redemptive light, and working as a communication that can find sympathetic readers. But Byron's own project depends upon his failure to recognize these possibilities as available to himself. Harold must refuse all offers of sympathy in order to keep his integrity, even his identity, intact. In no explicit way can Byron, through Harold, anticipate the human connection that his own words might facilitate, in the hands of the proper reader. Instead, he explains, his own wounds harden until his heart "wear[s] / That which disfigures it."[58] Writing, rather than working as a vehicle of human sympathy, itself becomes a scar, hardening experience into immobility.

Harold, then, is presented as a creature so individual that he not only fails to encounter human beings who might understand him to some degree; he cannot even recognize himself in others. Apart from the temperamental and biographical linkages we can make between Harold and Byron, Harold's limitations encourage us to read him as separate from Byron, a character that Byron has created and placed in a larger moral world, rather than a character who contains Byron's point of view entirely. But Byron comes to believe that the separation he attempts to maintain between Harold and himself draws more attention to himself as an author, rather than less. For this reason, in his prefatory note to Canto IV, Byron explains that he has done away with Harold's mediation altogether:

> With regard to the conduct of the last canto, there will be found less of the pilgrim than in any of the preceding, and that little slightly, if at all, separated from the author speaking in his own person. The fact is, that I had become weary of drawing a line which every one seemed determined not to perceive . . . [I]t was in vain that I asserted, and imagined that I had drawn, a distinction between the author and the pilgrim; and the very anxiety to preserve this difference, and disappointment at finding it unavailing, so far crushed my efforts in the composition, that I determined to abandon it altogether—and have done so . . . [T]he work is to depend on itself, and not on the writer; and the author, who has no resources in his own mind beyond the reputation, transient or permanent, which is to arise from his literary efforts, deserves the fate of authors.[59]

Counterintuitively, Byron believes that it is his determination to *separate* himself from the speaker of his poem that draws attention to himself and carries the danger that the reception of his work will depend upon himself instead of upon its literary merits. He concludes that casting the poem in his own voice will direct attention away from him and to the work itself. By suggesting that it is not speaking in one's own person, but speaking as a character close to oneself that exerts fascination, Byron comes close to theorizing charisma in the same terms that I have used here. Byron's finding of a dramatic counterpart in Harold, and Harold's finding (but failing to recognize) dramatic counterparts in the landscape of the poem heighten our awareness of the figure the poet cuts without giving us information about him that would allow us to subsume him into our own world. But at the same time, the character fails to find a narrative world that can contain him; his intense inwardness holds him in lyric isolation. This generic hybridism is a recurring condition of poetic charisma.

While Byron sends his characters to wander over vast landscapes, made vaster by the reminders they hold of the collective past, Sexton lives with her doubles on more intimate terms. Byron makes his claims to narrative on an epic scale, whereas Sexton's fictions are closer to traditional dramatic monologues. Nonetheless, she sustains a similar tension of connection and separation between herself and her speakers, and finds in this tension poetic resources and limitations parallel to those encountered by Byron. Her most famous borderline dramatic monologue, "Her Kind," posits and then undoes the separation between speaker and poet:

> I have gone out, a possessed witch . . .
> lonely thing, twelve-fingered, out of mind.
> A woman like that is not a woman, quite.
> I have been her kind.[60]

Somewhat like T. S. Eliot's Prufrock, this speaker is defined by her awareness of her own isolation. But rather than dissolving into a generalized and all-pervasive self-consciousness, Sexton's witch fails in a more specific way to coincide with herself. She is defined by her proximity to, but failure to embody, a particular type of social identity. To be a witch is to have a self that is not exactly a self, "twelve-fingered, out of mind"; to be a woman who is not quite a woman. What is unique about the situation that Sexton depicts here is that the role she takes on is itself split in two, between the desire to reproduce normalcy and the inability to do so. But rather than opening up a possible means of escape—after all, even Prufrock's oppressive self-consciousness opens up a space in which he can maneuver and try out different roles (Hamlet, Polonius, Lazarus)— the splitting of this identity serves only to wed Sexton more firmly to it.

In the stanza that follows, the witch's identity is again delimited and reinforced. She represents an alternative identity, but one that is peculiarly familiar. Rather than assemble gruesome potions or cast spells, the witch's task is to find shelter, fill it "with skillets, carvings, shelves," and make supper—in short not embodying but "rearranging the disaligned."[61] The witch is misunderstood not because she transgresses society's norms, but because she tries to reproduce them. If she were more clearly separate from the norm, she might provide a truly alternative identity for Sexton, one that would permit her to make a clear distinction between her troubled self and the powerful masks she wears. Instead, the witch reproduces Sexton's own difficulty in coinciding with herself in the normal, domestic first person. The most assertive self-definition, in the last stanza, is the most equivocal: the witch is no longer at the mercy of the misunderstandings of others, but only because she has been burnt at the stake. This self-claiming happens only on the condition of self-annihilation. Sexton can take on the witch's powers only if the witch takes on her own vulnerability. Speaker and poet are unified, but this unification not only liberates the witch into human self-expression; it also traps Sexton in the fictional world that she has created.

More characteristic of Sexton's work are poems in which the speaker is only barely marked off from the voice of the poet, and the power that these poems generate comes from the vibrations of this hair's-breadth distance. For example, in Sexton's mad-voiced poems, the regressive speech of the lunatic and the adult voice of the poet dwell in uneasy proximity. Her early poem "Music Swims Back to Me" mimics the disoriented, somewhat childlike voice of madness, but breaks this dramatic projection with glimpses of satirical insight:

> Wait, Mister. Which way is home?
> They turned the light out
> and the dark is moving in the corner.
> There are no sign posts in this room,
> four ladies, over eighty,
> in diapers every one of them.[62]

The childlike voice swerves into the knowing voice of the cynical, sane adult in the line, "in diapers every one of them." This voice can recognize that old ladies in diapers are incongruous and pathetic, and that this incongruity is part of the incongruity of the madhouse, which tries to stabilize or even normalize the frightening regressions of its patients. Four ladies in diapers are menacing in a different way than the dark moving in the corner. The beginning of the following stanza inverts this pattern: "Imagine it. A radio playing / and everyone here was crazy. / I liked it and danced in a circle." The imperative "imagine it" is clearly addressed to a sane listener, who can appreciate the incongruity of the radio being played for crazy people. But the "I" who likes it is absorbed back into the scene and into her own madness. These tonal shifts create the illusion of madness explaining itself to us, the madwoman in mesmerizing control of her own faculties, a charisma-effect that is possible only in poetic terms.

There are times, particularly in Sexton's later poems, when the small distance between speaker and poet collapses altogether, and, as Helen Vendler puts it, "we miss the complexity contributed by the double vision of fever taking its own pulse."[63] This collapse is not the usefully unattainable unification of speaker and poet that the would-be sincere poet seeks, but instead results in a contingent voice with no special purchase on the truth. Without the sense of a gap, however tiny, between speaker and poet, the tension goes out of the poetry, and it becomes true that if these poems are admired, it is because they are Sexton's, not because of an independent claim that they make upon us. But even in these later poems, Sexton occasionally achieves the hair's-breadth distance between poet and speaker that we find in the early poems. Like Byron's *Childe Harold's Pilgrimage,* Sexton's "The Hoarder" is a self-expressive poem that remains radically skeptical about the possibility or worth of self-knowledge. The poem exemplifies, and makes some attempt to analyze, the purposeless self-absorption that Sexton's harsher critics believe characterizes her poetry as a whole.

The poem consists of one long sentence enacting the process of digging into the psyche, but this digging is the opposite of the kind of excavation that would produce useful knowledge. Inquiry leads to breakage, not to a gain in understanding: as the speaker investigates the workings of Nana's clock, she breaks it and "didn't learn."[64] When the speaker encounters an object that she cannot identify as hers, such as a five dollar bill belonging to her sister, she rejects its reality altogether, declaring, "it wasn't mine was stage money,"[65] destroying any possible gain in knowledge and providing further evidence of her narcissism. But at this point we might ask, do the poem's own shape and its cunning in diagnosing the speaker's limitations themselves counter the insularity of the speaker's voice? The syntactic endurance of the poem, which creates a columnar shape that forces us to share the downward pressure of the speaker's experience, could be seen as the mark of a poetic intention separate from the needs of the speaker, an intention which indicates a slightly more enlarged perspective than that of the speaker. Or the suggestiveness of the examples that the poem presents, which raises them above the status of mere surrealist catalogue, could serve as evidence of the existence of a poet who is separate from the speaker. Even at this stage in the poem, it seems that we may be in the presence of two slightly differentiated voices instead of just one.

The poem eventually begins to make some chronological progress in its digging: the speaker remembers being in diapers and "the dirt thereof and my / mother hating me for it and me / loving me for it."[66] We appear to have reached a kind of knowledge after all, or at least to have discovered one of the origins of the speaker's self-hatred. But the poem, finally, does not permit this knowledge to serve a redemptive function; instead, it turns back on itself:

> . . . because
> of this I am a hoarder of words

I hold them in even though they are
dung oh God I am a digger
I am not an idler
am I?[67]

This question looks back to the epigraph from Ecclesiasticus at the begin-
ning of the poem: "An idler is a lump of dung; whoever picks it up shakes
it off his hand."[68] Hoarding words is a good description of what this
poem and many of Sexton's late poems do: images and metaphors prolif-
erate, sometimes without a distinguishable order, as if she cannot bear to
let anything go or cross anything out. The acknowledgment, at the end of
the poem, that this hoarding may be worthless functions as a kind of sec-
ond voice entering into the poem, a voice that suggests that the work of
digging may in fact be a form of idleness. This acknowledgment is not al-
lowed to cancel the poem out: instead, the poem's pressure inward simply
coexists with the possibility of critique. The digging voice and the ques-
tioning voice remain unassimilated to each other, as do the mad and sane
voices, the voice of the witch and the voice of normative domesticity, that
we have seen in other poems by Sexton. These unassimilated voices func-
tion like Harold's unrecognized others: we are confronted with many
possible mirrors of the poet, until we can no longer distinguish the liter-
ary characters, self-consciously constructed, from the living man or
woman, who barely escapes his or her literary embodiments.

The Other Becomes a Mirror

Both Byron and Sexton use poetry to produce estranged reflections of
themselves, literary counterparts that are separate from them not because
we can be sure that the poet is aware of his or her speaker's limitations,
but because of what may be strategic absences of awareness: forgetful-
ness in *Childe Harold's Pilgrimage,* and the unbridged gaps between
voices in Sexton's quasi-dramatic monologues. The charismatic effect
also entails the transformation of would-be interlocutors into projections
of the speaker within the boundaries of a given poem. The speakers in
Byron's and Sexton's poetry often search for others who have the same
level of reality as they themselves do, as if sensing that a genuinely mutual
relationship could give them an identity that would preserve both their
individuality and their humanity. But these self-other relationships con-
tinually threaten to collapse into self-self relationships, a mirror sliding
between the self and the desired original response. For example, Byron's
Manfred is set up as a drama, complete with a character list, settings,
acts, and scenes. But just as Childe Harold's journey to see the world is

curtailed into repeated confrontations with his unchanging character, Manfred's conversations with others simply serve to reinforce the impossibility of true dialogue for him, his entrapment in soliloquy.[69] Byron stages and then undermines dramatic conflicts in order to reinforce the idea that Manfred's only true struggle can be with himself. In the end, Manfred's very identity comes to be defined by his simultaneous proximity to and debarment from dramatic interaction.

Manfred finds himself in essentially the same condition as Harold: a terrible sin, which counterintuitively coexists with an overwhelming sense of superiority, has exiled him from normal human society. What experiences he has take place in concealment, internally:

> . . . in my heart
> There is a vigil, and these eyes but close
> To look within; and yet I live, and bear
> The aspect and the form of breathing men.[70]

The characters who attempt to interact with Manfred fall into two categories: human beings who fail to influence Manfred because he is superior to them, and spirits whose extraordinary powers are invoked only to be revealed as useless to Manfred's plight. In the first act Manfred conjures the spirits of the elements and the guiding star of his destiny. This star's speech to Manfred reveals the logic of power that will structure what follows:

> And thou! beneath its influence born—
> Thou worm! whom I obey and scorn—
> Forced by a power (which is not thine,
> And lent thee but to make thee mine)
> For this brief moment to descend.[71]

Obedience and scorn are not opposites in the world of this drama; instead they are simultaneous states of being. Manfred's power to conjure up the star is paradoxically granted him only to put him under the star's power. Under these circumstances, meaningful action is impossible, for acts of will only frustrate themselves further.[72] It is as if Manfred has been given so much power that it can only rebound upon itself: there is no empty space left in his universe for his power to fill or transform.

Like the speaker of *Childe Harold's Pilgrimage,* Manfred desires not knowledge or further power but forgetfulness. But this desire is especially difficult to achieve through an act of will; a conscious effort to make oneself forget something is likely only to engrave the memory more deeply.

As if reflecting this impasse, the spirits cannot fulfill Manfred's request for forgetfulness, only mirror it back to him. When the First Spirit asks Manfred what he wishes to forget, he replies, "Of that which is within me; read it there— / Ye know it, and I cannot utter it."[73] The Spirit responds, "We can but give thee that which we possess."[74] Manfred's request is literally unspeakable; it can barely be made under the conditions of dialogue. And the tenuous attempt at exchange is almost immediately shut down: the Spirits can endow Manfred with the powers they possess, but they cannot give him the one thing he desires—forgetfulness, a blank or gap in the will that would bring peace. This gap would make dramatic suspense and interaction possible; without it, the dramatic conventions invert into anti-drama. Manfred attempts to achieve the result he desires through a still more aggressive assertion of his will, commanding the spirits to "[a]nswer, or I will teach you what I am."[75] This threat, however, simply rebounds onto him, as if the greater the force exerted, the more rapidly and completely it will backfire on its agent. The Spirit replies, "We answer as we are answer'd; our reply / Is even in thine own words."[76] This response suggests not only the futility of dialogue, but also the impossibility of dramatic action in another sense. The contextual meaning of the Spirit's reply is that Manfred's insistence upon his own immortality answers his question about whether or not death will bring oblivion: the extent of Manfred's power rules out not only the possibility of forgetfulness, but of death itself. The absence of the possibility of death warns us of the impossibility of dramatic closure.

The play, however, continues into another two acts, falling into the pattern of serial repetition seen in *Childe Harold's Pilgrimage* (again, we have a hero who is literally incapable of learning), rather than coalescing into a true climax and dénouement. Manfred's encounter with the Witch of the Alps in the second act reveals another aspect of his inability to be transformed. He again asks for forgetfulness, and the Witch concedes, "It may be / That I can aid thee."[77] This exchange follows:

> *Witch.* . . . if thou
>   Wilt swear obedience to my will, and do
>   My bidding, it may help thee to thy wishes.
> *Man.* I will not swear—Obey! and whom? The spirits
>   Whose presence I command, and be the slave
>   Of those who served me—Never![78]

Manfred is incapable of giving up his own power, as incapable as he is of putting an end to his situation by an act of will. This incapacity is not only an index of Manfred's arrogance; his world-view is such that the idea that a goal can be achieved by a surrender of will is incoherent. Manfred's existence is so saturated with intention and will that there are no gaps in intention that make change possible: power is the absolute exercise of will, obedience the absolute frustration of it. Or to put it another way, Manfred's power is so seamless that he is entrapped inside it—he cannot give a lesser obedience to other beings, because his obedience to his own will is so complete.

To the extent that this play achieves something resembling a climax, it comes when Manfred finally faces Astarte, his partner in the fatal sin that has led to his impenetrable isolation. But even this original act seems not to have been an act exactly—instead, it appears that Manfred merely has had his power mirrored back to him yet again. He confesses to the Witch of the Alps, "I loved her, and destroy'd her!" The witch asks, "With thy hand?" and Manfred replies:

> Not with my hand, but heart—which broke her heart;
> It gazed on mine and wither'd. I have shed
> Blood, but not hers—and yet her blood was shed—
> I saw, and could not stanch it.[79]

The fateful crime was not committed through an act of will. Instead, both revealed hearts "gazed on" each other, as if on a mirror image, and disintegrated. This mirroring is repeated when Manfred is granted a vision of Astarte by another group of Spirits in the second act. When Astarte refuses, by silence, Manfred's request for either forgiveness or condemnation, he is stunned into one of his most vulnerable statements: "I know not what I ask, nor what I seek: / I feel but what thou art—and what I am."[80] Again, his heart gazes on hers, and the small possibility opens up that this gazing may go beyond destructive mirroring. But Astarte refuses to engage in dialogue, mirroring Manfred by repeating his name. The one message she delivers, "To-morrow ends thine earthly ills,"[81] is fulfilled only ambiguously at the play's close.

Astarte represents the failure of dramatic interaction in another way: Manfred's disclosures to the Witch of the Alps imply that incest was the original sin that has destroyed his life. This sin is, in a sense, a sin against dramatic interaction itself—what was supposed to be a relationship between a self and an other was corrupted into a relationship between a self and an almost-self. Manfred emphasizes the similarities between himself and his partner in crime: "She was like me in lineaments—her eyes, / Her hair, her features, all, to the very tone / Even of her voice, they said were like to mine."[82] In other words, even the one true other in Manfred's life is a mirror of himself. According to this reading, Manfred's original inability to define himself in relationship to another has become the template for all his future interactions. Not merely the subject matter, but the repetitive sameness of the dramatic structure of the play itself is incestuous.

At the play's close, after a failed suicide attempt, Manfred finally manages to die, but it is unclear whether even this change is a true transformation, because the Spirits have suggested that Manfred's death may not bring the forgetfulness he so desires.[83] Although Manfred wants to die, he fights the Spirit that has come to take his soul: "I am prepared for all things, but deny / The power which summons me."[84] He insists, "I . . . was my own destroyer,"[85] and though this assertion may be a triumph, it is also a defeat. It is unclear what death can mean in a world where Satan is the only character with real power; where, despite the efforts of the Abbot in the final scene, we cannot be sure of the alternative perspective of Heaven or of Adam and Eve. Manfred's death does not provide dramatic closure because it remains unclear whether this death is a successful act of dominance or a failed act of submission. This closing reinforces the perversity of Manfred's singular existence; dramatic structure is invoked only in order to be demolished more completely.

In Sexton's "The Double Image," guilt is not envisioned as an unimpeachable core of identity, but is instead more successfully dramatized as a function of the relationship between the self and others. The poem, however, shares the claustrophobia of *Manfred* because the guilt the speaker suffers makes it as difficult to maintain the boundaries of the self as it is to maintain a clear conscience. Though Manfred's problem is his isolation from others while the problem of the speaker of "The Double Image" is the danger of being incorporated into them, both poems face a similar psychological and aesthetic dilemma: how can the poet-speaker find an individual with whom he or she can interact meaningfully and communicate, an other who will not be revealed as another projection of the self?

"The Double Image" explores two different kinds of reproductions of the self: generational and aesthetic. The poem diagnoses generational reproduction as poisonous: it involves guilt that, once initiated, becomes an all-encompassing vicious circle. For example, Sexton's mother tells her, "I cannot forgive your suicide,"[86] and this remark in turn partly accounts for the speaker's second suicide attempt. Meanwhile, Sexton's mother begins to mirror her in a horrifying way:

> [M]y mother grew ill.
> She turned from me, as if death were catching,

as if death transferred,
as if my dying had eaten inside of her.
   . . . [S]he looked at me
and said I gave her cancer.
They carved her sweet hills out
and still I couldn't answer.[87]

The mother's mirroring of the speaker reinforces the speaker's guilt. We might expect that the next generation, represented by Sexton's daughter Joy, would hold the possibility of breaking this cycle, but the poison of generational mirroring extends into the future as well as the past.[88] The speaker closes the poem by admitting failure to her daughter: "this was my worst guilt; you could not cure / nor soothe it. I made you to find me."[89] Resemblance, by this logic, can only be the inheritance of guilt; there is no escape.

The alternative to this poisonous generational reproduction, reproduction by portraiture, at first does not appear very promising. The speaker's mother arranges to have the speaker's portrait painted, but the speaker takes this gesture as a refusal rather than an act of forgiveness:

I cannot forgive your suicide, my mother said.
And she never could. She had my portrait
done instead . . .
Your smile is like your mother's, the artist said.
I didn't seem to care. I had my portrait
done instead . . .
I wasn't exactly forgiven. They had my portrait
done instead.[90]

Despite her mother's hope, the portrait does not heal the speaker: "They hung my portrait in the chill / north light, matching / me to keep me well,"[91] but later she admits, "I rot on the wall, my own / Dorian Gray."[92] By implication, we can infer that Sexton's own making of a poem-portrait of the women of her family cannot be assumed to be redemptive. Making something into an artifact may only be a substitute for forgiveness, rather than the saving act itself. And yet the portrait seems to offer, even if only in a small way, the possibility of breaking the claims of resemblance. For a moment, the speaker can at least seem not to care that her smile resembles her mother's smile. The idea that portraiture is an alternative to recognition recalls Harold's refusal to recognize his potential doubles. Sexton borrows some of Harold's imperiousness here, a useful antidote to her own tendency to allow herself to be incorporated into the selves of others.

Breaking the spell of resemblance holds the promise of new opportunities for understanding. When Sexton's mother has her own portrait painted, Sexton addresses her: "you resembled me; unacquainted / with my face, you wore it."[93] Resemblance is imagined as the opposite of knowledge: without it, new acquaintanceships may be possible. This possibility is realized, in a tentative way, when the speaker stops to look at her own portrait:

> In north light, my smile is held in place,
> the shadow marks my bone.
> What could I have been dreaming as I sat there,
> all of me waiting in the eyes, the zone
> of the smile, the young face,
> the foxes' snare.[94]

For a moment, through the portrait, the speaker experiences herself as separate from herself. Her face has become other to herself, even an object of desire, as suggested by the full eyes, the smile, "the young face, / the foxes' snare." This newly found self-difference helps cancel out her resemblance to her mother, whose portrait the speaker goes on to describe:

> In south light, her smile is held in place,
> her cheeks wilting like a dry
> orchid; my mocking mirror, my overthrown
> love, my first image. She eyes me from that face,
> that stony head of death
> I had outgrown.[95]

The portraits thus give the speaker the distance from her relationship with her mother that she needs in order to "overthrow" her first image, to "outgrow" her suicide attempts. Understood as a "mocking mirror," the mother ceases to mirror.

Although the poem's ending ("I made you to find me") suggests that the generational multiplication of guilt has not been permanently thwarted, the last stanza of the penultimate section of "The Double Image" offers a final piece of evidence that the intervention of the portraits has permitted the destructive cycle to be broken, at least temporarily. The double image has been relegated to the past tense:

And this was the cave of the mirror,
That double woman who stares
At herself, as if she were petrified
In time—two ladies sitting in umber chairs.[96]

Now that the portraits have become fully unrecognizable, the double image can be replaced by the final image of the section, Joy kissing her grandmother: "You kissed your grandmother / and she cried."[97] Rather than reinforcing generational mirroring, this image suggests a new relationship, because kissing and crying are asymmetrical actions. The possibility of aesthetic detachment has, however briefly, broken the spell. But the poem's ultimate word on portraiture, and by extension on its own autobiographical procedure, is that such posing is double-edged. Sitting for a portrait carries the danger that the human body itself may become more like a portrait—Sexton writes, "I had my portrait done / holding my smile in place, till it grew formal."[98] The suspension of biographical time that this formality permits is both a kind of hope and a kind of death. Sexton's poems continually refigure this partial formalization, a charismatic flickering between speaking human woman and freeze-framed legend.

"The Double Image," then, follows the pattern that we have seen in Sexton's shorter lyrics: the act of making a portrait of oneself in a poem creates self-distance and potentially self-perspective, but this distance remains small and endangered. The artificiality of lyric address, like the artificiality of portraiture, opens a space where exploration and even a kind of forgiveness may be possible, but in Sexton's world, the artificial cannot be depended upon to remain artificial, for the boundary between life and literature has been eroded. The moral dangers of not being able to distinguish portraiture and maternal reproduction, artistic invention and lived experiences, other and self, are brought home in the poem's structure as an address to Joy. The information the poem conveys certainly could not be comprehended by four-year-old Joy at the time of its writing,[99] and if we understand the poem to be addressed to an older Joy, the pretense of the present tense is destroyed. Even under these circumstances it is difficult to accept this poem as a communication from mother to daughter. While lines such as "love your self's self where it lives. / There is no special God to refer to" sound like plausible advice, the rhetorical question that immediately follows, "[W]hy did I let you grow / in another place[?]"[100] is exactly the kind of question that Joy cannot, and should not be expected to, answer. To a degree, all lyric poems are cast as forms of address that would be impossible under other circumstances—this is one of poetry's functions. But in this poem, the boundary between what can be said in a poem and what can be said between actual human beings is porous: because we know that Joy is a real person with her own life history, the artificiality of the mode of address here becomes uncomfortably close to reality, with disturbing implications beyond the boundaries of the poem. Charismatic poetry transforms the generic problem of the relationship between the lyric first person and larger dramatic or narrative structures into one of personal urgency: finding an interlocutor is not just an aesthetic concern, but a task the poet makes us believe will define or destroy her own identity.

The Boundaries of the Charismatic Mode

As we have seen, the charismatic effects produced by Byron's and Sexton's poetry come in part from the incomplete differentiation between the poet and the protagonist or speaker who addresses us in their poems. Their poems offer us literary characters who also seem to be lived personalities, and living poets who take on the dramatic specificity and glamour of literary figures. In both Byron's and Sexton's bodies of work, we can find deviations from this pattern: most notably, Byron's best-known and most admired poem, *Don Juan,* makes a clear separation between the narrator and his protagonist. In many ways, *Don Juan* is the exception that proves the charismatic rule; as a persuasively dramatic narrative, its strategies throw into further relief the partial dramatizations I have described thus far. More fundamentally, though *Don Juan* presents stylistic and structural choices in contrast to the earlier poems, it operates under a logic similar to that which we saw operate in *Childe Harold's Pilgrimage* and *Manfred.*

At first glance, the dramatic structure of *Don Juan* has much in common with these earlier poems. Like *Childe Harold's Pilgrimage, Don Juan* is written in strictly rhyming stanzas that act as well-oiled engines generating a disorderly and endlessly proliferating series of digressions. The protagonist moves through a number of landscapes and situations, but does not face conflicts that lead to significant changes in his way of being. Like Harold and Manfred, Juan can be confused with Byron himself (Byron's reputation as a womanizer was well established by the time he wrote his poem, and his choice of hero was clearly meant to scandalize those who disapproved of its author). But unlike Harold, who is assimilated into Byron by the time the poem ends, or Manfred, who is set apart from Byron by the paraphernalia of theatrical convention, but whose point of view is in no way countered by the presence of a detached narrator, innocent Juan is kept at a distance from the worldly, ironic narrator of *Don Juan.* Whereas in the earlier poems, it is the protagonist's guilty secret that defines his identity and ensures his uniqueness, Juan has no true secrets, little capacity for guilt, and in a sense, no identity. We know that he is young, good-looking, and capable of meeting the challenges and opportunities that life offers him, but he remains essentially without personality.[101] This blankness becomes a tremendous resource for Byron.

Though Juan is far from innocent in terms of sexual experience, in a much more important sense he remains superlatively innocent: he is capable of undergoing experiences without being changed by them.[102] It is as if Juan effortlessly embodies the forgetfulness for which Harold and Manfred struggle. Multiple love affairs and participation in a brutal war leave him essentially unmarked. The narrator's dismay, late in the poem, when Juan finally shows a bit of wear, reads as one of the more heartfelt moments of the poem:

> Don Juan grew, I fear, a little dissipated;
> Which is a sad thing, and not only tramples
> On our fresh feelings, but—as being participated
> With all kinds of incorrigible samples
> Of frail humanity—must make us selfish,
> And shut our souls up in us like shell-fish.[103]

As if sensing that Juan's lack of worldliness must be kept intact for the poem to continue, the narrative quickly moves on: "This we pass over."[104] A more hopeful evaluation is given later:

> A little spoil'd, but not so altogether;
> Which was a wonder, if you think who got him,
> And how he had been toss'd, he scarce knew whither:
> Though this might ruin others, it did *not* him,
> At least entirely—for he had seen too many
> Changes in youth, to be surprised at any.[105]

The incident-rich rhythm of Byron's narrative, then, is meant to ensure that no event will be definitive—that all changes will leave the core of his protagonist untouched. While in *Manfred,* the character of Manfred supersedes the possibility of anything actually happening, the structure of *Don Juan* is the mirror opposite: a surplus of narrative events forestalls any definitive development of the hero. But we can already see the danger that the all-inclusiveness of *Don Juan* may ultimately amount to the same thing as the nothingness confronted by Manfred.

If Juan's freshness slowly fades over the course of the narrative, it is supplemented by a steady stream of hyperbolically innocent heroines. Once Juan has lost his virginity, he encounters Haidee, who "spoke not of scruples, ask'd no vows, / Nor offer'd any . . . never having dreamt of falsehood, she / Had not one word to say of constancy."[106] When Haidee and Juan are parted, she is replaced by Dudu, who possesses "perfect Innocence."[107] Even in the extreme absence of innocence that characterizes the battlefield, Juan rescues a child whose moral purity somewhat redeems the scene. It is as if Byron has determined that innocence is a necessary resource for his poem's survival, one that must be constantly replenished. In terms of narrative development, *Don Juan* refuses closure, but one way to explain the cessation of the poem is that the store of innocence is running out (as demonstrated in the questions the narrator raises about both Lady Adeline's and Juan's innocence in the last episode of the poem). In a more fundamental sense, one begins to wonder whether Juan's innocence is so very different from Harold's world-weariness.[108] Whether marked by extreme innocence or extreme guilt, Juan and Harold cannot be surprised or changed by the people and situations they encounter. In this sense, they are subject to the same kind of narrative logic.

In the end, the crucial difference between *Don Juan* and *Childe Harold's Pilgrimage* is not in the heroes of these poems, but in their narrators. While it would be nearly impossible to determine where Harold ends and Byron begins, Juan's innocence ensures that he remains differentiated from his author. Moreover, unlike Manfred, the narrator of *Don Juan* has found a worthy interlocutor: his conservative readers. Juan's "guilt," his loss of sexual purity, is invoked not to suggest a uniquely tragic destiny that provides the occasion for soliloquies, but instead to provoke the reader, and in turn to create the conditions for a conversation with a genuine and fully present audience. The narrator is not shocked by Juan's extramarital exploits, but they give him the opportunity to parry with his readers:

> Haidee and Juan were not married, but
> The fault was theirs, not mine: it is not fair,
> Chaste reader, then, in any way to put
> The blame on me, unless you wish they were;
> Then if you'd have them wedded, please to shut
> The book which treats of this erroneous pair,
> Before the consequences grow too awful;
> 'Tis dangerous to read of loves unlawful.[109]

Byron playfully insists on the reader's independence and, more crucially, on the reader's responsibility in determining what the moral of the poem may be. As he puts it, "gentle reader! When you gather meaning, / You may be Boaz, and I—modest Ruth."[110] But the narrator of *Don Juan* needs the moral censorship of his reader in order to give his own voice definition. Without that opposition, lines such as the following might be taken straight—a forbidding prospect:

> I therefore do denounce all amorous writing,
> Except in such a way as not to attract;
> Plain—simple—short, and by no means inviting,
> But with a moral to each error tack'd,
> Form'd rather for instructing than delighting,
> And with all passions in their turn attack'd.[111]

The reader that Byron projects (different from his real reader, who presumably recognizes the jokes), with his or her rigidly dependable expectations, is to Byron's narrative voice what rhyme is to his stanzas. The "you," as much as the "I," produces the coordinates for the narrator's personality.

Just as Juan's innocence begins to wear off as the poem ends, so does the distinction between narrator and protagonist that gives Byron the freedom to defy his readers. At the poem's close, Juan is coming more and more to resemble Byron:

> . . . he had that kind of fame
> Which sometimes plays the deuce with womankind,
> A heterogeneous mass of glorious blame,
> Half virtues and whole vices being combined;
> Faults which attract because they are not tame;
> Follies trick'd out so brightly that they blind.[112]

It is difficult to imagine a more exact description of the Byronic hero. The poem must end because the dramatic difference that made it possible, the distance between Byron and his protagonist, has eroded. We are gradually reentering the realm of Harold and Manfred, a realm in which narrative detachment is no longer possible. While *Don Juan* is by far the more critically acclaimed work, I believe that the more incomplete dramas that Byron stages come closer than *Don Juan* to the heart of his charismatic appeal—and after all, they created it.[113] The more characteristic Byronic mode is described in *Childe Harold's Pilgrimage*:

> 'Tis to create, and in creating live
> A being more intense, that we endow

With form our fancy, gaining as we give
The life we image, even as I do now.
What am I? Nothing: but not so art thou
Soul of my thought! with whom I traverse earth,
Invisible but gazing, as I glow
Mix'd with thy spirit, blended with thy birth,
And feeling still with thee in my crush'd feeling's dearth.[114]

It is not the creations that Byron achieves separation from, but the ones he remains "mix'd with" that radiate most insistently the Byronic glow.

In *Don Juan* Byron substitutes an extreme separation between poet and protagonist for the claustrophobic intimacy between the two in his earlier poems. Sexton undertakes a similarly extreme reversal in her collection of retold fairy tales, *Transformations,* in which she demonstrates a hyperbolic lack of identification with the perspectives of her characters.[115] The poems in this collection are experiments in the extent to which we can enjoy a story without feeling sympathy for its protagonist. For example, the queen in "Rumpelstiltskin," a typical heroine, is unappealingly "lovely as a grape" and is treated with mock-pity:

Poor grape with no one to pick.
Luscious and round and sleek.
Poor thing.
To die and never see Brooklyn.[116]

When she weeps, she weeps "of course, huge aquamarine tears."[117] We have seen that, in some of Sexton's poems, the tension between the speaker and the poet is in danger of collapsing altogether, with the danger of a loss of poetic force. Here, the opposite danger applies: the poet is often so dismissive of her protagonists that it is not clear why they should hold our attention. But while putting her projects in danger, Sexton's attraction to these extremes also makes possible her literary successes, in which she suddenly and unexpectedly resists the suffocating involvement or extreme detachment that her poem has been veering toward.

Rather than detailing the pleasures that these poems yield in spite of this vacuum of sympathy—the sharp transmutation of our childish suspension of disbelief into a recognition of the ugly connections between the fairy-tale world and our own, the slap-dash pace that speeds us through aptly flippant observations—I will focus on the one true transformation in a volume that might more accurately be titled *Anti-Transformations:* the movement in the closing poem from the externalized world of fairy-tale drama to the internal world of the narrator. This final

poem, "Briar Rose," permits us to witness the narrator's state of detach-
ment metamorphose with breathtaking speed into the most intimate in-
volvement.

In this poem, the well-known story of Briar Rose (or Sleeping Beauty)
is retold in the irreverent style Sexton uses in this volume, up to the famil-
iar point of the happy ending. But Sexton does not close, as she usually
does, with a few well-placed jabs at such endings. Instead, she continues:

> Briar Rose
> Was an insomniac . . .
> She could not nap
> Or lie in sleep
> Without the court chemist
> Mixing her some knock-out drops
> And never in the prince's presence.
> If it is to come, she said,
> Sleep must take me unawares
> While I am laughing or dancing
> So that I do not know that brutal place.[118]

Sleep is no longer a spell which comes once and then makes possible the
definitive rebirth, the transformation. Instead sleep, and its vulnerability
to spells and trances, becomes a perpetual problem. The larger implica-
tions of this passage are that Sexton can no longer control the moment of
transformation with derisive humor, and can no longer maintain the dis-
tance between herself and her heroines. Instead, this distance becomes a
spell that permits only fitful sleep, leaving her perpetually on the border-
line between sleep and waking, between dramatic externalization and
self-expression.

For the first time, the protagonist of one of the fairy tales begins to
speak in the first person:

> I wear tubes like earrings
> I lie as still as a bar of iron.
> You can stick a needle
> through my kneecap and I won't flinch.
> I'm all shot up with Novocain.
> This trance girl
> is yours to do with.[119]

The unreal body of the princess begins to come to life, as if her cartoonish
two-dimensionality were simply a spell she had been put under by the

narrator. Her vulnerability to the narrator's machinations, underlined in the last two lines of this passage, becomes the narrator's own vulnerability, permitting us to read the lack of sympathy extended by the narrator to the earlier characters as a lack of sympathy felt toward herself—narrative distance as a kind of self-hatred. Just as Juan acts essentially as Byron's puppet, less a dimensional character than a technique for unifying disparate scenes and episodes, Sexton's fairy-tale protagonists stand in for certain social roles and attitudes rather than behaving as fully dimensional beings. This kind of distance, readable as a form of impersonal detachment, is diagnosed here as a personal cry for help. Her poem demonstrates that fairy tales have power over us not because they are otherworldly, but because they are all too accurate about the drives and dangers that organize our own psychological worlds.

At this point, the poem tries to tell the personal story underlying the fairy-tale story. The narrator's assurance gives way to speculation—although in a sense, the "I" is telling us what she knows for the first time, what she knows is connected to what she cannot really know, an original experience of trauma (here, the trauma of paternal incest). We approach the kind of terrible secret that might have driven Harold and Manfred into exile. But instead of seeking forgetfulness, the speaker confronts the forgetfulness which cannot be willed, but which inheres in transformative, traumatic experience itself:

> There was a theft.
> That much I am told.
> I was abandoned.
> That much I know.
> I was forced backward.
> I was forced forward.
> I was passed hand to hand
> like a bowl of fruit.
> Each night I am nailed into place
> and I forget who I am.[120]

The experiences catalogued here summarize the transformations in the fairy tales Sexton has just narrated, but their strangeness (earlier flattened out by the narrator's nonchalant "of course") has been restored. The airless atmosphere of the fairy tales she has recounted becomes recognizable: it is the airlessness of her own childhood terrors, her own body being nailed into place, pressed flat, her own erased memory. The stories all become her story, but not in a way that flattens them into narcissistic mirrors—instead in a way that gives them back their missing life.

Sexton continues, rewriting the refrain of "Briar Rose," "Daddy! Daddy! / Presto! She's out of prison":[121]

Daddy?
That's another kind of prison.
It's not the prince at all,
but my father
drunkenly bent over my bed,
circling the abyss like a shark,
my father thick upon me
like some sleeping jellyfish.[122]

This passage is perhaps the most intimate and confessional moment in all of Sexton's poetry, and it apparently needed the preceding narrative flattening of the fairy tale in order to come into being. The kiss of the other does not wake the speaker—no longer princess—but suffocates her. The narrator's satirical recognition of the patriarchal bias of even the happiest of happy endings in traditional fairy tales is replaced by a genuinely terrifying representation of what that patriarchal bias may mean, personally, for one woman. The poet reveals the personal stake in what might otherwise seem to be a purely aesthetic decision. The poem—and the volume with it—ends on a rhetorical question addressed both to the young reader who might have understood the fairy tales in an innocent way and to the simplistically cynical narrator who recasts them as two-dimensional satire: "What voyage this, little girl? / This coming out of prison? / God help—/ this life after death?"[123] Coming back to life means entering not a happy ending but an unknown world that is even more uncanny and power-stricken than the world of fairy tales. The way in which this question is addressed to both us and herself exemplifies Sexton's powerfully incomplete dramatizations, the frightening and moving oscillation between poet and persona that makes for her charisma.

Byron and Sexton both exemplify the model of charismatic poetry developed here in their creation of speakers who are only barely separated from themselves as poets. But in their exploration of the implications of speaking as delimited characters—the breakdown of narrative into serial repetitions, the flattening of others into projections of the self—they move beyond this model. To a degree, both poets not only exemplify, but also theorize the charismatic effect of their poetry, writing allegories of the predicament of being simultaneously a delimited personality with an unalterable destiny and a fully dimensional human being capable of choice and surprise. The insularity of Harold's and Manfred's identities and the ultimate sterility of their worlds work as an analysis of the limits of charismatic originality. Similarly, "The Hoarder" and "The Double Image" demonstrate an acute awareness of the limits of speaking from the perspective of uniquely individual guilt. Whether we should credit these poets with purposefully constructing these allegories, rather than merely acting them out, remains an open question. And in the end, the formal similarities we have discovered in Byron's and Sexton's poems can only partially explain the charismatic effects of their poetry. To an extent, "charisma" must stand as a name for the irreducible remainder of the personal impact of poetry, the appeal that resists all theorization of it.

CHAPTER FIVE

Agnostic Sincerity

The Poet as Observer in the Work of Keats,
Bishop, and Merrill

THE FORMS OF SINCERITY we have encountered thus far offer themselves as compromised but still luminous presences: the fully human being attempting to articulate an integrated vision of the world, the voice struggling to strip all artificiality from its language, the character who promises to reveal his or her true nature to us, the charismatic personality staged against our ordinary ways of being. Is it possible, in contrast, to imagine a sincerity built around absence instead of presence, a sincerity that entails forgetfulness of the self or absorption in another rather than the consolidation of the self or the performance of a personality? The inspiration for this question comes from Keats's concept of negative capability, which he defines as being "capable of being in uncertainties, Mysteries, doubts, without any irritable reaching after fact & reason."[1] In this chapter I apply Keats's off-the-cuff coinage to any poetic attempt to suspend the organizing, interpreting functions of consciousness in favor of a different, and hypothetically more authentic, engagement with the external world. We can immediately see why this strategy would appeal to poets discouraged by other approaches to sincerity: if it is impossible to grasp the self with a consistency that indicates truth has been obtained, then perhaps one could achieve greater self-understanding by abandoning the effort of grasping altogether. At this point, it is perhaps too easy to see how any such attempt is doomed by the omnipresence of self-consciousness—Keats's sense of the necessity of his new term in itself attests to the mind's stubborn habit of "reaching after fact and reason"; and any conscious attempt to elude consciousness is bound to negate itself in the very act. But Keats's idea of negative capa-

bility retains its power, both in his poetry and in the poetry of Elizabeth
Bishop and James Merrill, through the ways in which their attempts to
relinquish the inventing, controlling mind in favor of new encounters
with the outside world coexist with their determination, more or less ex-
plicit, to make sense of their experiences.

Keats, Bishop, and Merrill share the intuition that the self may be as
well expressed by losing itself in contemplation of an object or scene as
by finding itself in some way. Their poetry inhabits a borderline between
self-expression and description of the outside world. They generally write
in their own person and imply that their subject matter arises from their
own experiences, but they often are more interested in watching them-
selves experiencing external phenomena than in exploring their feelings
about themselves or others or constructing autobiographical narratives.
It could almost be said that they practice an ekphrastic mode of self-ex-
pression, locating themselves in their contemplation of a work of art or a
world that possesses the detail, beauty, and metaphorical suggestiveness
of a work of art. We can witness the complexity of this simultaneous
commitment to relinquishing the self and being true to its perceptions in
Keats's letters, in which he describes the poetry of negative capability in a
number of memorable phrases: "A Poet is the most unpoetical of any
thing in existence: because he has no Identity—he is continually in for—
and filling some other body";[2] the "camelion poet" [sic], as distinguished
from the poet of "the wordsworthian or egotistical sublime" is "not it-
self—it has no self—it is every thing and nothing—It has no character."[3]
But despite this stated opposition to the Wordsworthian model of sincer-
ity, Keats remains attracted to and influenced by what he understands as
Wordsworth's ability to "think into the human heart"[4] and acknowl-
edges a Wordsworthian type of genius that serves as an exception to his
own definition: "Men of Genius . . . have not any individuality, any deter-
mined character."[5] In terms of his own practice, Keats's definition of po-
etic genius might lead us to expect him to write something like dramatic
monologues or plays (which he did attempt) or even novels, when in fact
the poems by which he is known are written in his own person—and not
only in his own person, but in his person as a poet, suggesting that the
poet is after all a creature of interest to poetry. These contradictions re-
main unresolved, and to a large extent determine the texture of his odes.

Similar contradictions operate less visibly in the poetry of Bishop and
Merrill. Both poets make statements that recall Keats's idea of negative
capability. For example, Bishop explicitly shares Keats's belief that a poet
is someone who attempts to perceive the world without preconceptions,
effacing rather than asserting individual identity: "What one seems to

want in art, in experiencing it, is the same thing that is necessary for its creation, a self-forgetful, perfectly useless concentration."[6] In somewhat different terms, James Merrill argues, "You hardly ever need to *state* your feelings. The point is to keep the eyes open. Then what you feel is mimed back at you by the scene . . . I'd go a step further. We don't *know* what we feel until we see it distanced by this kind of translation."[7] This quotation encompasses several different beliefs simultaneously: it begins with the assumption that poetry is primarily a medium for self-expression and suggests that what we feel is automatically projected upon the environment around us. But in the second part of the quotation, it is observation itself that produces the feeling to be expressed. Finally, Merrill uses the metaphor of translation: instead of directly mirroring our feelings back to us, our environment somehow translates them to us during the act of observation, so that we only know our feelings in this foreign language. The poems we will encounter in the following pages dwell in this uncertain region, in which it cannot be said which takes precedence, feeling or seeing, self-expression or the effacement of the self.

Bishop's and Merrill's employment of negative capability can be seen most clearly in their attraction to the trope of reading. Again and again in their poems, these two poets present themselves not only as observers of objects but also as readers, by which I mean not only literal readers (of the book of "2,000 Illustrations," of *The National Geographic,* of the Ouija board) but also interpreters of more or less obscure phenomena. Merrill, referring to Bishop's poem "A Miracle for Breakfast," comments, "She tended to identify not with the magician on his dawn balcony but with the onlookers huddled and skeptical in the bread-line below."[8] In his poem dedicated to Bishop, "The Victor Dog," which sums up the "dog's life" to which art has committed them both, Merrill depicts the poet's task as "[l]isten[ing] long and hard as [one] is able," without judgment, even without movement. At the expression of violence or passion, the artist-dog "doesn't sneeze or howl; just listens harder."[9] The poet's task, in other words, is primarily to perceive external phenomena as unflinchingly as possible, rather than to color a scene with his or her feelings or to produce something new. With this unswerving and apparently neutral attention, Bishop's speakers read maps and paintings, monuments and geographies; Merrill's speakers read architecture and statues, puzzles and everyday objects that, to his eye, present the complexity of aesthetic artifacts. Merrill's *Changing Light at Sandover* announces the culmination of his career as the epic of the poet-as-reader (here, reader of the Ouija board). The premise of *Sandover,* in which the poet must interpret the enigmatic messages of various spirits, is designed to give new urgency to the central questions of reading: When and in what senses can I believe the author(s)? How can I detect the presence of external or self-censorship? How am I to sort out literal from metaphorical truth?

For each of these three poets, the relationship between observing or reading the world and the discovery of truth is cast somewhat differently. Keats's relationship to the world is mediated by his experience of beauty: "What the imagination seizes as Beauty must be truth";[10] "I never can feel certain of any truth but from a clear perception of its Beauty."[11] In theory, Keats's concept of beauty unites subjective and objective perspectives, sincerity and the loss of the self in observation: the individual, emotional experience of beauty is proof that we are seeing and interpreting the world properly. In practice, the possibility of beauty further destabilizes the already complicated relationship between individual perception and the greater world by removing any illusion of emotional detachment or neutrality, and for the poet further troubles an already fraught relationship between encounter and invention. The poet exercising negative capability commits to encountering scenes and objects independent from himself; to invent the scene or object encountered would be to close down the possibility of genuine mystery. By emphasizing the importance of beauty, however, Keats endangers the distinction between invention and encounter by opening the question: Is the beauty we discover in the world made or found? The destabilizing function of Keats's idea of beauty can be seen more clearly in contrast to Bishop's relative lack of interest in beauty for its own sake: in her poetry, any claim to truth instead rests implicitly upon an accurate observation of the world. Compared to Keats's odes, the surfaces of her poems are relatively untroubled, but at the same time she denies herself a number of Keats's poetic resources. Merrill, possessing both a Keatsian attraction to gorgeous objects and language, and a curiosity and skepticism that align him with Bishop, could be located at the stylistic midpoint between these two poets.

To consider the negative capability to which all three of these poets commit themselves as a form of sincerity provides a new perspective on the selves that we encounter in their poetry. First of all, I do not mean to imply that the only way to think about the sincerity of these poets is by conceiving it as self-effacement or absence—one could certainly identify sincerities based on presence as well: for example, the scrupulous honesty that causes the warm-hearted Keats to admit to a friend his occasional emotional coldness—"I assure you I sometimes feel not the influence of a Passion or Affection during a whole week—and so long this sometimes continues I begin to suspect myself and the genuiness of my feelings at other times";[12] or his belief that "[n]othing ever becomes real till it is experienced";[13] or his hard-earned impatience when he commands,

"Give me this credit—Do you not think I strive—to know myself?"[14] In Bishop's poetry, we could identify as sincerity her sense of proportion, the assurance she imparts that no single feeling or experience will be allowed undue influence. In Merrill's work, we could claim to find sincerity in his constant willingness to inquire to what degree his positions are also poses. (Of course, each of these definitions of sincerity as presence would be as vulnerable to the paradoxes of self-consciousness as the other forms we have encountered thus far.) But instead of following up these possibilities, I attempt to follow these poets' own procedure of bracketing the question of personal sincerity and looking instead for experiential truth in their perceptions of the external world.

This perspective brings into focus a John Keats, Elizabeth Bishop, and James Merrill in some ways counter to their reputations. Reading Keats's poems in the context of his letters renders him a much more autobiographical poet than he would be considered based on the evidence of the poems alone. By seeking sincerity as a form of negative capability in his poems rather than attending to the more confessional sincerity of his letters, we find a cerebral, disinterested Keats. If this perspective on Keats reveals a latent (and to my mind bracing) coolness in some of his odes, I would like to think that it renders Bishop and Merrill rather warmer than their critical reputations sometimes imply. These two poets have been both admired and condemned for their reticence, the scrupulousness and indirection with which they include details from their personal life in their poetry, and their formal control and restraint. Harold Bloom summarizes the negative connotations of this stance neatly: it "too readily can be mistaken for a psychic remoteness or a stylistic coldness."[15] One could speculate about the personal reasons for Bishop's and Merrill's relatively impersonal interest in the phenomenal world,[16] but I prefer to draw attention to their attraction to the trope of reading as a means of bringing into question the distinction between personal and impersonal itself. Their supposed reticence can be understood as a consequence of their highly developed sense of the ways in which everything in the world, including themselves, responds unpredictably to the pressure of interpretation.

By turning to the external world, these poets escape some of the ravages of self-consciousness. But they cannot help noticing themselves among the objects they examine, and under the pressure of their gaze this world itself takes on the instability we associate with self-consciousness. In this chapter, I examine these poets' special awareness of the intractability of the world's stubborn surfaces, and of the tendency of these surfaces to give way unexpectedly to interpretive depths, which may in turn be revealed to be still more surfaces. Things that could be metaphors insist on their uncannily literal existence, and things singled out for their concreteness are revealed as insubstantial without stabilizing into symbols for human experience, until the physical world comes to seem as unpredictable as the psychological one.

Observation as Dissolving

The idea of negative capability suggests two distinct activities: the relinquishment of an overly assertive, controlling self and the absorption of that self in perceiving the external world. It is always possible for the poet to claim to unite these two movements simply by projecting consciousness outward into the world instead of inward upon the self. But what makes Keats's "Ode to a Nightingale" an exemplary and also enduringly troublesome poem of negative capability is his decision to depict these two activities separately. The poem offers both a negative capability defined by the speaker's state of mind, a semi-conscious, receptive state; and a negative capability founded upon the speaker's imaginative flight to join the nightingale. To complicate matters further, the status of the nightingale remains unresolved in the course of the poem—it is both imagined creature and real bird, both of this earth and otherworldly. The poignancy of the speaker's desire to fly from "[t]he weariness, the fever, and the fret" of daily life and the incomparable mellifluousness of Keats's language do not conceal the poem's disjointedness, its inability or refusal to marry the receptive state of mind in which the speaker finds himself and the identification with the nightingale that he names as this state's cause.[17] By trying out multiple versions of self-loss and imaginative identification, instead of telling a single story about the relinquishment of the self to the perceivable world, Keats's Ode provides a catalogue of stances available to later poets of negative capability.

The disconnection between receptive semi-consciousness and what that consciousness receives is pressed upon the reader from the very first stanza. We are introduced to a speaker whose equivocal state of consciousness at first appears to have no cause:

> My heart aches, and a drowsy numbness pains
>   My sense, as though of hemlock I had drunk,
> Or emptied some dull opiate to the drains
>   One minute past, and Lethe-wards had sunk.[18]

Keats here depicts a characteristic mood, balanced precariously on the boundary between consciousness and unconsciousness. If we think of negative capability as a kind of willed unconsciousness, this passage draws our attention to the difficulty of maintaining such a state, temporally limited to the fleeting moment before unconsciousness takes hold completely. The borderline realm between consciousness and unconsciousness threatens to disappear altogether when the speaker describes numbness as painful; the movement of the heart toward unconsciousness contradictorily intensifies feeling rather than diminishing it.

As if this receptive passivity cannot be maintained on its own, the poem abruptly seeks an external reason for it in order to secure the speaker's flickering mind:

> 'Tis not through envy of thy happy lot,
>> But being too happy in thine happiness,—
>>> That thou, light-winged Dryad of the trees,
>> In some melodious plot
> Of beechen green, and shadows numberless,
>> Singest of summer in full-throated ease.[19]

But the state of mind in the first part of the stanza and the "light-winged Dryad" retrospectively assigned as its cause remain disconnected. The speaker claims that his figuratively suicidal numbness comes not from the distance he experiences from the nightingale (not from "envy"), but from his union with it ("being too happy in thine happiness"). But the painful, drowsy, deathlike numbness of the first part of the stanza and the hyperbolic happiness, summer lushness, and ease of the second part of the stanza remain distinct; and the nightingale, failing to serve its role as a bridge between the two, becomes peculiarly superfluous.[20] The mind, left open, can neither stay nor fly, and this indecision governs the remainder of the poem.

The following stanza confirms that the empathetic union between poet and nightingale that has just been claimed has not yet actually taken place, as the speaker states his desire to "fade [with the nightingale] away into the forest dim."[21] If union with the nightingale is the speaker's goal, the poem at the same time resists this goal by continually raising the question: When can I be entirely sure that the desired poetic experience has occurred? When am I both poetically active (conscious) and passive (unconscious) enough to receive true inspiration? This stanza and the next give further alternatives for achieving conscious unconsciousness, or versions of negative capability: in stanza 2 through drunkenness ("O, for a draught of vintage!")[22] and in stanza 3 by defining it against its opposite, "[t]he weariness, the fever, and the fret" of human existence.[23] The latter alternative suggests that the receptiveness of negative capability could be achieved simply by escaping consciousness of the pains of lived experience, but this alternative threatens to reduce semi-consciousness to mere unconsciousness. In the course of these two stanzas the nightingale is all but absent, and the poem courts an almost Byronic forgetfulness. But then Keats swiftly reorients his poem to the other side of negative capability: its promise of absorption in an external object or being.

Rejecting escapism, the speaker reasserts his will, abruptly insisting that the desired union between himself and the nightingale will occur and then has occurred:

> Away! Away! For I will fly to thee,
>   Not charioted by Bacchus and his pards,
> But on the viewless wings of Poesy,
>   Though the dull brain perplexes and retards:
> Already with thee![24]

If "Already with thee" is successful, it is successful in a strangely self-thwarting manner.[25] The "brain" is abandoned in favor of "poesy," but this same "dull brain" is likely an instrument that the poet must use to imagine the union of himself and the nightingale. Although relinquishing his own consciousness may help the poet be completely "with" the nightingale, he needs this consciousness in order to assert his will and summon the language that makes the claim "Already with thee!" possible. This assertion undercuts itself in another sense: the metaphorical association of the nightingale with "the viewless wings of Poesy" encourages our suspicion that the nightingale is a convenient figure of thought, almost literally a mere vehicle, rather than a genuinely independent creature that can provide an external destination for the poet's consciousness, as if the poet uses "poesy" to return full circle to "poesy." The passage is an elaborate demonstration of the difficulty of achieving unconsciousness through heightened self-consciousness.

But as if to prove the unpredictability of the poetry of negative capability, the ways in which forced passivity can give way to an open-ended alertness, pyrrhic success to a fortunate failure, the poem here discovers a new way of perceiving the world:

>   . . . tender is the night,
> And haply the Queen-Moon is on her throne,
>   Cluster'd around by all her starry Fays;
> But here there is no light,

Save what from heaven is with the breezes blown
   Through verdurous glooms and winding mossy ways.

I cannot see what flowers are at my feet,
   Nor what soft incense hangs upon the boughs,
But, in embalmed darkness, guess each sweet
   Wherewith the seasonable month endows
The grass, the thicket, and the fruit-tree wild;
   White hawthorn, and the pastoral eglantine;
      Fast fading violets cover'd up in leaves;
         And mid-May's eldest child,
The coming musk-rose, full of dewy wine,
   The murmurous haunt of flies on summer eves.[26]

What has been achieved is not exactly union with the nightingale, nor is it a poetry of pure observation. The poet is neither experiencing the world as a nightingale would nor looking at the bird, but using a partial identification with the nightingale to alter and heighten his mode of perception. The poet may be unified with the nightingale in the sense that he is experiencing a kind of nightingale-consciousness, but if this is the case, the main feature of this consciousness is its limitations. The speaker's sense of feeling remains only in an abstracted form (enough to register the night as "tender"), and his sense of sight has been reduced to pure speculation—he can no longer say for sure whether the moon is out or not.[27] Light cannot be seen, only felt as "breezes blown," and the "embalmed darkness" forces the poet to guess, rather than identify, the features of his surroundings. We can now see that the nightingale's true function is not as an external object of address or praise, but as a method of strategic self-blinding. Unexpectedly, this self-blinding becomes the experience that makes visual description possible: the last seven lines of the stanza reproduced above, subsumed under the category of "guessing," are the most visually and sensually realized of the poem. This paradoxical blend of speculative uncertainty and empirical detail is the poem's most successful mixture of consciousness and unconsciousness, but apparently it cannot be maintained. As the poet's vision accumulates sensual detail (moving from the pared-down "grass" and "thicket" to the musk-rose, whose characteristics are elaborated over three lines), he loses touch with the nightingale, the vehicle of his imaginative self-blinding and unconsciousness, and by the end of the stanza, we wonder if the poet has not become too wakeful.

If this part of the poem represents a successful absorption of the self in the external world, the external world is here represented not by the nightingale, but by the other features of the poet's environment. The nightingale becomes a third, mediating party—separate from the poet but also part of him; real but also mythic; encountered as an independent being but also, at least in its figurative status, invented. The poem, rather than halting at this achieved vision, goes on to heighten these conflicts: the nightingale maintains its independence as a singer "pouring forth [its] soul abroad / In such an ecstasy!"[28] but then becomes a figure of thought in its imagined immortality. At the same time, the distinction between consciousness and unconsciousness becomes more extreme, as the speaker begins to court unconsciousness in the form of death. Poetry, it would seem, is designed neither to anticipate the poet's final, complete unconsciousness in death nor to imagine and praise the nightingale's super-conscious immortality; neither to sustain unconsciousness nor to permit complete absorption in a separate being—it must inhabit a space defined by the interplay and contradictions of these two possibilities.

It is to this space that the poem returns in its final stanza. Ostensibly a complaint against the "deceit" of the poet's fancy, which permitted his temporary but unsustainable imaginative union with the nightingale, this stanza in fact reaffirms the experience that the imaginative flight with the nightingale made possible: the blending of consciousness and unconsciousness. The stanza rejects the most explicit form of self-consciousness, in which the poet suddenly becomes aware of his own voice—"Forlorn! the very word is like a bell"[29]—in favor of a more implicit form in the stanza's closing lines: "Was it a vision or a waking dream? / Fled is that music;—Do I wake or sleep?"[30] Here we come full circle to the beginning of the poem, feeling numbness becoming conscious sleeping. Rather than serving as a distinct location to which the poet's consciousness can "fly," or an object that can be observed and described, the nightingale remains a shadowy harbinger of that which is outside of the poet. The nightingale does not make it possible for the poet to move forward from the threshold between consciousness and unconsciousness, the place of his never-completed initiation into poetry; he can only return to it again and again.[31]

Elizabeth Bishop's poem "In the Waiting Room" introduces us to a world as far from Keats's Ode as it is possible to imagine. In contrast to Keats's lush language and imagery, we find a stunning renunciation of the resources of poetry, and in their place what at first appears to be an undistinguished catalogue of ordinary American life:

In Worcester, Massachusetts,
I went with Aunt Consuelo

> To keep her dentist's appointment
> And sat and waited for her
> In the dentist's waiting room.[32]

But this refusal of sonic and metaphorical richness works somewhat in the way that Keats's deliberate blinding of his senses in stanzas 4 and 5 of his Ode does: unexpectedly, it precipitates a new way of seeing. As in Keats's Ode, Bishop's poem includes two movements of negative capability: the absorption of the self in external phenomena and the loss of the self in swooning semi-consciousness. But instead of juxtaposing different versions of each of these conditions, Bishop's poem dramatizes the uncontrollable transformation of the former state into the latter. In spite of its end-stopped abruptness, "In the Waiting Room" is more seamless than Keats's Ode in its gradual progression from casual self-possession to an immersing alienation. Bishop's poem could be described as both less and more a poem of negative capability than "Ode to a Nightingale": less in its determined wakefulness, the belief it imparts that we can be accurate about our states of being in the same way that we can be accurate about the objects we observe; and more in the way it permits us to watch the poem unnerve the poet, as if the loss of self that accompanies the examination of the world takes her completely by surprise.

The experiences that define Keats's Ode are intoxication, meditation, empathy, and imaginative identification; in Bishop's poem, these experiences are summed up in the act of reading. Reading governs the poem literally, in the sense that the young girl's coming-to-consciousness interrupts a long passage in which she is portrayed reading the *National Geographic;* and procedurally, if we think of the poet's seemingly unselective cataloguing of the girl's environment as analogous to the girl's unselective reading of her magazine. Like the poem's protagonist, Bishop reads her environment "straight through," not omitting "the yellow margins, the date," almost as if she were "too shy to stop."[33] The act of reading, whether perusing a magazine or registering the aspects of a room, at first appears to be an act in which the distance between the self and what is observed remains stable. The words on the page and the objects in the room can be depended upon to remain discrete, and the reader can exert a certain amount of control over them. But this poem becomes a poem of negative capability when Bishop uses the trope of reading to prepare for a loss of control and absorption into another being. Reading is shown to be the ground upon which involvement and detachment, recognition and strangeness can become unexpectedly interchangeable.

The child's reading of the *National Geographic* establishes the mixture of recognition and alienation that will later structure her onset of self-consciousness. First of all, reading in the most basic sense already involves a puzzling combination of sameness and difference. In order to read, the child must be familiar with letters and words—one could almost go so far as to say that we can only read what we already know. But at the same time, new combinations of words and letters impart new information. The images that the child encounters in the *National Geographic* exhibit an analogous familiarity and newness:

> A dead man slung on a pole
> —"Long pig," the caption said.
> Babies with pointed heads
> wound round and round with string;
> black, naked women with necks
> wound round and round with wire
> like the necks of light bulbs.
> Their breasts were horrifying.[34]

In this passage, the familiar and unfamiliar coexist in uncomfortable proximity because, unlike the adult whose interpretive skills are more developed, the child does not select or ignore certain details that she encounters. She recognizes men, women, babies, clothing, wire, and light bulbs, but these familiar objects have been dislocated from the contexts in which she knows them. In the most extreme instance, one man's body has become so dislocated that it signifies "meat" instead of humanness. The preliminary attempt at interpretation, "Their breasts were horrifying," similarly hovers between familiarity and unfamiliarity, for it is not clear whether the breasts are horrifying because they are "exotic" breasts or because the child understands them to be breaking a more familiar taboo against sexual display. Reading is the experience in which the distinction between self and other gives way to a series of signifiers that are both and neither.

It is in the midst of this act of reading that the crisis of the poem comes: the speaker hears "an *oh!* of pain" and cannot tell whether it is coming from herself or her aunt: "Without thinking at all / I was my foolish aunt, / I—we—were falling, falling." And at this moment a new and more disturbing form of reading is forced upon the speaker—she learns to read herself as a set of italicized signifiers: "I felt: you are an *I*, / you are an *Elizabeth*, / you are one of *them*." The child must trade her masterful eye for a vulnerable body; after the moment of revelation, she flinches from observation for the first time—"I scarcely dared to look / to see what it was I was"[35]—because looking at herself destroys the comforting illusion of invisibility. But as Marjorie Levinson suggests, we may be surprised that here "coming to consciousness [does] not take the form familiar to us from the long history of both Cartesian and German philosophies of the subject, 'where the subject makes itself subject by constructing itself objectively to itself.' . . . The shaping moment in "In the Waiting Room" is not equated with separation but convergence."[36] To expand upon this insight, Bishop implicates separation and convergence in one another. It is the speaker's sense of convergence with her aunt and with humankind more generally that forces her to look at herself; she comes to examine herself as an object because she discovers that this self belongs to a larger group of objects (other social selves) from which the examining self feels separate. Her emerging self-consciousness simultaneously entails a sense of isolation—"the sensation of falling off / the round, turning world / into cold, blue-black space"—and engulfment—"[the room] was sliding / beneath a big black wave, / another, and another."[37] She is both newly familiar to herself and utterly strange.

The mixture of the all-too-familiar and the irrecoverably foreign that guides the child's reading cannot be limited to the *National Geographic;* it comes to define her entire world. Or as the child puts it, in both reading and living, what she experiences as superlatively "unlikely" is the experience of likeness or recognition.[38] Negative capability is identifiable in the poem as the surprise of likeness, or the way that looking at exterior objects can unexpectedly give way to a pressure toward reading oneself. (This pressure is something that Bishop will both court and resist over the course of her career.) Bishop does not invite unconsciousness in the way that Keats does, but she finds it all the same at the heart of the ordinary act of reading. We are made to understand that casting poetry as an act of observation, however seemingly unselective, open, and innocent, does nothing to stabilize poetry, or to rescue the poet from the quicksands of the self.

James Merrill's "An Urban Convalescence" in a number of ways picks up where Bishop's poem leaves off. The poem shares Bishop's urge to catalogue the surface of her world, and like Bishop, Merrill finds that such cataloguing is as likely to dissolve as to reaffirm the observing, interpreting self. Forgetfulness, loss, and unconsciousness come without being sought, and, as Keats suggested in "Ode to a Nightingale," they cannot be seamlessly transmuted into an abandonment of the self to the experience of the world. We find in Merrill's poem a speaker who understands that the rips he perceives in the visual fabric of his urban environment portend the gaps in his memory and in his ability to make sense of his surroundings, just as Bishop's speaker comes to understand the foreignness she perceives outside of herself as a harbinger of her own foreignness to herself. What Merrill's poem adds is an explicit consideration of the relationship between negative capability and self-knowledge. He casts doubt upon the familiar poetic situation in which losing oneself in the contemplation of a landscape or scene climaxes in the achievement of self-knowledge.

The poem introduces itself as a depiction of what the speaker sees "[o]ut for a walk, after a week in bed," but what is seen soon becomes mixed up with what can no longer be seen. The fragility of the physical world, the tricks that memory plays, and the intermingling of actual and represented worlds conspire to confound presence and absence, as the speaker attempts to remember the building that once stood on his block:

> Wait. Yes. Vaguely a presence rises
> Some five floors high, of shabby stone
> —Or am I confusing it with another one
> In another part of town, or of the world?—
> And over its lintel into focus vaguely
> Misted with blood (my eyes are shut)
> A single garland sways, stone fruit, stone leaves,
> Which years of grit had etched until it thrust
> Roots down, even into the poor soil of my seeing.
> When did the garland become part of me?
> I ask myself, amused almost,
> Then shiver once from head to toe.[39]

The speaker's attempt to conjure up the missing building is thwarted not only by his lapses in memory but also by other insistent presences: the emphatic garland and his own body, strikingly represented by the inside of the eyelid. (As in the case of Bishop's newly self-conscious speaker in "In the Waiting Room," the body cannot help perceiving itself as well as the outside world.) Meanwhile, the difference between represented and actual garlands, and between the eye of the speaker and what it observes, is eroded by the startling idea that the garland has "thrust / Roots down, even into the poor soil of [the viewer's] seeing." The "amused" distance of the unimplicated observer gives way to genuine fear as the speaker "shiver[s] once from head to toe." Reading, or here the interpretation of visual data, creates shifting ground upon which detachment gives way to helpless involvement and vice versa.

As the poem continues, Merrill increasingly insists upon the impossibility of distinguishing between reality and representations of reality;

more and more, it appears that the world is shot through with implicit interpretations from the beginning, rendering the speaker's own interpretations secondary at best. The garland that he remembers becomes associated with the memory of "a particularly cheap engraving of garlands."[40] Here, we might expect to be squarely on the side of representation, but in a surprising reversal, this piece of paper bearing a representation of plants is used to wrap the dripping ends of actual plants. Memory transforms the material world into representations, but in this memory a representation itself becomes material, suggesting that memories can unsettle us with their concreteness as well as their ghostliness. Meanwhile, the woman who holds the flowers in the speaker's memory becomes "toppled under that year's fashions. / The words she must have spoken, setting her face / To fluttering like a veil, I cannot hear now."[41] In this world, faces and veils (of words) refuse to remain separate. By implication, it is difficult to determine how "veiled" the poet is in this poem, not because he is determined to hide himself but because nothing exists but veils, layers of visual input, artistic representations, and memories that can be pulled aside only to reveal still more layers.

The speaker makes an apparent effort to organize these layers by summing up:

> Well, that is what life does. I stare
> A moment longer, so. And presently
> The massive volume of the world
> Closes again.
>
> Upon that book I swear
> To abide by what it teaches:
> Gospels of ugliness and waste,
> Of towering voids, of soiled gusts,
> Of a shrieking to be faced
> Full into, eyes astream with cold
>
> With cold?
> All right then. With self-knowledge.[42]

In contrast to the implicit hope that an undesigning openness to the world produces true knowledge both of the world and of the self, this passage offers a particularly graphic depiction of the disjunction between perception and self-knowledge. We notice first the equivocal language of the passage. The book of the world has not been opened to facilitate reading; rather, it has been opened in a more violent sense through the opening of a gap in the physical world accomplished by the destruction of a building in the speaker's neighborhood. This book can be sworn on, and self-knowledge claimed, only once it is closed again, placing knowledge and vows in opposition to the poem's vision of destruction. Even more vividly, Merrill's image of "eyes astream . . . with self-knowledge" heightens our sense of the incommensurability of the eye's physical being (here an organ of touch as much as an organ of sight) and our ability to gain meaning from the visible world. Negative capability as openness to the world (represented here by the vulnerability of the exposed eyeball) offers the poet experience that refuses to be translated into knowledge.

These choices of language suggest that we should be suspicious of what seems to be the literal meaning of the passage: that "self-knowledge" indicates a knowledge of the world's destructibility, an acceptance (signaled by the speaker's tears) of the ugly gaps that continually open in the physical world and in human memory and consciousness. This knowledge is not exactly empirical knowledge, for in the passage preceding the conclusion—"that is what life does"—the speaker describes his own home crumbling, while we know that it still stands. It is also not entirely accurate to say that the speaker has achieved the metaphysical knowledge that the world is destructible, ridden with "ugliness and waste," "voids" and "gusts," because, as we have seen, the world is as troubled by its abundance of presences (the insistence of the physical world, layered over with the ghostly representations of the past) as its absences. "What life does" is as much refuse destruction as accomplish it—as Merrill puts it in another poem, "nothing *either* lasts *or* ends."[43] To the extent that this passage describes self-knowledge as resignation to the harsh realities of the world, it expresses at best a partial self-knowledge, one that fails to acknowledge the equally insistent and unasked-for gifts the world offers. Ultimately, in this passage, "self-knowledge" becomes a marker for its impossibility—the self can definitively "know" neither the presences of its world nor its world's absences, because each tends to transform into the other.[44]

For a time, the word "self-knowledge" represented the dead end of the poem—Merrill could not decide what kind of closing to add.[45] But later he ends the poem in a way that brings us full circle to one of the questions raised by Keats's Ode: What is the place of the poet's inventiveness in a poetry of negative capability? When can we be certain that the poet encounters a reality independent from herself rather than a reality she has imagined? Just as Keats's identification with the nightingale is destroyed when he hears himself pronounce the word "Forlorn," Merrill turns upon his own tendency to wrap literary language around the mysteries of experience:

> . . . The sickness of our time requires
> That [the new buildings] as well be blasted in their prime
> . . .
> There are certain phrases which to use in a poem
> Is like rubbing silver with quicksilver. Bright
> But facile, the glamour deadens overnight.
> For instance, how "the sickness of our time"
>
> Enhances, then debases, what I feel.[46]

Here, Merrill extends his reading of the world to a reading of his own language, but this self-consciousness can no more produce stable self-knowledge than Keats hearing himself speak the word "Forlorn" can put him firmly on the side of sleep or wakefulness. The falsifying phrase, "the sickness of our time," can be crossed out, but the unpredictable alternation of enhancement and debasement cannot be evaded. (The poem reestablishes its ongoing attraction to "glamorous" language in subsequent phrases, such as "that honey-slow descent / Of the Champs-Elysées.")[47] By reading himself, the poet does not provide the definitive interpretation of his poem, but instead adds one more layer of reading to a scene already overlaid with multiple interpretations. Under these circumstances, the distinction between invention and encounter breaks down: both activities are in thrall to the flickering alternation of presence and absence, embellishment and nakedness. Replete with meanings, the world refuses to render up a unified metaphorical meaning that the poet could create or control.

Surface Tension

The internal resistance that Merrill's "An Urban Convalescence" generates against its own impulse to interpret what he has seen as offering self-knowledge is part of a larger desire, identifiable in each of these three poets, to cling to the surface of what they perceive while resisting the urge to immediately interpret it or make it into metaphors for the self's epiphanies. In this version of negative capability, Keats, Bishop, and Merrill develop strategies to keep their eyes arrested at the sensual or decorative surface of things in order to avoid turning surfaces into depths, substituting the self for the world. Thus far I have treated visual observation and reading as if they were the same activity, but a number of Keats's, Bishop's, and Merrill's poems explore possible tensions between these two acts, particularly if we understand "seeing" to denote scanning a surface visually and "reading" to connote a second-order interpretation that designates metaphorical or symbolic meaning. Readers have long admired Bishop as a poet of description and noted her resistance to attributing supersensory significance to what she observes.[48] Merrill exhibits less of this resistance, particularly in his earlier poetry, but he too finds ways to register his own ambivalence about the ways in which reading interferes with seeing. As Bonnie Costello comments in relation to Bishop, all three poets "spread subjectivity out across a visual surface rather than centering it in opposition to the visual as something absolute which can endow it with meaning."[49] Together, these three poets chart how surfaces give way not to depth or significance, but to still more surfaces, which are as likely to resist as give way to the inquiring subject.

In Keats's "Ode on Indolence," the poet's resistance to attributing allegorical significance to the figures he encounters is directly linked to the semi-conscious receptiveness that characterizes the negative capability developed in "Ode to a Nightingale." As the poem opens, both the poet and we are faced with three figures whose status is unclear:

> With bowed necks, and joined hands, side-faced;
> . . . one behind the other stepp'd serene,
>   In placid sandals, and in white robes graced:
> They pass'd, like figures on a marble urn
>   When shifted round to see the other side;
>   They came again, as when the urn once more
> Is shifted round, the first seen shades return;
>   And they were strange to me.[50]

These beings hover on the boundary between the literal and the metaphorical. They have human forms, and thus seem to be of the same order of reality as the poet, an impression reinforced by the fact that they share his environment with him, but he does not hail them as fellow men and women. Instead, the stylization of their costumes and poses places them in the world of art. They appear to move freely, as autonomous creatures, but then the poet describes them as resembling figures on an urn. This image implies that the figures also inhabit a borderline between what the poet encounters and what he invents: if the figures move of their own accord, they are independent visitations; but if they move because an urn has been rotated to create the illusion of movement, then we are reminded in a strikingly literal way that these images are in the poet's hands. It is as if Keats is saying to us that even the poet of negative capability cannot help inventing the world he wishes to encounter, wrenching that world into metaphorical significance. But he can create a counter-current to his own powers of creation and claim to inhabit a mysterious world where invented and encountered, literal and metaphorical blur.

The suspension of these figures in the literal realm, achieved by their apparent reluctance to reveal their allegorical meaning, allows the poet to dwell in the realm of unanswered questions, the place where he ended in "Ode to a Nightingale" ("Do I wake or sleep?"), and the place to which he will return in "Ode on a Grecian Urn":

> How is it, shadows, that I knew ye not?
> > How came ye muffled in so hush a masque?
> Was it a silent deep-disguised plot
> > To steal away, and leave without a task
> My idle days?[51]

Though they hint of interpretive depths to be plumbed ("deep-disguised plot"), these lines skim the surface of the figures, postponing their inevitable translation into allegory. The poet's refusal to recognize his own metaphors is in an important sense a fiction—he "knows them not" because he is pretending not to know them. The willfulness of this refusal of acknowledgment underlines the poet's investment in maintaining the surface texture of his vision. Similar in function to the nightingale, the liminal presence of these figures creates the conditions for a version of negative capability, a kind of conscious unconsciousness:

> Ripe was the drowsy hour;
> > The blissful cloud of summer-indolence
> > > Benumb'd my eyes; my pulse grew less and less;
> Pain had no sting, and pleasure's wreath no flower.
> > O, why did ye not melt, and leave my sense
> > > Unhaunted quite of all but—nothingness?[52]

The final rhetorical question helps explain the necessity of the figures: despite his claim to desire otherwise, they make the poet's borderline state possible. Without this haunting, the tension between consciousness and unconsciousness would be lost. The speaker implies that if the figures did not haunt him then "nothingness" itself must, unless he is to become nothing.

But because this semi-consciousness is an unstable state, liable to slide into a more definitive sleep or wakefulness, the moment in which the figures are recognized and named cannot be put off forever. The poet af-

firms what we have suspected all along, that these creatures are poetic fig-
ures or metaphors that he has invented:

> . . . I knew the three:
> The first was a fair maid, and Love her name;
> The second was Ambition, pale of cheek,
> And ever watchful with fatigued eye;
> The last, whom I love more, the more of blame
> Is heap'd upon her, maiden most unmeek,—
> I knew to be my demon Poesy.[53]

If this poem set out in search of others rather than the self, it has circled
fully back in on itself, the act of writing poetry ending in the discovery of
Poesy. This almost perverse circularity, echoing the identification of the
nightingale with Poesy, works as an explanation of why negative capabil-
ity is necessary to the poet. Without the possibility of an encounter with
the unknown, the poet finds only himself, his powers of invention barren.
As if to prove that the animating tension of the poem depended upon the
suspension of this moment of recognition, the poem slowly self-destructs
once the moment has occurred. The figures fade, and even though the
poem continues for three more stanzas, it can do little other than recon-
firm, again and again, this loss. Keats must devise new means to linger
over the surface of his experience.

Bishop's "At the Fishhouses" deploys observation against epiphany
with less difficulty than Keats's "Ode on Indolence," in part because she
sidesteps the question of the relationship between encounter and inven-
tion by clearly marking the phenomena she observes as external. (Her
poem is less troubled than Keats's, but it also loses a dimension that
Keats found it possible to include.) The poem is structured as a gradual
accumulation of visual detail that builds to what appears to be a super-
sensory epiphany, but is in fact, I will argue, an anti-epiphany. In this
sense, "At the Fishhouses" is unusually explicit in its resistance to turning
an observed object into a metaphor; Bishop's poems more commonly ex-
ert this resistance in quieter ways, through tonal effects as much as narra-
tive movement. In its atypical exemplarity, "At the Fishhouses" could be
read as an allegory of these subtler effects.

The poem opens with forty-six lines of minutely detailed observation,
apparently governed solely by the speaker's roving eye, which takes in an
old man netting, the architecture of the five fishhouses surrounding him,
the smaller paraphernalia of the fishing industry (benches, lobster pots,
masts, fish tubs, wheelbarrows), the capstan on the slope behind the

houses, the old man's knife, and tree trunks at the water's edge. The shifting of focus and scale here feels realistically arbitrary: the things close up are not necessarily more important than the things that are far away, nor are the things represented in detail more important than the things left in outline. But one aspect of the scene comes to be emphasized:

> All is silver: the heavy surface of the sea,
> swelling slowly as if considering spilling over,
> is opaque, but the silver of the benches,
> the lobster pots, and masts, scattered
> among the wild jagged rocks,
> is of an apparent translucence
> like the small old buildings with an emerald moss
> growing on their shoreward walls.
> The big fish tubs are completely lined
> with layers of beautiful herring scales
> and the wheelbarrows are similarly plastered
> with creamy iridescent coats of mail,
> with small iridescent flies crawling on them.[54]

This description presents a paradox: the silver that we know is translucent—the water of the sea—looks opaque, while the silver that we know is opaque—the benches, pots, and small old buildings—appears translucent. This paradox implies a more general set of questions: To what extent can we "see through" (decode or interpret) objects? What if what seems opaque, realistic, a thing-in-itself, is actually translucent, a medium for transmitting light, a surface partially revealing something behind it? And what if the object that seems to be a mere screen or signifier for something else asserts its own materiality? By describing the objects around her as uniformly silver (down to the iridescent flies), Bishop heightens our sense of the world as a metal-plated surface that resists interpretive penetration (covered as it is in a "coat of mail").[55] But at the same time, we are surprised by an "apparent translucence" that extends even to the sturdy moss-covered buildings.

This shifting movement between opacity and translucence becomes increasingly urgent as the speaker turns to the sea itself, a body that is surface and depth at once. She approaches the sea with the words, "Cold dark deep and absolutely clear, / element bearable to no mortal," and then instinctively backs away from this inhuman and absolute clarity, this transparency that destroys all surfaces. She, and we, are temporarily distracted by the mediating appearance of a seal who does, in a more literal sense, find the sea inhabitable. But she remains irretrievably drawn to the sea's extra-literal portent and begins again, "Cold dark deep and absolutely clear, / the clear gray icy water . . ." She again turns away, this time physically turning backwards toward the fir trees that line the shore. But it seems that even in the ordinary, human world she looks toward, thoughts of transcendent meaning are unavoidable, so that looking at the seal leads to thoughts about baptism and looking at the fir trees reminds her of Christmas.[56]

Finally, she faces the sea fully, and apparently accepts the invitation to epiphany it has presented all along:

> . . . The water seems suspended
> above the rounded gray and blue-gray stones.
> I have seen it over and over, the same sea, the same
> slightly, indifferently swinging above the stones,
> icily free above the stones,
> above the stones and then the world.
> If you should dip your hand in,
> your wrist would ache immediately,
> your bones would begin to ache and your hand would burn
> as if the water were a transmutation of fire
> that feeds on stones and burns with a dark gray flame.
> If you tasted it, it would first taste bitter,
> then briny, then surely burn your tongue.
> It is like what we imagine knowledge to be:
> Dark, salt, clear, moving, utterly free,
> Drawn from the cold hard mouth
> Of the world, derived from the rocky breasts
> Forever, flowing and drawn, and since
> Our knowledge is historical, flowing, and flown.[57]

The force and satisfaction of this closing depend upon the revelation of the sea as a metaphor for knowledge: suddenly, the poet has decided to interpret the sea for us, to make it mean something more than it has meant up until now. But this passage resists its own movement toward meaning in a number of ways. The metaphor of the sea for knowledge depends upon our ability to recognize the senses in which the observable qualities of the sea—darkness, saltiness, clarity, movement—also characterize the abstract idea of knowledge. But these qualities of the sea are not exactly perceivable. It is difficult to look at the ocean: it seems to be transparent (so that the speaker can see the stones below) but also opaque, "suspended / above" what it covers, as if the surface of the sea were a suspended solid rather than part of the element of suspension. It is difficult as well to assess the qualities of the ocean by touching it: the physical experience inaccurately suggests great heat instead of great coldness, and later the movement of the sea reminds us that we can never touch the same ocean twice (in counterpoint to the earlier repetition of "same"). It is difficult to taste the ocean, because the taste changes on the tongue and then turns to burning touch. Empirical observation is untrustworthy: sensory input creates the metaphorical association of the sea with fire rather than providing literal knowledge about its qualities.

Under these circumstances, if the sea is "like what we imagine knowledge to be" (phrasing that underlines the metaphorical and speculative nature of this equivalence), then what we imagine knowledge to be is in an important sense unknowable. The sea is like knowledge not in its present qualities but in its elusiveness, its refusal to present either a stable surface to be mapped or a depth to be plumbed.[58] The sea-as-knowledge cannot be accurately perceived by human beings—it is entirely "indifferent" to and "free" from them, an indifference that is emphasized by the inhuman nature of the "cold hard mouth" and "rocky breasts" from which it is drawn and derived.[59] The "knowledge" offered at the end of the poem is contentless; like the "self-knowledge" of "An Urban Convalescence" it is a marker of absence rather than presence. The epiphany to which Bishop's observations have led turns out to be a recognition that empirical observation cannot justify abstract equivalences—in other words, a recognition that her own epiphanic leap from observation to insight is groundless.[60] The poem's attraction to metaphorical depths serves only to reinforce its own surfaces.

Merrill more readily than Bishop gives into the temptation of ascribing metaphorical significance to perceivable objects, but he too voices his resistance to this activity. His early poems in particular are often emblem poems, seizing upon objects with metaphorical potential to be exploited by the poet. But from the beginning, one of the main things that these objects come to represent is their own resistance to metaphorical representation. For example, the first poem of *First Poems,* "The Black Swan," includes the observation:

> Though the black swan's arched neck is like
> A question-mark on the lake,
> The swan outlaws all possible questioning:
> A thing in itself.[61]

The speaker simultaneously notes the resemblance of the swan to a question mark and the inappropriateness, in a sense the meaninglessness of this resemblance—the swan's being and the poet's questions remain separate. However fanciful and uninformative it may be, the poetic attraction to resemblances continues to be irresistible; the young poet is not content to leave the swan as a "thing in itself," and it is immediately transformed into "[a] thing in itself, like love, like submarine / Disaster"[62]—but the resistance to such equations remains on record.

By insisting upon observable surfaces and delaying or countering these surfaces' tendencies to give way to depths, Bishop and Merrill implicitly question the opposition between surface and depth as a metaphor for subjectivity. They are anticipated in this questioning by Keats's "Ode to Psyche," which tries to remake Psyche's shrine in the depths of the poet's own mind, a depth in turn to be penetrated by the "warm Love" of Cupid;[63] but the poem ends up dismantling the distinction between inside and outside altogether, rendering the poet's mind as yet another picture plane. In Romantic terms, according to the dichotomy that opposes surfaces to depths, our social self is sometimes understood as a surface self, while our "private" self is understood as our more authentic, deep self. Or, in Freudian terms, our manifest consciousness both cloaks and represents our deeper unconscious drives. In psychosexual terms, the penetrability of the body's surfaces becomes a crucial marker of identity. Bishop challenges this last idea in "Brazil, January 1, 1502," in which she stages a conflict between the hyperbolically detailed surface of the jungle, "every square inch filling in with foliage,"[64] and the European conquerors who wish to tear through this tapestry and, as a logical extension of this act, rape the indigenous women. But rather than simply protesting against the violent penetration of surfaces and insisting upon the sanctity of depths, Bishop enacts an uneasy identification with the conquerors as well as their victims. Like the Portuguese, she has been raised in a Christian tradition that nurtures the impulse to select and give symbolic meaning to individual items of this seamless surface, but like them she is also halted and baffled by the surfaces she confronts. The poem ultimately suggests that identity is not defined by the ability to penetrate or to be penetrated; instead, all human beings are destined to be arrested by surfaces that render penetration beside the point.

But the most explicit challenge to the opposition of surfaces to depths as a model of subjectivity comes in Merrill's "Mornings in a New House," a poem which, rather than depicting the devices of repression as surfaces concealing the depths of what must be repressed, portrays both these devices and what they are supposed to conceal as arresting surfaces, until the difference between what is repressed and the external forms of repression becomes impossibly blurred. At the beginning of the poem, a fire has been lit in the speaker's new house, "[b]y whom a cold man hardly cares,"[65] a phrase with a double meaning that economically prepares us for the ambiguities to come. Does the man fail to care who lights his fire because he is emotionally cold, or because he is so physically cold that he can only warm himself, lacking any extra energy to feel curiosity about the identity of his helper? Is the problem here too little need (the effect of repression), or too much (which may require repression)? Similarly throughout the poem, the act of repression and feelings needing to be repressed, violence and suffering, love and hate occupy a single line.

The fire that has been placed between the speaker and his humiliating needs serves as both cure and reminder of those needs, and the speaker explains that now "[h]abit arranges the fire screen," as if this screen serves as a protective shield against his physical and emotional vulnerability. But the screen is not a blank surface; it too represents feelings that have been repressed. The screen, stitched by his mother, is "crewelwork," cruel work (the question of whether cruelty is being suffered or inflicted left deliberately open) in part because it serves as a reminder of the need for repression, indirectly indicating the presence of the fire that it shields. But it is also cruel work because it represents his mother's displaced rebellion against her own mother: "His mother as a child / Stitched giant birds and flowery trees / To dwarf a house, *her* mother's."[66] The mother also experiences unruly desires that are both expressed and repressed through her representation of her house. The fire of the poem cannot be contained, just represented—it is not only shielded but also reproduced, in the form of a chimney, on the screen that covers it.

The poem works to make fire and screen increasingly indistinguishable. The "[i]nfraradiance" of the fire "enters each plume-petal's crazy weave," suggesting that the difference between repression and what is repressed is being further undone. The poem ends with a scene from "deep indoors"—inside the new house where the speaker makes a home, inside the familial house represented on the screen, and inside the speaker's own unconscious: "[B]lood's drawn / The tiny needlewoman cries, / And to some faintest creaking shut of eyes / His pleasure and the doll's are one."[67] The speaker confronts his violent and sexual impulses towards his mother—her penetration and pain become his (and his surrogate, the doll's) pleasure. But this Oedipal narrative is complicated by correspondences that circumvent the opposition of surface and depth upon which the theory of repression depends.[68] For example, the speaker identifies with the mother against whom he also harbors hostile impulses. Just as he defines himself against his mother by setting up a new home, his mother defines herself against her mother by weaving her own image of a house. As Merrill expresses and displaces his latent hostility toward his mother by writing this poem, his mother expresses and displaces her hostility against her mother by weaving the fire screen. When Merrill's mother drops the doll or baby that stands in for Merrill, it is not clear whether she or the baby "[h]owled when his face chipped like a plate," and the "tiny needlewoman" in the concluding stanza is Merrill's mother but is also identified with Merrill as a child through her doll-like stature.[69] One cannot merely say that Merrill carries on a partially repressed argument with his mother in this poem, for in some important ways Merrill *is* his mother in this poem.

At this point in the poem, there is no place where reading can definitively stop. Merrill makes it almost too easy for us to decode the stereotypically Oedipal feelings he is repressing; but once we have achieved this decoding, we have not satisfactorily translated the surface of the poem into a more authentic depth, for the screen itself possesses both a surface—the ornamental depiction of birds, trees, and house—and a depth—the coded message of Merrill's mother's desire to "dwarf" the house of her mother. Because the screen depicts a fire, we can imagine that the depicted fire also has its screen, which depicts yet another fire, and so forth—the surfaces available for reading multiply endlessly. Merrill offers us yet another reading of the scene at hand in the form of a footnote appended to the poem, which transforms the fire itself into a screen:

> Days later. All framework & embroidery rather than any slower looking into things. Fire screen—screen *of* fire . . . Flames masking that cast-iron plaque—"contrecoeur" in French—which backs the hearth with charred Loves & Graces. Some such meaning I might have caught, only I didn't wait, I settled for the obvious—by lamplight as it were.[70]

The fire screen is reimagined as a "screen *of* fire": flames, or repressed desires, are not only things concealed by a mask; they themselves mask. What they mask here is not a depth, but yet another surface, the cast-iron plaque at the back of the hearth, which itself is ornamentally engraved with "Loves & Graces." Though this plaque is the final layer that the poem uncovers, it is not the "heart" of the poet or the poem; it is "against the heart" in French, as if what finally can be figured is not any kind of ultimate reality or meaning, but an inherent resistance, in life and in language, to human desire and self-expression.

The footnote itself appears to deliver the poet's definitive judgment of what he has written, but in truth it only adds another reading to a scene that has already been interpreted and reinterpreted. To describe this poem as "all framework and embroidery rather than any slower looking into things" is not only unnecessarily harsh self-criticism; it simply seems untrue of a poem that has already revealed so much (many other Merrill poems are more vulnerable to this criticism). Merrill admits as much himself when he closes the footnote with a concession that it is futile to wish that the poem had proceeded differently: "Oh well. Our white heats lead us no less than words do. Both have been devices in their day."[71] If both passion and language are "devices," then it is useless to complain that here passion has been subjugated to the devices of poetic language. Our identity is determined as much by the topography of the manifest as by that of the latent. Merrill does not revise his poem; he instead adds one more reading of what has occurred, as if there is only reading, reading that makes claims to penetrate surfaces and discover depths but encounters only another surface. The essence of an experience is, as Bishop puts it in "Brazil, January 1, 1502," "retreating, always retreating, behind it."[72]

Readers of Reading and the Disalignment of Perspective

By foregrounding their own processes of reading objects and experiences, dramatizing the difficulty or even impossibility of making the transition from observation to insight, from surface to depth, Keats, Bishop, and Merrill align themselves with the readers of their poems—we all occupy a similar position of bafflement. The poet approaches experience in a way analogous to the way in which the reader approaches the poem: with a good deal of preexisting information, the initiative to hunt for clues, and various learned methods for decoding, which may be as much hindrances as helps. This stance creates a mirror-effect in that the readers of Keats's, Bishop's, and Merrill's poetry discover themselves doubled by the readers in the poems. This doubling produces intimacy between poet and reader—we both must overcome our initial puzzlement and develop at least a provisional interpretation of the objects that we encounter. But we approach the surface of Keats's, Bishop's, and Merrill's poetry at a substantially different angle from that at which they encounter the surfaces of their worlds. First and most obviously, the poets know more about their experiences than we do—for example, we must speculate about the details of Merrill's relationship with his mother when we read "Mornings in a New House," while these details are well known to the poet. The difference between our sensitivity to obscurity when reading a poem by Keats, Bishop, or Merrill and the poet's sense of obscurity when assessing his or her experiences creates yet another layer between experience and any definitive poetic interpretation of it. In the end, when the speaker of a poem is positioned as a reader, the gap between his position as a reader and our position as actual readers of the poem makes the poem, and the experience it represents, more, not less, difficult to read. Our ability to read is in a sense blocked, for the poet's refusal of authority means there is no masterful intention that we can attempt to access. With the proliferation of readers, the authorizing self disappears.

This difference between readers in poems and us as readers is always implicitly present, but at times our awareness of it becomes heightened. For example, the child speaker of "In the Waiting Room" assures us parenthetically, "I could read,"[73] and we are startled by the gap this assurance opens up between the speaker of the poem and its reader, who must to some degree take the act of reading for granted. When the child reads the *National Geographic,* we cannot literally read over her shoulder—Bishop can represent the images the child encounters, but not, except through direct quotation, the language she reads. In an important way, the experience of reading is unrepresentable. Similarly, Merrill's "An Urban Convalescence" contains a reference to an external text, *The White Goddess,* but his reading of this text is in a key sense inaccessible to the reader. Although we can examine *The White Goddess* in a way that we cannot examine the construction site that is the occasion for Merrill's poem, we still cannot be certain that we read this work in the same way that Merrill does.[74] The public availability of the reference holds the promise that its presence in the poem can be interpreted thoroughly, but this promise cannot be entirely fulfilled. In addition to these fleeting reminders of the difference between the poet-as-reader and the readers of poems, each of these three poets write poems that exploit this difference at length.

Keats writes the poem that defines this subgenre. His "Ode on a Grecian Urn" is a poem of negative capability that develops strategies in contrast to those he uses in "Ode to a Nightingale." Here, what teases the poet out of thought is not a semi-mythical bird, but a solid object. But rather than confirming the concrete existence of the object, the language of the poem erodes it, and one of the poet's main tools of erosion is the disjunction between his relationship to the object described and our own as readers of the poem.[75] The question of whether the poet invents or encounters what he describes takes on a new urgency, as we struggle to see what he seems to see. The first stanza lyrically compresses these two possibilities: first, that the urn is available to the poet and, through his mediation in language, to us; and second, that the urn does not exist and therefore can only be recovered by us to the extent that the poet invents it.

In the first four lines of the poem, the poet confidently wreathes the urn in epithets: bride of quietness, foster child, historian. But then, unexpectedly, this assurance that the urn can be seized for poetic purposes gives way to an almost pointless series of questions:

> What leaf-fringed legend haunts about thy shape
>   Of deities or mortals, or of both,
>   In Tempe or the dales of Arcady?
>   What men or gods are these? What maidens loath?
> What mad pursuit? What struggle to escape?
>   What pipes and timbrels? What wild ecstasy?[76]

These questions, which provide the reader with some details of the urn's decoration while rendering these details equivocal, straddle a boundary between information and its lack. The poet can see the urn well enough to catalogue some of its carvings: there are male creatures pursuing female creatures in a bacchanalian scene. But he gives this information in the form of questions that highlight the limits of his knowledge—he does not know if the anthropomorphic creatures are men or gods, and he cannot settle on their geographic location. It would be possible to take Keats exactly at his word here, and assume that he is simply laying out in a straightforward manner what he does and does not know about the object that stands before him. But to my mind, the effect of this list of questions—some of which could be answered if more information were available, but some of which are mainly rhetorical (it is clear, at least in sexual terms, what "mad pursuit" and "struggle to escape" this is)—is to bring into question the urn's physical existence, especially when contrasted with the confident salutation that precedes it. To Keats's list of questions, the reader is tempted to reply, do you not know? The urn is right before you, is it not? As with the poet's hesitation to name the figures that confront him in the "Ode on Indolence," his withholding of information or his actual ignorance allows him to hover on the surface of what he describes.

What has been enacted so far is the negative capability of dwelling in questions—questions that, in order to remain unanswered, must refuse to fully declare themselves actual or rhetorical questions, while at the same time the urn refuses to declare itself either an external and accessible point of reference or a projection of the poet's mind. The poem then turns briefly to consider a more uncomplicated version of negative capability, in which the poet enters into a direct communion with the urn that transcends observation: "Heard melodies are sweet, but those unheard / Are sweeter."[77] If silent communication is more satisfying than spoken communication, these lines suggest, then the poet's silent communion with the urn may be more satisfying than an active naming or interpretation of it. But here we see the importance of at least the possibility of the urn's separate being, its refusal to communicate directly. Without questions to ask of the urn, the poet is left merely to affirm its existence, exclaiming, "More happy love! more happy happy love!" as if he is slamming language against its unyielding surface. Language, which opened the poem as a powerful resource that could seize and explain the urn, hardens into an object itself, a blunt tool of limited use. The poet has no choice but to move back to the poem's dominant mode, the semi-rhetorical question.

At this point, the questions are permitted to move beyond the scene depicted on the urn, into pure speculation:

> Who are these coming to the sacrifice?
>   To what green altar, O mysterious priest,
> Lead'st thou that heifer lowing at the skies,
>   And all her silken flanks with garlands dressed?
> What little town by river or sea shore,
>   Or mountain-built with peaceful citadel,
>   Is emptied of this folk, this pious morn?[78]

This seamless movement, from questioning the object present to asking speculative questions about what cannot be seen, temporarily dissolves the surface of the urn by extending the imaginative surface of the poem. If this transformation is a poetic triumph,[79] it also marks a faltering of the tension that has held the poem together so far. The urn, both demanding and resisting interpretation, must reassert itself for the poem to continue.

This reestablishment takes place in the final stanza, where the poet-speaker again greets the urn with descriptive language: "Attic shape! Fair attitude!" This language is considerably more abstract than the epithets that opened the poem, suggesting a readjusted balance between what can confidently be asserted about the urn and what must be left open to question. The urn is a form or outline that at most suggests an unnamed attitude. The penultimate line of the poem tells us that the urn represents "beauty" itself, but only in the guise of the most difficult problem of reading that the poem has yet presented. The idea of beauty as truth is the link between negative capability and sincerity in Keats's oeuvre. The state of mind that can perceive beauty will be true to the world and to the self. But, in one of the most famous interpretive cruxes in English literature, the uncertain placement of quotation marks leaves us to wonder whether Keats or the urn believes that "Beauty is truth." To what degree does this phrase demand to be interpreted, with shades of doubt and uncertainty allowed in? What in our world must be put in quotation marks and handed over to our skepticism? The ending of this poem suggests that no matter how unmistakably or beautifully objects offer themselves to us, they will always remain vulnerable to our questioning. We have been initiated into the readerly world.

Bishop's "The Monument" reads as a splintery reply to the "Ode on a Grecian Urn." Like Keats's Ode, the poem explores the relationship between poetic language and a visual artifact, and sets up an implicit competition between the two, in which the status of the admired object is brought into doubt by the poet's strategies of interpretation. As in Keats's Ode, the speaker in Bishop's poem sometimes gives us reason to believe that she may be inventing what she describes rather than simply depicting an encountered object. This ambiguity is extended further by the fact that the poem is addressed to a "you" rather than to the object itself, who may or may not have his or her own access to the object, and who both represents and usurps the place of the reader of the poem. The reader is included in but also excluded from the scene of the poem through the shifting position of the speaker in relationship to her addressee.[80]

The poem begins with an abrupt, uncontextualized address to this "you":

> Now can you see the monument? It is of wood
> built somewhat like a box. No. Built
> like several boxes in descending sizes
> one above the other.[81]

The question that initiates the poem suggests that the "you" is standing next to the speaker-guide, but the guide's description implies that the "you" is dependent upon her for basic information. Adding to this ambiguity, the speaker's self-correction ("No") brings into question even her own authority, suggesting that unified sources of information are always in danger of fracturing further and further into dissenting dialogue. Meanwhile, the reader of the poem is left uncertain whether the speaker is describing something that the poet invents as she goes along or something that exists independently from her. (Although the poem was inspired by a wood rubbing by Max Ernst,[82] its referent as an ekphrastic poem is never mentioned. The rubbing does not serve as a point of origin that will permit us to decode the poem.) The line between invention and interpretation, along with the line between speaker and reader, is deliberately obscured.

This condition is worsened, not eased, as the speaker begins to impart information with greater confidence:

> Then on the topmost cube is set
> a sort of fleur-de-lys of weathered wood,
> long petals of board, pierced with odd holes,
> four-sided, stiff, ecclesiastical.
> From it four thin, warped poles spring out,
> (slanted like fishing-poles or flag-poles)
> and from them jig-saw work hangs down,
> four lines of vaguely whittled ornament
> over the edges of the boxes
> to the ground.[83]

At the beginning, it was fairly easy to picture what the speaker was describing: boxes stacked in descending sizes catty-corner upon each other. But soon "the sheer number and complexity of details begin to disorient rather than clarify."[84] Language, almost parodically, is shown to produce imprecision as it attempts to achieve increasing visual precision. Qualifications such as "sort of," "fishing-poles *or* flag-poles," and "vaguely" communicate a commitment to accuracy while denying the possibility of visual accuracy in language. Meanwhile, possible interpretations of what the monument may commemorate or mean are blocked by its simultaneous material presence and vagueness, its obscure concreteness. Bishop has invented another way of lingering over the surface of what she observes.

The "you" in the poem and the reader of the poem are temporarily conflated at this baffling moment, but the question of the place of the reader within the scene and within the poem returns with startling specificity in the lines that follow:

> The monument is one-third set against
> a sea; two-thirds against a sky.
> The view is geared
> (that is, the view's perspective)
> so low there is no "far away,"
> and we are far away within the view.[85]

At this point, "in order to place the tower spatially, Bishop sacrifices its third dimension";[86] because the speaker has fixed the horizon, it is no longer possible for us to inspect the monument by walking around it. "We" are now firmly located below sea level, looking up so that the sea takes up one-third of the horizon and the sky takes up two-thirds of it, with the monument in the foreground. This description reminds us of what perspectival visual art wishes us to forget: when we look at a flat representation of three dimensions, the picture is in a sense "looking" at (or is "geared" toward) us at the same time that we are looking at it. The presented scene has anticipated us, just as Bishop's poem anticipates us in the placeholder "you." The perspective implied by this scene creates intimacy (there is no "far away"; we are so low that we are right at the base of the monument, oriented vertically within the scene rather than horizontally outside of it) but at the same time alienates the viewer because she cannot literally stand within the represented scene: she is far away *from herself* within the view.[87] In the same way, Bishop's inclusion of the reader inside the poem permits the reader to recognize herself, but only at the cost of a self-division, the division between the reader in the poem and the reader of the poem. When placed alongside "In the Waiting Room," this position of being "far away within the view" suggests a definition of the experience of art, which takes us out of ourselves and restores us to ourselves only after we have been made strange.

We are not permitted to rest in this stable, albeit divided point of perspective, however, for suddenly the scene that looked three-dimensional on the flat picture plane is revealed as even more two-dimensional—sea, monument, and sky are all made of wood.[88] The scene immediately becomes both less sculptural (flattened as it is) and more so (the sea is no longer distinguished from the sky by a dividing line but by the contrasting textures of the wood composing each, a tactile rather than a visual difference). We cannot possibly any longer be "inside" the picture, for we are not made of wood; but the "you" that has been silent thus far is moved to ask, "Why does that strange sea make no sound? / Is it because we're far away?"[89] We seem to be both inside and outside the scene at hand, and our surrogate's questions (which begin to pick up momentum at this point) raise the more fundamental question: what can we ask of any representation set before us? (As David Kalstone puts it, and as could be said of Keats's poem as well, Bishop is "not so much providing answers as initiating us into the mysteries of how questions are asked.")[90] To what extent may we question the scene from the inside, as something we find familiar enough to refer to our own experience (as if to ask, "The sea usually makes a sound; why does this sea not make a sound?"), and to what extent must we question it as utterly foreign ("What is this strange thing made of wood?")? In the terms of "In the Waiting Room," how do we sort out the mixture of familiarity and foreignness that any act of reading involves?

The question-and-answer dialogue that forms the middle section of the poem raises more questions about the comparative knowledge and access to information of the speaker and the "you" to whom she explains things. As if she has not heard the speaker's explanation that the sea and sky are made of wood, the "you" complains, "But that queer sea looks made of wood . . . What is that?" The speaker responds tautologically, "It is the monument"—objects are objects (in Keats's loftier terms, "Beauty is truth"); interpretation is impossible or irrelevant. When the addressee complains that the monument is "cracked and unpainted," the guide answers speculatively, but not as if she has full authority to explain: "all the conditions of its existence / may have flaked off the paint." Finally, the "you" asks in exasperation, "what can it prove?"[91] These questions in their near pointlessness serve a function similar to that of the rhetorical questions in Keats's "Ode on a Grecian Urn," simultaneously gesturing toward but failing to fully interpret the object that faces them. We are left to share with the "you" the sense that what is given does not fully answer the question, "What is that?"

At the end of the poem, the resistances to finally saying what the monument is, carefully accumulated over the preceding fifty-eight lines, are released with breathtaking swiftness. The monument "is the beginning of a painting, / a piece of sculpture, or poem, or monument"—that is, a metaphor for art more broadly. This naming exhibits the circularity of Keats's discoveries that the beings he pursues are Poesy: to an extent, rather than learning something new, we have been sent back to where we started. The speaker-guide confirms this return when she refuses to give a fully authoritative explanation. The statement that "wood holds together better / than sea or cloud" suggests the artisan's commitment to purposeful creation with the tools of her trade, but at the same time the monument is given an organic life of its own, as if the speaker merely stumbled upon it: "It chose that way to grow and not to move." The decorations of the monument, not its creator, are described as "having life, and wishing: wanting . . . to cherish something."[92] The guide finally tells us explicitly that it is not necessary or even appropriate to wonder where the "bones" of the creator are located: the human origins of the monument "after all / cannot have been intended to be seen."[93] In the end, it is the reader who is "far away within the view," not the bones of the artist-priest, which may be inside the artifact or out of it. The origin of the poem is with us, not the artist; it is the reader's ordinary and mysterious search for information and meaning and not the impulse to immortalize or elegize the poet that is the engine of the poem. More explicitly than anywhere else in Bishop's oeuvre, making art is subsumed here under the larger, shared problem of interpreting artifacts.

In Merrill's body of work, the connection between the simultaneous engagement and bafflement of the reader and the poet's own ambivalent experience of reading himself is established most consistently and memorably in "Lost in Translation." A poem about a puzzle, "Lost in Translation" is also a poem about the necessity and rewards of puzzlement. Though full of double meanings, the poem avoids any strict binaries (any premature abandonment of surfaces in favor of depths) by seeing multiply, creating not just one but several layers of signification. (The complicated surface that any Merrill poem presents to the reader, its attraction to every kind of doubling from puns to metaphor to symbolization, prevents any one kind of double seeing from being definitive.) In "Lost in Translation," we accompany the speaker as he undertakes difficult reading in many different guises: as a child he attempts to read his own confusing circumstances; as an adult he attempts to read the past; the puzzle the child pieces together is read as a representation of reality; the adult tells us of his reading of Valéry's "Palme"; the act of reading is challenged by the presence of foreign languages; and so on. At the same time, the poem presents a highly complex linguistic surface that must be read by us. More exactly, the poem cannot simply be read by us—it must be re-read multiple times for its meanings to fall into place, just as Merrill must continually reinterpret his past, and there appear to be few limits to the number of connections and associations we may accumulate.

The poem opens with a sketch of the child's life. Under the care of his French Mademoiselle (his parents are absent), he waits for a puzzle "which keeps never coming." The speaker comments, "A summer without parents is the puzzle, / Or should be. But the boy, day after day, / Writes in his Line-a-Day No puzzle."[94] We are alerted from the beginning that some things should be puzzles, and that looking for one kind of puzzle (like the child who writes "No puzzle") can mean ignoring other puzzles that may be more important. If a poem is like a puzzle, there is a danger that the reader will choose false puzzles, or solve them too easily. (Like the boy, we may be susceptible to waiting for puzzles that we can solve rather than tackling the more intractable puzzles at hand.) But to decide that "a summer without parents" is the ultimate puzzle of the speaker's childhood or of the poem that describes it is itself a tempting but false solution (rather like deciding that the fire screen simply suppresses the fire), for solving this mystery does not begin to solve the poem.

The poem periodically reinforces the importance of puzzlement. At one point, the child peeks at a letter his caretaker has been writing to a friend about the parental absence that should be puzzling him. The adult

speaker comments, "Fearful incuriosity of childhood!"[95] This line can be
interpreted to mean that the child is incurious about the contents of his
Mademoiselle's letter because he is fearful of knowing the truth about
his parents' absence, but an equally plausible reading is that the adult
speaker finds the child's incuriosity fearfully inadequate. At another
point in the poem, concerned that his child self and his nurse are complet-
ing their puzzle precipitously, the speaker warns, "Not so fast."[96] What
follows is the most obscure passage in the poem, almost perverse in its
determination to prevent the puzzle-poem as well as the puzzle from be-
ing pieced together too easily.

While the child waits for his puzzle, we are given what in hindsight will
be pieces of the bigger puzzle of the poem. The description of the card ta-
ble where the puzzle will be put together as a "tense green oasis" can sub-
sequently be pieced together with Valéry's "Palme," palm-shaped puzzle
pieces, and the oasis portrayed by the puzzle, which in turn can be pieced
into other lines of association (the table linked to the parents' gambling,
the Valéry poem to the library and to the "self-effacing tree" at the
poem's close, the palm-shaped puzzle pieces to the piece of the puzzle
that is lost, the oasis to the family romance suggested by the completed
puzzle, and so forth). Such correspondences can be almost endlessly de-
lineated, but like the puzzle itself, what they add up to is closer to an ever-
expanding flat picture plane than a hierarchy of meaning. It would be dif-
ficult to prove that the poem is really about the particular circumstances
of the speaker's childhood or Valéry's "Palme" or languages or memory
itself—all of these motifs and more are present, but none of them can
claim precedence.[97]

When the puzzle the child awaits finally arrives, we are made aware of
yet another complexity. Not only will the puzzle represent a scene once it
is put together; even its individual pieces are representative. The puzzle is

> A superior one, containing a thousand hand-sawn,
> Sandal-scented pieces. Many take
> Shapes known already—the craftsman's repertoire
> Nice in its limitation—from other puzzles:
> Witch on broomstick, ostrich, hourglass,
> Even (surely not just in retrospect)
> An inching, innocently branching palm.
> These can be put aside, made stories of.[98]

The broomstick, ostrich, hourglass, and palm can be put into their own
stories regardless of the images printed on their surfaces. Similarly, the

poet's images signify in multiple ways, their surface placing them in one narrative, their shape in another. But this multiple representation remains in important ways two-dimensional: the images are more like flat emblems than round symbols; as in Bishop's "The Monument," we remain in a world of two-dimensional planks of wood. We inhabit a space in which multiple stories are possible—some when we assemble a picture plane by putting pieces together, another when the pieces are considered individually—but one story is not necessarily more true than another; they are not arrested in a hierarchy of significance.

There are limits to the poem's accrual of complexity, however, for the poet's images are also "nice in their limitation," and the poem itself remains obligingly interpretable, susceptible to being pieced together in various ways. Merrill does not proliferate complexity for its own sake, or as a general program of postmodernist difficulty; nor does he believe that complexity is a necessary sign of emotional depth. For example, he writes of a missing puzzle piece, encountered under mysterious and theatrical circumstances in adulthood:

> ". . . hidden here is a freak fragment
> Of a pattern complex in appearance only.
> What it seems to show is superficial
> Next to that long-term lamination
> Of hazard and craft, the karma that has
> Made it matter in the first place.
> Plywood. Piece of a puzzle."[99]

The pattern on the puzzle piece is "complex in appearance only" first of all because it is the fragment of a larger picture. Once it is fitted into place, the shapes and colors that perplex will now find their place in a larger representation. In this way, the poem recognizes the influence of coherence as well as fragmentation. Life does, after all, have a way of "fall[ing] piecemeal into place."[100] By extension, we are reminded that human truths at a certain level of generalization are often common and ordinary. The complexity of living comes not from some existential resistance to pattern or coherence, but from the accidents and felicities that make up an individual life, "that long-term lamination / Of hazard and craft," what the poet later will call "the color of context."

The poem warns us, however, that coherence is not the same as truth, any more than the patterns of this poem prove that the poet has finally understood his own life. Though he cannot solve the other puzzles of the poem, the child finishes his puzzle, and it is just as quickly pulled apart:

> . . . All too soon the swift
> Dismantling. Lifted by two corners,
> The puzzle hung together—and did not.
> Irresistibly a populace
> Unstitched of its attachments, rattled down.
> Power went to pieces as the witch
> Slithered easily from Virtue's gown.[101]

This completion and dismantling feel arbitrary, suggesting that while unified picture planes and coherent stories do occur, such coherence should not be given undue significance. Stories are also given to falling apart, the witch given to slithering from Virtue's gown. Each story that we might tell about this poem, following one line of association or another, may cohere, but it is not necessarily truer than the other stories that might be told, and coherence in a world of dissolving surfaces itself is not a quality to be trusted.

At this point, the missing puzzle piece alluded to earlier in the poem reappears:

> Before the puzzle was boxed and readdressed
> To the puzzle shop in the mid-Sixties,
> Something tells me that one piece contrived
> To stay in the boy's pocket. How do I know?
> I know because so many later puzzles
> Had missing pieces.[102]

The idea that some loss incurred during childhood has left the adult speaker with missing pieces in his emotional life is plausible and poignant, but what is strange about this passage is that the piece of the puzzle is not lost to the child but retained by him. The problem is not (only) that we are missing pieces of our lives, the poem suggests, but that we carry extra pieces with us, pieces that may or may not complete the puzzles that later confront us. The possibility that we have too many puzzle pieces, rather than too few, informs the luminous abundance of the poem's closing:

> Lost, is it, buried? One more missing piece?
>
> But nothing's lost. Or else: all is translation
> And every bit of us is lost in it

(Or found—I wander through the ruin of S
Now and then, wondering at the peacefulness)
And in that loss a self-effacing tree,
Color of context, imperceptibly
Rustling with its angel, turns the waste
To shade and fiber, milk and memory.[103]

There is no one authentic interpretation of a life, only its translations into languages and contexts. Memory imposes continual losses and discoveries, and this alternation cannot be resolved by finding a definitive truth; instead all that can be found are still more patterns of losing and finding. This means that all is loss, but at the same time nothing is: the ruin of the parents' marriage, the love affair with "S," the childhood no longer possessed, are also oases of remembered image and nuance. By recreating the past as a complex of dissolving surfaces, the poem restores the world to its speaker and to us.

By presenting themselves as readers of the world, Keats, Bishop, and Merrill do not write a more objective or detached poetry than that of their more explicitly autobiographical contemporaries. Instead, as we have seen, the translations involved in the poet's reading of his or her world and the reader's reading of the poet are shifting and precarious, to the extent that it would be impossible to label this reading as subjective or objective, personal or impersonal. This poetry of negative capability can be embraced as a truly modern form of sincerity, because it expresses a fundamental agnosticism about whether and in what sense the self can be known. What appears to be personal reticence can be read as a resistance to the premature or false assignation of meaning to experience. If sincerity as an ideal is to be saved, these poets suggest, it can be saved only by its careful abandonment. The self-expressive poet is a reader, too; and no one can limit the puzzlement that we face together.

Conclusion

WHAT IS POETRY? If we begin with the idea that poetry is uniquely sincere self-expression, we discover that poetry is the realm in which an ardent desire for truthful self-expression comes up against not only the limits of language but also the limits of self-consciousness itself. The poet who wishes most to be humanly, morally present refigures herself as an inanimate instrument, himself as a hovering but unaccountable presence; the poet who wishes to communicate most transparently and naturally can only permit artificiality to invade the intimate recesses of her being, or wander the ruins of old forms. If we assume, on the contrary, that poetry creates fictional selves instead of documenting a true one, we find that poetry is the place where invented characters point us toward a human complexity greater than any individual characterization, and where the difference between inventing and invented self begins to dissolve. If we propose that poetry is the expression of an utterly unique sensibility, we are confronted instead with a poetry in which the dramatization of uniqueness implodes under the pressure of its own insularity. Finally, if we decide that poetry is the meticulous description of the world outside the self, marked by a refusal to sacrifice sensual surfaces to the poet's impulse to fabricate metaphors and the self's desire for reflective depths, poetry reveals itself as the scene of the most difficult reading, in which what seems to be an objective surface gives way to subjective depths, and depths reveal themselves to be yet more surfaces. Poetry is the place of sudden reversals, boundless frustration, and the constant possibility of delight, discovery, surprise.

The poems we have encountered live under the shadow of the ideal of sincerity in no single sense, but meet and surpass the multiple definitions of "shadow" provided by Webster's dictionary: "a reflected image," "shelter from danger or observation," "an imperfect and faint representation," "an attenuated form or vestigial remnant," "an inseparable companion or follower," "a source of gloom or unhappiness," "a pervasive and dominant influence," "a state of ignominy or obscurity," and, most literally, "the dark figure cast upon a surface by a body intercepting the rays from a source of light." Lyric poetry is potentially both an image of sincerity and a method for avoiding self-scrutiny. Poetry can be sincerity's compromised representation or remnant; the motive of sincerity remains poetry's pervasive but discredited influence, its fellow traveler or ghost. Above all, poetry is as likely to usefully obstruct the self's illuminations as to serve as their conduit. It figures self-revelation as the trace of an opaque shape blocking a source of light, a halo around an absence.

The categories developed in this book are not intended to harden into subgenres of the lyric poem, but to suggest patterns of self-consciousness available to any poet. The opposition of the moral sincerity of Adrienne Rich to the charismatic sincerity of Anne Sexton is useful in countering the habit that would place them both under the heading of "confessional" poetry and thus distort each of their achievements, but both of these kinds of sincerity can be located in the work of a variety of poets. Each poet that I have placed under a single label here writes poems that belong in other categories, and each category describes possible modes of reading as well as writing. It would be possible to locate examples of Wordsworthian sincerity in every poet that this study explores, to examine Merrill for evidence of Byronic charisma, to assess Rich in terms of agnostic sincerity, and so forth. Contemporary poetry—I think especially of the work of John Ashbery and Jorie Graham—offers increasingly complex hybrids of these kinds of self-consciousness with newer forms.

The problem of sincerity is central to the questions that the experience of self-consciousness raises, but it does not exhaust these questions. There are at least two other forms of poetic self-consciousness that have been crucial to the development of Romantic and post-Romantic poetry, and especially to American poetry since the 1980s: metapoetic and what could be called linguistic self-consciousness. A poet exercising metapoetic self-consciousness writes poetry about being a poet or about the nature of poetry itself, as, for example, Keats does in his Odes and Wallace Stevens does in a large proportion of his work. Under the related but distinct conditions of linguistic self-consciousness, the poet becomes explicitly aware of the ways in which language—a relatively closed, self-referential system, bearing the marks of history and inflected with political power—shapes her perceptions of the world.[1] This second type of self-consciousness adds a new possible definition of poetry to those listed above: poetry is a field for experimenting with language's materiality—what Jean-Paul Sartre calls the "attitude which considers words as things and not as signs"[2]—and disrupting the otherwise imperceptible and potentially coercive ways in which it structures our lives. The influence of this concept of poetry can be seen in different ways from the modernism of Pound and Stein to the Projective verse theorized by Charles Olson to the LANGUAGE poetry of the 1980s. We have glimpsed these forms of self-consciousness in the preceding pages, but it would of course take a separate study examining a different group of poets to do them justice. What I want briefly to suggest here is that even these seemingly more impersonal forms of self-consciousness are disrupted by the inherent contradictions of self-consciousness, and are not as divorced from the problem of sincerity as they initially appear to be.

The poem "Cliff Notes" (1986) by Bob Perelman, for example, exhorts us to "Pay attention to the flatness of the screen now!"[3]—the flattening effect of certain and perhaps all languages and forms of representation, and particularly of both language that attempts to "wash . . . the body free of any monetary transaction"[4] and language that "consist[s] entirely of dirty jokes about money."[5] Even before we enter into the particular difficulties that this poem raises, we can anticipate a difficulty inherent to the poem's consideration of its own language. By choosing to be self-conscious about its own operations in language instead of about the emotional, psychological, or moral being of the poet writing, this poem would seem to place itself on firmer ground than a poem that takes self-expression as its main goal. If the would-be sincere poet faces the problem of locating a "self" to which he or she can be true, the poet practicing metapoetic or linguistic self-consciousness can at least be sure that the poem, the language on the page, is present. But just as the self to which a self-consciously sincere poet attempts to be true refuses both to remain stable enough to be consistently observed and to be absorbed fully into the consciousness of the poet doing the observing, the poetic form or language that the poet wishes to examine will neither remain separate from nor totally unite with the poetic form or language used to examine them.

That Perelman is aware of and even gladly accepts this situation is suggested by the ways the poem intensifies this slipperiness through its ambiguity of tone. The poem expresses disapproval of the flatness of the "private" languages of compartmentalized suburbia but connects this flatness to a more general problem of the "humanized body," which is inevitably "pinned to . . . forces outside our control," and explains that this flatness is not the fault of modern forms of language and representation but goes "back before the / alphabet,"[6] leading us to wonder to what degree the intelligence organizing the poem must partake of what it deplores. The poem critiques Plato's theory of ideas by suggesting that the material world comes "back to haunt him in the form of crude jokes / about his square calves at unprestigious dinners," but under these circumstances it is difficult to decide whether Plato or his critic is more responsible for the flattening effects of representation, more likely to reduce language to "dirty jokes about money."[7] The task of sorting out which kinds of language the poem embraces and which it dismisses is made more difficult by the title "Cliff Notes," which may indicate either that the entire poem is an example of a debased summary or that such a summary is simply its subject matter. At no point in the work can we be certain whether we are encountering the poet's criticism of language or an example of language to be criticized, a theory of poetry or an actualized poem.

We may be tempted to resolve (or at least delimit) these ambiguities by trying to guess what the poet's precise intentions are. But the poem is as clear as it can possibly be that the problem of a language's biases and implicit values cannot be resolved through an appeal to one individual's personal intentions. It opens with the warning that no privately developed language can counter the larger political and historical forces of language and representation:

> Because the languages are enclosed and heated
> Each one private a separate way
> Of undressing in front of the word window
> Faces squashing up against it
> City trees and personal rituals of sanitation
> Washing the body free of any monetary transaction
>
> The parts of the machine take off their words and die away.[8]

The desire to domesticate a corner of language for oneself here appears to be critiqued as a debased exhibitionism, with the naked body and the peering faces of strangers separated only by a sliver of glass. Instead, the poem seems to suggest, we should abandon our illusion that we can possess a personal language free from the taint of political or mercenary self-interest—just as the poet seems to have abandoned his—in favor of a larger, possibly more responsible or freer understanding of the regimes of representation under which we live. But here the seeming impersonality of the poem's considerations of its own procedures, its self-reflexivity that appears almost to operate without a human agent, breaks down. The poem offers us, if not a personal language, then an individualized one nonetheless. Its argument for the coerciveness of language, or at least certain languages, is brought into question by its own elaboration of a style that apparently to some degree escapes this coercion. To put it differently, its metapoetic self-consciousness, which focuses our attention on the poem's (and, inevitably, the poet's) own procedures, conflicts with its linguistic self-consciousness, which insists upon language's relative autonomy and power. (This potential conflict inherent in the combination of metapoetic and linguistic self-consciousness could be analyzed in the many postmodern poems that include both forms.) For this reader at least, the combination of the poem's commitment to political critique—which after all is meaningful only with reference to individual human beings capable of feeling and thought and choice—and the obscurity that results from its purposeful rejection of our usual ways of constructing meaning, makes an interest in the personal motives and intentions of the poet more rather than less inevitable. In any case, the existence of the poet, or, at a bare minimum, the existence of a reader who must read the poem as if it were a deliberate communication, means that the self-reflexivity of the poem cannot replace or absorb the questions raised by personal forms of self-consciousness. The poem's vision of the impersonal omnipotence of language and representation implies an equally vivid vision of the human limits to this omnipotence.

As Perelman's poem demonstrates, American poetry that emphasizes metapoetic and linguistic self-consciousness has often explicitly opposed itself to the poetry of self-expression. Perelman is representative in his impatience with what he understands as a dominant mode of contemporary American poetry based on "a highly distinct individuality," "sensibility and intuition." In this poetic tradition, according to him, "The poet as engaged, oppositional intellectual, and poetic form and syntax as sites of experiment for political and social purposes—these would not be found. The confessional poets were the model: Lowell, Plath, Sexton, Berryman. Poems were short, narrative, focused on small or large moments of crisis or optimism. Whether the form was free verse or rhymed iambic stanzas, the tone was conversational."[9] Alice Fulton makes a similar critique, expressing her belief that this "confessional" model has dominated into the 1990s: "Rather than being concerned with conscience, responsibility, power, cruelty, or *form*, in practice American poetry is relentlessly concerned with the self. Its investigations are not ontological or epistemological so much as solipsistic."[10] The poems that these writers have in mind, which Fulton aptly describes as "failed short-short stories rather than failed poetry,"[11] are immediately recognizable—the less ambitious or thoughtful of the so-called confessional poems, and the poems of the past forty years that assume that a relatively superficial sincerity (a sincerity that succeeds too easily instead of rigorously, beautifully failing) is enough to ensure their claim on us. But this minor subgenre of the lyric is too often conflated with all poetry that explores the challenges that human self-consciousness poses to the desire for self-knowledge. We have seen that the putatively personal forms of self-consciousness necessarily force the poet to confront various forms of impersonality: the question of what human beings can be assumed to have in common, the question of the responsibility of the individual to history, the question of which values can be taken for granted and which must be interrogated, and the question of which forms of self-consciousness exclude and which help us to embrace other people. As John Ashbery succinctly puts it in "Self-Portrait in a Convex Mirror," "This otherness, this / 'Not-being-us' is all there is to look at / In the mirror."[12] Similarly, poetry that explores more impersonal forms of self-consciousness (such as linguistic or metapoetic forms) cannot help facing the personal questions of how, for example, the poet is to position herself against the larger forces of language and history and on whose behalf the critique of misuses of power is to be made. The divisions we can make between varying poetic styles and priorities should not obscure the ways in which all poets writing today must confront the same basic and unanswered questions: Is self-knowledge possible, and if so, on what terms? If I must claim a self-understanding that I cannot fully verify, what are my responsibilities in taking this action? What are the uses of whatever provisional self-knowledge we can achieve? Larger than our differences is our shared perplexity in the face of these questions.

In her memoir *A Dialogue on Love*, Eve Kosofsky Sedgwick gets to the heart of this perplexity: "One of the big features of being [human] is that you articulate quite an elaborate inner space, full of all kinds of voices. Not to say the voices don't come from anywhere, they do—but they don't come *directly* from anywhere. There's a lot of time and echoey, experimental space for them to take on a life of their own. There are all the fearful—and worse, hopeful—gaps between what you'd want to say and what you can . . . manage to say. There's the insuperable problem of *as whom* or as what one can say anything."[13] Lyric poetry is the echoey, experimental space in which the question of what forms of being we are able to take and have a right to claim is most open-ended. In spite of modern experiments in communal authorship, writing poetry remains one of the most individual of acts, and yet, because it provides the ground upon which the paradoxes of self-consciousness can move most freely, one of the acts most skeptical about the authority of any individual claim to self-understanding. What is more, poetry is the place where the authority of even this skepticism remains an open question, asking, as in particular contemporary poetry does: What kinds of selves or voices can be invented that "know" what they know about the impossibility, or at least the instability and unverifiability, of self-knowledge? In undertaking its experiments, poetry may separate itself from certain contexts (economic, political, historical), but is itself as local and concrete as these contexts, an experience as well as a meditation on our experiences. In its particularity, its flexibility, its sensual and sonic complexity, its consideration of the extra-rational experiences of pleasure and desire, and above all in the ways in which it speaks with both more and less authority, more and less presence than an actual human voice, poetry offers us the experience of the unknown at the core of proposed self-knowledge. This is lyric poetry's enduring—though not sole—claim on us.

Notes

Introduction

1. Samuel Taylor Coleridge, "Dejection: An Ode," lines 85–93, in *The Collected Works of Samuel Taylor Coleridge,* vol. 16 (Princeton: Princeton University Press, 2001).
2. See Roland Barthes, "The Death of the Author," for the most famous version of this argument (in *Image-Music-Text,* trans. Stephen Heath [New York: Hill and Wang, 1977]).
3. Tennyson, *In Memoriam* 5.3–4.
4. These problems and more that attempts at sincerity encounter are described in detail in the book-length studies devoted to the subject, including David Perkins's *Wordsworth and the Poetry of Sincerity* (Cambridge, Mass.: Harvard University Press, 1971), Lionel Trilling's *Sincerity and Authenticity* (Cambridge, Mass.: Harvard University Press, 1971), Henri Peyre's *Literature and Sincerity* (New Haven: Yale University Press, 1963), and Leon Guilhamet's *The Sincere Ideal: Studies on Sincerity in Eighteenth Century English Literature* (Montreal: McGill-Queen's University Press, 1974).
5. Donald Davie, "Sincerity and Poetry," *Michigan Quarterly Review* 5.1 (Winter 1966): 3–8.
6. The continuing importance of "sincerity," despite its failures to function as a positive analytical tool, is easily demonstrated by a casual perusal of the jacket copy of poetry books published in the 1980s and 1990s. For example, Sharon Olds's *The Gold Cell* is praised for its "candor" (New York: Knopf, 1992), Stephen Dunn's "mere living, with eyes that see everything and a heart that misses nothing" recommends his *Between Angels* to the reader (New York: W. W. Norton, 1989), and Marie Howe is credited with "a poetry of intimacy, witness, honesty, and relation" (*What the Living Do* [New York: W. W. Norton, 1998]). "Sincerity" is obviously a meaningful category for readers; the challenge is to define or delimit the term in a way that also makes it meaningful for the theorist.

7. Davie, "Sincerity and Poetry," p. 7.

8. Ibid., p. 8.

9. Jerome McGann, *Fiery Dust: Byron's Poetic Development* (Chicago: University of Chicago Press, 1968), p. 26.

10. Lawrence J. Starzyk, *The Dialogue of the Mind with Itself* (Calgary: University of Calgary Press, 1992), p. 3.

11. Although Descartes represents the optimistic view of self-consciousness, he is still troubled when he attempts to take himself as an object of his thinking: "I am something real and really existing, but what thing am I? I have already given the answer: a thing which thinks. And what more? . . . I am not this assemblage of members which is called a human body; I am not a rarefied and penetrating air spread throughout all these members; I am not a wind, [a flame,] a breath, a vapor or anything at all that I can imagine and picture to myself" (*Discourse on Method and Meditations,* trans. Laurence J. Lafleur [Indianapolis: Bobbs-Merrill, 1960], p. 84). Eventually he confesses, "I cannot keep myself from believing that corporeal things, images of which are formed by thought and which the senses themselves examine, are much more distinctly known than that indescribable part of myself which cannot be pictured by the imagination" (p. 86). In other words, even the philosopher who places the autonomous self at the center of his enterprise doubts our ability to *know* that self. The persistence of this mixture of certainty and doubt in both his followers and his critics suggests that this instability is a structural component of self-consciousness itself.

12. Ernst Tugendhat describes this regress, though he disputes its relevance: "If the knowledge that I am in such and such a conscious state is itself a conscious state, it appears to follow that I also must know that I know that I am in such and such a conscious state, and so on" (*Self-Consciousness and Self-Determination,* trans. Paul Stern [Cambridge, Mass.: MIT Press, 1986], p. 16).

13. Zachary Mayne, *Essay on Consciousness* [*Über das Bewußtsein*], English-German ed. (Hamburg: Felix Meiner Verlag, 1983). Mayne is not entirely correct in his claim of priority: according to the *Oxford English Dictionary,* the term "self-consciousness" was first used in 1688, and John Locke consistently used the term "consciousness" in his account of personal identity in 1690 (Howard Caygill, *A Kant Dictionary* [Oxford: Blackwell, 1995], p. 126).

14. Mayne, *Essay on Consciousness,* p. 10.

15. Ibid., p. 16.

16. Ibid., p. 46; emphasis in original.

17. This argument is put forth in the Transcendental Dialectic of the *Critique of Pure Reason* (Book II, Chapter 1). Here, Kant writes, "One may therefore say of the thinking I (the soul), which represents itself as substance, simple, numerically identical at all times . . . that it *does not know itself through the categories,* but knows the *categories* only, and through them all objects, in the absolute unity of apperception, *that is, through itself.* It may seem no doubt self-evident that I cannot know as an object that which is presup-

posed in order to enable me to know an object, and that the determining self (thought) differs from the self that is to be determined (the thinking subject), like knowledge from its object. Nevertheless nothing is more natural or at least more tempting than the illusion which makes us look upon the unity in the synthesis of thoughts as a perceived unity in the subject of thoughts. One might call it the surreptitious admission of an hypostasised consciousness" (*Critique of Pure Reason,* trans. F. Max Müller, 2nd ed. [New York: MacMillan, 1927], pp. 324–325; emphasis in original). Of course, it is Coleridge who introduces German philosophies of self-consciousness into British Romantic literature. His thinking represents the double nature of self-consciousness—like Mayne, he understands it as an essentially unifying force (see, for example, Chapter 12 of the *Biographia Literaria*), but he also recognizes that "consciousness is impossible without distinction" ("On Consciousness and Self-Consciousness," in *Collected Works of Samuel Taylor Coleridge,* vol. 2, ed. H. J. Jackson and J. R. de J. Jackson [Princeton: Princeton University Press, 1995], p. 427). In terms of self-consciousness, consciousness would entail a distinction between the self observing and the self observed.

18. Pierre Keller, *Kant and the Demands of Self-Consciousness* (Cambridge: Cambridge University Press, 1998), p. 2.

19. For example, the philosopher who focuses most diligently upon Kant's conception of self-consciousness, Johann Fichte, reproduces the familiar tension between self-consciousness as an experienced principle of unity and self-consciousness as an intractable problem. The first kind of self-consciousness, which Fichte understands as a development of Kant's transcendental apperception, he calls the "self-positing subject," or "absolute I." This self-consciousness accompanies all of our acts of consciousness, like the Cartesian "I think." But Fichte is aware that this type of self-consciousness cannot include conscious self-reflection. As Frederick Neuhouser explains: "Reflective self-consciousness [i.e., self-consciousness that takes the self as its object] cannot be understood simply as an explicit awareness of the same content that is present, though only implicitly, in the subject's immediate self-awareness. For if the distinction between the two forms of self-consciousness is to halt the infinite regress that constituted Fichte's initial problem, then they must also differ in *structure* and not merely in degree of awareness. This point is simply an implication of Fichte's basic claim that the subject's self-positing, in contrast to reflective self-consciousness, may not exhibit the structure of representational consciousness" (*Fichte's Theory of Subjectivity* [Cambridge: Cambridge University Press, 1990], p. 83; emphasis in original). Kantian apperception, or Fichte's self-positing subject, must be structurally different from reflective self-consciousness (the kind that takes the self as its object and might be thought to produce self-knowledge) if it is to avoid the infinite regress of self-consciousness. Fichte's Romantic development of the theory of self-consciousness thus emphasizes rather than resolves the division between self-consciousness as self-awareness and as self-dispossession.

20. Rodolphe Gasché, *The Tain of the Mirror: Derrida and the Philosophy of Reflection* (Cambridge, Mass.: Harvard University Press, 1986), p. 21. To put it another way, Hegel understands the doubling involved in self-consciousness to be "meaningful only with respect to a totality," a presupposed unity that will be reinstated in a final synthesis (ibid., p. 27). Against Kant, Hegel argues that this unity is objectively valid, rather than merely a feature of the way in which we experience the world (Robert Pippin, *Hegel's Idealism: The Satisfactions of Self-Consciousness* [Cambridge: Cambridge University Press, 1989], p. 8).

21. Jacques Derrida, *Of Grammatology,* trans. G. C. Spivak (Baltimore: Johns Hopkins University Press, 1976), p. 36.

22. Because psychoanalysis constitutes the most comprehensive network of theories about consciousness, it is obviously an indispensable part of the foundation of my project. I have decided not to use Freudian or Lacanian terminology systematically because I believe that if I were simply to decontextualize and apply psychoanalytic terms, these terms would lose their own literary richness. But I would like to think that my project comes out of the same urgency that causes Lacan to ask, given the symbolic nature of language, "Who is speaking?" ("The Freudian Thing," in *Écrits: A Selection,* trans. Alan Sheridan [New York: W. W. Norton, 1977], p. 123).

23. Slavoj Žižek provides a laundry list of contemporary opponents of the self-recuperating tendencies of the Cartesian subject, including "the postmodern deconstructionist (for whom the Cartesian subject is a discursive fiction, an effect of decentered textual mechanisms); the Habermasian theorist of communication (who insists on a shift from Cartesian monological subjectivity to discursive intersubjectivity) . . . the cognitive scientist (who endeavors to prove empirically that there is no unique scene of the Self, just a pandemonium of competing forces) . . . the critical (post)-Marxist (who insists that the illusory freedom of the bourgeois thinking subject is rooted in class division); and the feminist (who emphasizes that the allegedly sexless cogito is in fact a male patriarchal formation)" (*The Ticklish Subject: The Absent Center of Political Ontology* [New York: Verso, 1999], p. 1).

24. Susan Baur writes, "As recently as thirty years ago, the talking cure was a cottage industry practiced by a small number of analysts and therapists on a tiny fraction of the population, but today it is big business. In 1990, for example, it is estimated that Americans spent some $10 to $12 billion for office visits to their therapists" (*The Intimate Hour: Love and Sex in Psychotherapy* [Boston: Houghton Mifflin, 1997], p. 160).

25. Mikhail Bakhtin suggestively though disapprovingly describes poetic language as language "saturated with intention" (*The Dialogic Imagination,* trans. Carl Emerson and Michael Holquist [Austin: University of Texas Press, 1981], p. 293).

26. Roman Jakobson helpfully defines "the poetic function of language" as "focus on the message for its own sake." In other words, poetry heightens language's inherent self-referentiality (*Language in Literature,* ed. Krystyna

Pomorska and Stephen Rudy [Cambridge, Mass.: Harvard University Press, 1987], pp. 69–70).

27. James Engell writes, "In its postclassical phase poetry runs into several countervailing pressures. It becomes both more and less specialized. It revolts against poetic diction but champions poetic knowledge. Its 'language' may in one sense be viewed as essentially that of prose—the doctrine of poetic diction wanes—but its function and meaning are more than ever potentially separated from fact and systematic understanding" (*Forming the Critical Mind: Dryden to Coleridge* [Cambridge, Mass.: Harvard University Press, 1989], p. 222). As Michael O'Neill puts it, "Romantic poetry lays radically altered emphasis on poetry as a way of knowing. In poems of the period, it is evident that poetry becomes the, at times uneasy, rival of philosophy, theology, and science. Poetry's being is no longer defined by the serving of traditional purposes" (*Romanticism and the Self-Conscious Poem* [Oxford: Clarendon Press, 1997], p. xxiii).

28. The simultaneous ambition and vulnerability that these conditions produced are summarized by Raymond Williams, who writes, "At a time when the artist is being described as just one more producer of a commodity for the market, he is describing himself as a specially endowed person, the guiding light of the common life" (Williams warns against seeing this response as mere self-interest on the part of the poet). *Culture and Society 1780–1950* (New York: Columbia University Press, 1958), p. 36.

29. In Yeats's "Ego Dominus Tuus," he describes this repetition in despairing terms:

> *Hic.*   . . . I would find myself and not an image.
> *Ille.*   That is our modern hope and by its light
> We have lit upon the gentle, sensitive mind
> And lost the old nonchalance of the hand;
> Whether we have chosen chisel, pen, or brush
> We are but critics, or but half create.

The Collected Poems of W. B. Yeats, ed. Richard J. Finneran (New York: Macmillan, 1989), p. 160.

Yeats's "Ille" is right—modern poetry is doomed to repeat, again and again, the Romantic loss of "nonchalance," and the Romantic discovery of the "gentle, sensitive" or critical mind, but we can offer him the comfort that the experience of discovery is never complete but ever before us, and that self-consciousness is a tremendous resource for lyric poetry as well as a limitation.

30. Jerome McGann, *The Romantic Ideology* (Chicago: University of Chicago Press, 1983), p. 134.

31. Marjorie Levinson, more polemical than McGann in her willingness to describe Romantic poetry's orientation toward history as "mystified," "opportunistic," and "escapist," is also more frank about her own orientation when she describes herself as "a lapsed Romanticist—the purest form of our breed" ("Picturing Pleasure: Some Poems by Elizabeth Bishop," in

What's Left of Theory, ed. Judith Butler, John Guillory, and Kendall Thomas [New York: Routledge, 2000], 192–239, p. 197).

32. Alan Liu, *Wordsworth: The Sense of History* (Stanford: Stanford University Press, 1989), pp. 35 and 39.

33. Thomas Pfau, *Wordsworth's Profession: Form, Class, and the Logic of Early Romantic Cultural Production* (Stanford: Stanford University Press, 1997), p. 266.

34. James Chandler, *England in 1819* (Chicago: University of Chicago Press, 1998), p. 4.

35. John Keats, Letter to J. H. Reynolds, 22 November 1817, in *Letters of John Keats,* ed. Robert Gittings (Oxford: Oxford University Press, 1970), p. 40.

1. The Personal Universal

1. Lionel Trilling, *Sincerity and Authenticity* (Cambridge, Mass.: Harvard University Press, 1971), pp. 12–13.

2. As David Perkins writes of Wordsworth, "The mind of a great poet . . . assimilates and integrates all its experience; it is complete and ready. But the assimilating and integrating can be fully carried out only when they are grounded in truth, only when our inward impressions correspond to outward realities" (*Wordsworth and the Poetry of Sincerity* [Cambridge, Mass.: Harvard University Press, 1964], p. 39).

3. Perkins explains, "A great poem, Wordsworth thinks, does its work . . . as an example in living, an engagement of the whole being of the poet—his imagination, but also his conscience and intellect—in the whole of his experience" (ibid., p. 111). Or, as Charles Altieri says of Adrienne Rich, "The desire to unite speaker and writer [means that] the actual self is always responsible for its fantasies and projections" (*Self and Sensibility in Contemporary American Poetry* [New York: Cambridge University Press, 1984], p. 176).

4. This definition of sincerity has perhaps its closest critical precursor in I. A. Richards's development of the term. Richards insists upon the importance of sincerity: "Whatever it is, it is the quality we most insistently require in poetry" (*Practical Criticism* [New York: Harcourt, Brace, 1929], p. 282), and he comes to define it as "self-completion . . . The completed mind would be that perfect mind . . . in which no disorder, no mutual frustration of impulses remain" (p. 285). M. H. Abrams's discussion of sincerity also underlines its "moral connotations": "Even in its use as aesthetic norm, good poetry is a test of character" (*The Mirror and the Lamp* [New York: Oxford University Press, 1953], p. 319).

5. Although there are many conceivable examples of sincere poetry before that of Wordsworth (such as Shakespeare's or Milton's sonnets, or Herbert's meditative verse), Wordsworth's sincerity has more at stake because of the newly unstable and important status of the self in the Romantic period. Rich is also historically unique in her deployment of sincerity as a moral touchstone: she dwells more consistently and thoughtfully than any other

modern poet on the possibility that self-reflection can be taken as a guiding aesthetic and moral principle. As Charles Altieri argues, she offers a model of self-scrutiny remarkable for its persistence in resisting the dominant modern stance of self-irony (*Self and Sensibility,* p. 180).

6. All quotations from Wordsworth's Preface are from the 1850 version in *The Prose Works of William Wordsworth,* vol. 1, ed. W. J. B. Owen and Jane Worthington Smyser (Oxford: Clarendon Press, 1974); this quotation from p. 127.

7. *The Prose Works of William Wordsworth,* vol. 2, ed. W. J. B. Owen and Jane Worthington Smyser (Oxford: Clarendon Press, 1974), p. 70.

8. Ibid., p. 57.

9. This contrast is not meant to imply that Wordsworth was uninterested in the political roles and responsibilities of the individual—there is ample evidence that he was—only to suggest that in Rich's poetry, this concern is more consistently explicit.

10. Adrienne Rich, *Blood, Bread, and Poetry* (New York: W. W. Norton, 1986), pp. 199–200; hereafter abbreviated as *BBP.*

11. Adrienne Rich, *On Lies, Secrets, and Silence* (New York: W. W. Norton, 1979), p. 40; hereafter abbreviated as *LSS.*

12. Ibid., p. 47.

13. Wordsworth, Preface, p. 129.

14. Adrienne Rich, *What Is Found There* (New York: W. W. Norton, 1993), p. xiv; hereafter abbreviated as *WFT.* In one of her few references to Wordsworth, Rich seems to recognize this connection between her time and his. In the poem "Long Conversation," which attempts to determine which "old books" are useful and relevant to the end of the twentieth century, she quotes:

> 1799, Coleridge to Wordsworth: *I wish*
> *you would write a poem*
> *addressed to those who, in consequence*
> *of the complete failure of the French Revolution*
> *have thrown up all hopes*
> *of the amelioration of mankind*
> *and are sinking into an almost epicurean*
> *selfishness, disguising the same*
> *under the soft titles of domestic attachment*
> *and contempt for visionary philosophes*

(*Midnight Salvage* [New York: W. W. Norton, 1999], p. 63; italics in original).

15. Joyce Carol Oates is one of the few critics to recognize this quality in Rich, writing, "If a certain impulse to 'confession' remains, it is almost totally refined and in a sense depersonalized" ("Evolutions," *Modern Poetry Studies* 2.4 [1971]: 190–191, p. 191). When Rich does finally address her father and her late ex-husband in a confessional style in the long poem "Sources," it is in the 1980s, long after this type of address was fashionable, and these

sections of the poem are in prose, as if she felt that this kind of naked address was not appropriate to poetry proper (*Your Native Land, Your Life* [New York: W. W. Norton, 1986], pp. 9, 19, 25).

16. *LSS*, p. 47.

17. See Helen Dennis, "Adrienne Rich: Consciousness Raising as Poetic Method," pp. 178–180 for an uncritical but useful description of consciousness raising in Rich's work (in *Contemporary Poetry Meets Modern Theory*, ed. Antony Easthope and John O. Thompson [New York: Harvester Wheatsheaf, 1991], pp. 177–194). Altieri argues that "Rich's basic strength is not in the complexity of her self-consciousness but in its rigorous intensity and her determined effort to test beliefs by their practical, ethical consequences" (*Self and Sensibility*, p. 19). But I contend that this intensity produces a uniquely complex self-consciousness, which I outline here.

18. *BBP*, p. 171.

19. *WFT*, p. 216.

20. *BBP*, p. xii.

21. Ibid., p. 137.

22. Ibid., p. 123.

23. Ibid., p. 97.

24. Recent work on identity politics suggests that this tension between the impulse to claim a marked identity and the desire for a freer, unmarked identity is an unavoidable part of identity politics itself. Denise Riley argues, "A lack of fit between my self-description as a social subject and my presence as a political subject is not disappointing but benevolent, insofar as the subject of political language actually requires a certain impersonality, or a non-identity, to be able to circulate productively at all" (*The Words of Selves: Identification, Solidarity, Irony* [Stanford: Stanford University Press, 2000], p. 5). In Rich's case, we can read "poetic subject" for political subject. But she does not experience this tension, as Riley does, as benevolent and easily discharged by postmodern irony. Instead, her work treats this tension as an urgent, even if irresoluble, problem.

25. *The Fact of a Doorframe: Poems Selected and New 1950–1980* (New York: W. W. Norton, 1984), p. 215; hereafter abbreviated as *FDF*.

26. Ibid., p. 230.

27. Ibid., p. 304; italics in original.

28. Here I follow Altieri in suggesting that we should "concentrate on the qualities of consciousness" that Rich's political commitments produce rather than the content of those commitments (*Self and Sensibility*, p. 167), which is not to imply that Rich's politics are unattractive or unpersuasive. But too often criticism of Rich's work from the 1960s to the present has focused on her political stances, either to welcome them or to criticize them as damaging to the aesthetic impact of her work. In an early and helpful article, Susan Van Dyne points out a common mistake in such criticism: "Critics who attempt to measure her poetic success . . . by how completely fused her personal and political life appear in any poem or volume mistakenly assume that the person and the poet are, or should be in a poetry as authentically

reportorial as Rich's, exactly or only one" ("The Mirrored Vision of Adrienne Rich," *Modern Poetry Studies* 8 [1977]: 140–172, p. 144). Instead, Van Dyne recognizes Rich's tendency "to remove herself intentionally, if only momentarily, from any type of involvement whatsoever. Although the habit of keeping her distance has been repeatedly a source of personal suffering and guilt, it has nevertheless served throughout her career as an essential poetic advantage" (p. 143). It is this distancing, the "splitting" entailed by self-consciousness, that I explore here. Rosemary Tonks also notes this quality of detachment, remarking upon Rich's poetry's "anonymous appearance," "impersonal quality," and "objective effects" ("Cutting the Marble," in *Reading Adrienne Rich: Reviews and Revisions 1951–81*, ed. Jane Roberta Cooper [Ann Arbor: University of Michigan Press, 1984], 232–237, p. 232). But Tonks understands these qualities as a weakness of a subject-matter-driven poetry, preferring the more "personal" poetry of "psychological survival" (p. 235), rather than exploring the ways in which these two modes are linked.

29. *FDF,* p. 229.
30. Ibid., p. 228.
31. This leaves open the question of whether that same kind of self-distance could destroy a moment of pure joy or transcendence just as it destroys suffering, a question taken up by Wordsworth.
32. *FDF,* p. 228; italics in original.
33. Ibid., p. 155.
34. *LSS,* p. 47.
35. *FDF,* p. 114.
36. Ibid., pp. 114–115.
37. Audrey Crawford rightly observes that "the sense that the world is 'split'" is a central dilemma in Rich's poetry, and she suggests that technologies are useful for bridging this split: "Technologies are significant in this endeavor since they are a means of constructing and managing space and time, as well as of traveling and communicating across space and time" ("'Handing the Power-Glasses Back and Forth': Women and Technology in Poems by Adrienne Rich," *NWSA* 7.3 [Fall 1995]: 35–53, p. 38). But here, technology is part of the problem of splitting—it is something that separates the observer from what she observes. Rich addresses this problem not by using the instruments of technology, but by becoming an instrument herself.
38. *FDF,* p. 116.
39. Ibid., p. 115. Judith McDaniel argues that here, because the poet is no longer "the passive receptacle of others' descriptions of her," she "becomes an active agent of change" ("'Reconstituting the World': The Poetry and Vision of Adrienne Rich," in *Reading Adrienne Rich,* ed. Cooper, 3–29, p. 14). But this reading accepts too quickly Rich's contention that seeing is automatically a way to change oneself, and fails to register the passivity of the woman bombarded by signals.
40. *FDF,* p. 164.
41. Ibid., p. 163.

42. Ibid., pp. 163–164.
43. Cheryl Walker touches on this quality of "Diving into the Wreck" when she observes that it "is utterly personal but there is nothing in it which draws away into private life" ("Trying to Save the Skein," in *Reading Adrienne Rich,* ed. Cooper, 226–231, p. 229). James McCorkle comments, "The 'I' . . . in 'Diving into the Wreck' is a disembodied marker and does not establish an identity or ethos" (*The Still Performance: Writing, Self, and Interconnection in Five American Poets* [Charlottesville: University of Virginia Press, 1989], p. 109).
44. Thomas Weiskel makes this point, observing that the buoyancy of spirits that follows the statement quoted below "depends neither on [Wordsworth's] own self-understanding nor the successful communication of his history in the terms of 'knowledge'" (*The Romantic Sublime* [Baltimore: Johns Hopkins University Press, 1976], p. 168).
45. *The Fourteen-Book Prelude,* ed. W. J. B. Owen (Ithaca: Cornell University Press, 1985); lines I.621–631.
46. As Frank McConnell describes it, *The Prelude* continually seeks and stages "evidences of election" (*The Confessional Imagination: A Reading of Wordsworth's "Prelude"* [Baltimore: Johns Hopkins University Press, 1974], p. 5). More recently, Thomas Pfau has described in detail the ways in which "the representation of subjective 'growth' and self-disciplining throughout . . . *The Prelude* is by definition a very conspicuous, public, and hence in large measure transpersonal act" (*Wordsworth's Profession: Form, Class, and the Logic of Early Romantic Cultural Production* [Stanford: Stanford University Press, 1997], p. 269). While Pfau focuses on the sociopolitical aspects of this "transpersonality," I attempt to describe some of its formal aspects determined by the structure of self-consciousness more generally.
47. A reputation described at greatest length in David Perkins's *Wordsworth and the Poetry of Sincerity.*
48. Lines I.21–99.
49. Lines I.135–139.
50. *BBP,* p. 171.
51. Alan Liu, for example, explains that during the Romantic period the idea of universal truth was endangered by contingent historical truths. He argues that in response, "the Romantics reasserted nature's universal truth against that of history in the new form of individuality: the 'original' or transcendentally non-conventional self" (*Wordsworth: The Sense of History* [Stanford: Stanford University Press, 1989], p. 11). Succinctly put, this new "ideology of self," exemplified by Wordsworth, is his "greatest denial of history" (p. 388).
52. *FDF,* p. 329.
53. See, for example, Marjorie Levinson's well-known critique of "Tintern Abbey" (in *Wordsworth's Great Period Poems* [Cambridge: Cambridge University Press, 1986]).
54. Liu, for example, recognizes an "objective subjectivity" in Wordsworth's

poetry, "a mind knowing itself only in the impersonal" (*Wordsworth: The Sense of History,* p. 23).

55. This crisis is expressed in New Historicist criticism in the puzzling but prevalent claim that Wordsworth is somehow quintessentially historical in his putative anti-historicism. Marjorie Levinson, for example, argues that Wordsworth's poetry "perversely advertises its occasional, topical character" at the same time that it suppresses this character (*Wordsworth's Great Period Poems,* p. 5). Liu more categorically states that "denial [of history] is also the strongest kind of engagement with history" (*Wordsworth: The Sense of History,* p. 35). What keeps such claims from being simple contradictions is Wordsworth's own tendency to make denial and admission indistinguishable. It is this tendency that I explore here.

56. *Lyrical Ballads and Other Poems, 1797–1800,* ed. James Butler and Karen Green (Ithaca: Cornell University Press, 1992); lines 13–19.

57. Lines 20–22.

58. Lines 39–40.

59. Lines 40–45.

60. Lines 51–53.

61. For a recent recapitulation of Freudian readings of "Nutting," see Janice Haney Peritz's "Sexual Politics and the Subject of 'Nutting': Questions of Ideology, Rhetoric, and Fantasy," *Studies in Romanticism* 38 (Winter 1999): 559–595, pp. 588–589. While a number of studies of this poem devote themselves to decoding the latent content of "Nutting," none to my knowledge addresses the problem that the supposedly latent sexual content is actually on the poem's surface.

62. Lines 45–50.

63. *Lyrical Ballads and Other Poems;* lines 123–124.

64. Lines 50–51.

65. Lines 24–25.

66. Galperin suggests that Wordsworth produces this effect consciously, in order to manipulate the reader into accepting his point of view (*Revision and Authority in Wordsworth* [Philadelphia: University of Pennsylvania Press, 1989], pp. 81–82). But I contend that it is precisely the question of whether Wordsworth is self-consciously manipulative or unself-consciously exposing himself that remains crucially unanswerable. In any case, once Wordsworth makes himself vulnerable to questions about his sincerity, he cannot control how and where these questions are posed.

67. Line 92.

68. Lines 28–30.

69. Lines 37–42.

70. Lines 43–50.

71. Jerome McGann, *The Romantic Ideology* (Chicago: University of Chicago Press, 1983), p. 88.

72. This distinction must be qualified by Wordsworth's very real anxieties, through much of his career, about how his poetry of sincerity would be received, and the public acclaim and support that Rich's poetry has received.

But it is undeniable that white male experience has historically been accepted as "universal," while the experiences of women, particularly women who actively oppose the cultural dominance of men, have been labeled as merely "personal."

73. *FDF*, p. 103.

74. As Don Bialostosky puts it, "a Romanticist in the [19]70s and 80s, especially a Wordsworthian, was also singularly implicated in the field of 'theory,'" particularly in poststructuralist theories of language (*Wordsworth, Dialogics, and the Practice of Criticism* [New York: Cambridge University Press, 1992], p. xiii).

75. See Geoffrey Hartman's *Wordsworth's Poetry 1787–1814* (New Haven: Yale University Press, 1964); Paul de Man's "Rhetoric of Temporality" in *Blindness and Insight* (Minneapolis: University of Minnesota Press, 1983); Thomas Weiskel's *Romantic Sublime;* and Frances Ferguson's *Wordsworth: Language as Counter-Spirit* (New Haven: Yale University Press, 1977).

76. See Charles Altieri's "Wordsworth's 'Preface' as Literary Theory," *Criticism* 18 (1976): 122–146; Don Bialostosky's *Wordsworth, Dialogics, and the Practice of Criticism;* Edward Duffy's "The Romantic Calling of Thinking: Stanley Cavell on the Line with Wordsworth," *Studies in Romanticism* 37 (Winter 1998): 615–645; and Brad Sullivan's *Wordsworth and the Composition of Knowledge* (Boston: Peter Lang, 2000).

77. Appendix to the Preface (1802), in *The Prose Works of William Wordsworth,* vol. 1, ed. W. J. B. Owen and Jane Worthington Smyser (Oxford: Clarendon Press, 1974), p. 160.

78. Preface, p. 127.

79. This essay is often overlooked by Wordsworth's critics, an important exception being Frances Ferguson's *Wordsworth: Language as Counter-Spirit,* which takes the theory of language suggested by the "Essay upon Epitaphs" seriously.

80. "Essay upon Epitaphs," p. 85.

81. Ibid., p. 70.

82. Ibid., pp. 68–69.

83. Ibid., p. 69.

84. Ibid.

85. Ibid., p. 70.

86. As Ferguson puts it, "The truth of poetry for Wordsworth . . . is ultrahuman, in any normal or individualized conception of the human. For, in the formulation of the 'Essay upon Epitaphs,' the truth of poetry involves neither particular language nor particular individuals but rather a perception of the supplementarity between language and individual consciousness—and the perception that the supplementarity is always greater than the sum of its parts" (*Wordsworth: Language as Counter-Spirit,* p. 33).

87. "Essay upon Epitaphs," p. 93.

88. Ibid., p. 96.

89. Joanne Feit Diehl explains, "Rich turns away from the outspoken word, the power of voice, to advocate a language that borders on silence" ("'Car-

tographies of Silence': Rich's *Common Language* and the Woman Poet," in *Reading Adrienne Rich,* ed. Cooper, 94–110, p. 101).

90. Rich, *Midnight Salvage,* p. 69.
91. *FDF,* p. 133. While Rich's insistence upon language as a tool belonging to the oppressor may be overstated or unpersuasive, she is raising a question familiar from Wordsworth's thinking: what are we to do about language's cultural accumulations? How do we take language that has been appropriated by a political or cultural elite and make it newly relevant to ordinary people's lives?
92. *FDF,* p. 133.
93. Ibid., p. 103.
94. Ibid.
95. Ibid., pp. 103–104.
96. Ibid., p. 119.
97. Ibid., p. 116.
98. Ibid., p. 117.
99. Ibid., p. 119.
100. Ibid., p. 117.
101. Ibid.
102. Ibid., p. 118.
103. Ibid., p. 119.
104. Altieri reads this ending as one of utter despair: "The forces of oppression ultimately reduce the poem to prose and prose to obsessive repetition among associations" (*Self and Sensibility,* p. 175). Yet Altieri's admiration of the unity of pathos and style here suggests a kind of redemption: we can read this pathos in quotation marks and hence imagine an escape from it.
105. McDaniel, "'Reconstituting the World,'" p. 15.
106. The issue of verification was suggested to me in part by Rich's paraphrase of Muriel Rukeyser, who "spoke of two kinds of poetry: the poetry of 'unverifiable fact'—that which emerges from dreams, sexuality, subjectivity—and the poetry of 'documentary fact'—literally, accounts of strikes, wars, geographical and geological details, actions of actual persons in history, scientific invention" (*WFT,* p. 21).

2. Before and After

1. Appendix to the Preface to the *Lyrical Ballads* (1802), in *The Prose Works of William Wordsworth,* vol. 1, ed. W. J. B. Owen and Jane Worthington Smyser (Oxford: Clarendon Press, 1974), p. 160; emphasis in original.
2. Preface to the *Lyrical Ballads* (1850), in *The Prose Works of William Wordsworth,* vol. 1, p. 123.
3. Samuel Johnson, *Selected Writings,* ed. Patrick Cruttwell (New York: Penguin, 1968), p. 409.
4. The most influential version of this question is posed by T. S. Eliot, who famously wonders whether Shakespeare finds the appropriate "objective correlative" for what he wishes to express in *Hamlet* ("Hamlet and His Prob-

lems," in *Selected Essays 1917–1932* [New York: Harcourt Brace, 1932], pp. 124–125). In similar terms, Paul Lacey suggests that poetic form "gives shape to experience" (*The Inner War: Forms and Themes in Recent American Poetry* [Philadelphia: Fortress Press, 1972], p. 9); Robert Phillips explains that "the aesthetic process must transform [personal] motifs" (*The Confessional Poets* [Carbondale: Southern Illinois University Press, 1973], p. xv); Steven K. Hoffman contends that personal "experience must be transformed into images, the images into rhythmic patterns, the patterns, finally, into dramatically convincing poetic incidents which become the joint possession of poet and reader" ("Impersonal Personalism: The Making of a Confessional Poetic," *ELH* 45 [1978]: 687–705, p. 696); and Alan Williamson argues that the main challenge of contemporary poetic style is finding "a kind of equivalent for consciousness" (*Introspection and Contemporary Poetry* [Cambridge, Mass.: Harvard University Press, 1984], p. 5). Similar examples can be found in virtually any criticism written about personal lyric poetry. The point is not that any of these statements is wrong in its practical application, but that the implicit and repeated assumption that consciousness or experience is something that precedes form tells at best half the story.

5. This bias can be seen most starkly in the confusion generated by the category of "confessional" poetry. Coined by M. L. Rosenthal to describe the turn to autobiographical subject matter in Robert Lowell's free-verse *Life Studies*, the label soon gained a pejorative meaning, connoting formal incompetence. As Linda Wagner explains, the term "signalled the end of control, the opposite of craft" (Introduction to *Sylvia Plath: The Critical Heritage*, ed. Linda W. Wagner [New York: Routledge, 1988], 1–24, p. 12). Steven Hoffman summarizes the effects of this connotation: "To those who have chosen to attack the [confessional] mode on fundamental grounds, the term conjured visions of the kind of solipsistic self-advertisement disparaged by Eliot and his heirs, and has therefore become a token of derision or outright contempt. Equally burdened by an all too literal application, even the movement's defenders have been forced into a quandary: either to glorify the courageousness of self-exploration in the face of grave psychic risks, and its potentially therapeutic value, or to rise to the righteous defense of a particular favored poet against the ominous taint of the label" ("Impersonal Personalism," p. 687).

6. Lacey, *Inner War,* p. 9. Similar accounts of the relationship between "confessional" poetry and the New Critics are given by Marjorie Perloff (*The Poetic Art of Robert Lowell* [Ithaca: Cornell University Press, 1973], p. 83), Robert Phillips (*Confessional Poets,* pp. 5–9), Ralph J. Mills, Jr. (*Cry of the Human: Essays on Contemporary American Poetry* [Chicago: University of Illinois Press, 1975], p. 4), Steven K. Hoffman ("Impersonal Personalism," p. 687), Diane Middlebrook ("What Was Confessional Poetry?" in *The Columbia History of American Poetry*, ed. Jay Parini [New York: Columbia University Press, 1993], 632–649, p. 634), and many others.

7. Stephen Cushman also studies the metaphors American poets use for form,

arguing that American poets tend to "overestimate the synecdochic rela-
tionship between . . . formal aspects [of their art] and various ideas of
America" (*Fictions of Form in American Poetry* [Princeton: Princeton Uni-
versity Press, 1993], p. 5).

8. Adrienne Rich, *On Lies, Secrets, and Silence* (New York: W. W. Norton,
1979), pp. 40–41; hereafter abbreviated as *LSS*. In similar terms, Robert
Duncan describes formal control as a "prophylactic genius against experi-
ence" ("Ideas of the Meaning of Form," in *Claims for Poetry*, ed. Donald
Hall [Ann Arbor: University of Michigan Press, 1982], 78–94, p. 80).

9. Steven Gould Axelrod, "Robert Lowell: From Classic to Outlaw," Intro-
duction to *The Critical Response to Robert Lowell*, ed. Axelrod (Westport,
Conn.: Greenwood Press, 1999), 1–26, p. 1. Using similar imagery, A.
Alvarez writes that Sylvia Plath "bore[d] through the crust of mere crafts-
manship and release[d] the lava below" ("Poetry in Extremis," in *Sylvia
Plath: The Critical Heritage*, ed. Linda W. Wagner [New York: Routledge,
1988], 55–57, p. 56). Hugh Kenner concurs in less flattering terms, writing
that Plath's poems demonstrate "naked negation spilling down the sides of
improvised vessels" ("Sincerity Kills," in *Sylvia Plath: New Views on the
Poetry*, ed. Gary Lane [Baltimore: Johns Hopkins University Press, 1979],
33–44, p. 42).

10. James Breslin, "From Modern to Contemporary: *Life Studies*," in *The Crit-
ical Response to Robert Lowell*, ed. Axelrod, 91–97, p. 96. Lowell uses
analogous imagery when he describes his own wrestling with conventional
form: "Meter plastered difficulties and mannerisms on what I was trying to
say to such an extent that it terribly hampered me" (interview with Freder-
ick Seidel, in *Collected Prose*, ed. Robert Giroux [New York: Farrar, Straus,
& Giroux, 1987], p. 244; hereafter abbreviated as "Seidel"). In similar
terms, Ralph Mills writes of "an intense imaginative liberation, achieved at
great personal cost, in which the poet, like a snake shedding his dead skin,
frees himself of the weight of imposed styles and current critical criteria to
come into the place of his own authentic speech" (*Cry of the Human*, p. 3).
Less approvingly, John Hollander writes of "a somewhat militant esthetic
position equating strict prosody with a kind of literary repression—a poetic
Reichian character armor, so to speak, and demanding a more 'natural' na-
tional mode of poetic expression" ("Robert Lowell's New Book," in *Critics
on Robert Lowell*, ed. Jonathan Price [Coral Gables, Fla.: University of Mi-
ami Press, 1972], 66–70, p. 66).

11. Among many possible examples, see J. D. McClatchy, who writes that, with
the *Ariel* poems, Plath "was prompted to free her work of the inhibitions,
both psychological and stylistic, that had restricted her first book" ("Short
Circuits and Folding Mirrors," in *Sylvia Plath: New Views on the Poetry*,
ed. Gary Lane [Baltimore: Johns Hopkins University Press, 1979], 19–32,
p. 24), and Charles Newman ("Candour is the Only Wile," in *The Art of
Sylvia Plath*, ed. Newman [Bloomington: Indiana University Press, 1970],
21–55, p. 49).

12. Kenner, "Sincerity Kills," p. 41. Kenner criticizes those who equate this sui-

cidal drive with a new kind of sincerity, but his implicit agreement that *Ariel* is the more authentic book underscores the connection between Plath's newfound formal freedom and genuine self-expression.

13. See also Elizabeth Hardwick, who writes that Plath's verse exhibits "an uncanny control of language, sound, rhythm, and metaphor that is the very opposite of madness" ("On Sylvia Plath," in *Ariel Ascending*, ed. Paul Alexander [New York: Harper & Row, 1985], 100–115, p. 106).

14. Appendix to Preface, p. 160.

15. "Shakespeare's Judgment Equal to his Genius," in *Coleridge's Shakespearean Criticism*, vol. 1, ed. Thomas Middleton Raysor (Cambridge, Mass.: Harvard University Press, 1930), p. 224.

16. "Talking with Adrienne Rich," *Ohio Review* 13 (1971): 28–46, pp. 30–31.

17. Admittedly, in the essay at hand Coleridge is thinking about literature as mimesis rather than as self-expression. But his theory of organic form has implications for the expressive turn in poetry that coincided with his critical writings.

18. When Rich states that the poet's task is to reveal the innate shape of experience, she imagines a significantly diminished role for the poet. Her comment comes in the course of a discussion of a line she had written: "the notes for the poem are the only poem" ("Talking with Adrienne Rich," p. 30). If the poet can never completely grasp the shape that inheres in experience, then perhaps the poet can never truly write "the poem," only tentative notes on the conditions in which such a grasping or revelation might take place. Tellingly, this vision of the poet's role is difficult to distinguish from the language Rich uses to describe her earlier, nonorganic uses of poetic form. Of her second book, she writes, "I was already dissatisfied with these poems, which seemed to me mere exercises for poems I hadn't written" (*LSS*, p. 42). The difference between her earlier, mechanical use of form and what she sees as her later, organic commitment to experience does not necessarily mean that she can now write the real poem for which other poems have been exercises; instead, she commits herself to continue writing exercises that are notes toward the organic form that can never be fully bodied forth in an individual poem.

19. Williamson, *Introspection*, p. 12.

20. Other examples include Steven K. Hoffman's defense of so-called confessional poems: "Far from loosing a torrent of personal feeling, they offer emotions fused to images and objectified" ("Impersonal Personalism," p. 698). Jon Rosenblatt writes that Plath's poetry "reorders personal experience into patterns that obtain an objective character through repetition, allusion, and symbolic enactment" (*Sylvia Plath: The Poetry of Initiation* [Chapel Hill: University of North Carolina Press, 1979], p. 15). William Bedford makes explicit the moral judgment underlining claims of objectivity when he argues that Lowell's formal poetic achievements amount to both objectivity and moral goodness ("The Morality of Form in the Poetry of Robert Lowell," *Ariel* 9.2 [January 1978]: 3–17, p. 16).

21. T.S. Eliot, "Tradition and the Individual Talent," in *Selected Essays 1917–1932* (New York: Harcourt Brace, 1932), pp. 7–8.

22. Ibid., p. 10.

23. See Brian Lee, *Theory and Personality: The Significance of T. S. Eliot's Criticism* (London: Athlone Press, 1979), for an exhaustive and unforgiving analysis of the ways in which the style of "Tradition and the Individual Talent" works against its message. Lee writes, "It has to be said that part II of 'Tradition and the Individual Talent' [the part about impersonality] is itself an escape, from the implications of [the part about tradition]; and that in so far as it is an escape, it is sentimental" (p. 62).

24. Eliot, "Tradition and the Individual Talent," p. 7.

25. Ibid., p. 10.

26. Ibid., p. 6.

27. Ibid., p. 8.

28. Ibid., p. 10.

29. Maud Ellmann makes an argument similar to mine in somewhat different terms, concluding, "Eliot is attacking expressivism with its own weapons, and he reinstates the feeling subject at the center of the process of creation at the same time as he attempts to circumscribe his will" (*The Poetics of Impersonality: T. S. Eliot and Ezra Pound* [Brighton: Harvester, 1987], p. 41). Gareth Reeves extends Ellmann's analysis into Eliot's writings on Valéry, demonstrating that the seemingly impersonal self-reflexivity that Eliot admires in Valéry becomes difficult to distinguish from the kind of self-absorption Eliot finds distasteful ("'The Present Self-Conscious Century': Eliot on Valéry," *Yeats-Eliot Review* [Summer 1994]: 42–47).

30. Eliot, "Hamlet and His Problems," pp. 124–125.

31. This is to say nothing of the more obvious problem that Eliot's formulation presents: it seems simply wrong to assume that "a set of objects, a situation, a chain of events" will reliably invoke the same emotional effect in every reader, unless you believe (as Eliot does) that something like "tradition" guarantees that all (properly educated) readers will experience identical responses. Needless to say, it is ever more difficult to maintain this belief as the readership of English literature becomes increasingly diverse and the English literary canon becomes more open to question.

32. "Hamlet and His Problems," p. 125; emphasis in original.

33. Ibid., p. 125.

34. Ibid.

35. Ibid., p. 126.

36. "Essay upon Epitaphs," in *The Prose Works of William Wordsworth*, vol. 2, ed. W. J. B. Owen and Jane Worthington Smyser (Oxford: Clarendon Press, 1974), p. 58.

37. Ibid., p. 59.

38. Ibid., p. 57.

39. Ibid., p. 77. We may be given pause by the fact that Pope's own body of work includes similar insistences upon the sincerity of the writer, for exam-

ple, "He best can paint 'em, who shall feel 'em most" ("Eloisa to Abelard," line 366).

40. "Essay upon Epitaphs," p. 76.
41. Ibid., p. 77.
42. Ibid.
43. Ibid., p. 78.
44. Ibid., pp. 77–78.
45. Ibid., p. 78.
46. Ibid., p. 58.
47. Ibid.
48. Wordsworth also becomes entangled in what he disparages as false discrimination in a polemical way, as he comments on his own procedure with Pope's epitaph: "Minute criticism is in its nature irksome, and as commonly practiced in books and conversation, is both irksome and injurious. Yet every mind must occasionally be exercised in this discipline, else it cannot learn the art of bringing words rigorously to the test of thoughts" ("Essay upon Epitaphs," p. 78). The essay in its entirety wavers between trying to educate the reader's taste through reasonable expostulation and insisting that "if the unction of a devout heart be wanting everything else is of no avail" (ibid., p. 83), an ambivalence that reproduces at an organizational level the blurring of overintellectualization and emotional sincerity that Wordsworth attempts to avoid in his discussion of Pope.
49. "Essay upon Epitaphs," p. 59.
50. *The Fourteen-Book Prelude*, ed. W. J. B. Owen (Ithaca: Cornell University Press, 1985); lines I.147–157.
51. T. S. Eliot, "The Metaphysical Poets," in *Selected Essays 1917–1932* (New York: Harcourt Brace, 1932), p. 248; emphasis in original.
52. Seidel, p. 244.
53. "Robert Lowell in Conversation," with A. Alvarez, in *Robert Lowell: Interviews and Memoirs*, ed. Jeffrey Meyers (Ann Arbor: University of Michigan Press, 1988), 74–78, p. 75.
54. R. P. Blackmur, "*Land of Unlikeness*," in *The Critical Response to Robert Lowell*, ed. Steven Gould Axelrod (Westport, Conn.: Greenwood Press, 1999), 25–28, p. 25; emphasis in original.
55. Randall Jarrell, "From the Kingdom of Necessity," in *The Critical Response to Robert Lowell*, ed. Axelrod, 30–37, p. 35.
56. Robert Lowell, *Selected Poems*, Revised Edition (New York: Farrar, Straus, & Giroux, 1977), p. 11.
57. For example, the opening line of the poem, "This Easter, Arthur Winslow, less than dead," is stitched together with "s," "r," "l," and "w" sounds, achieving symmetry at its center with "Winslow" and "less," which reverses the "sl" pattern in "Winslow." Only the "d's" in "dead" are left unmatched (or match only themselves), appropriately mirroring death's abrupt intrusion. Again, the exception of "dead" proves the prosodic rule.
58. Lowell, *Selected Poems*, p. 11.
59. Ibid.

60. Ibid., pp. 72–73.

61. Ibid..

62. Ibid., p. 72.

63. Laurence Lerner, "What Is Confessional Poetry?" *Critical Quarterly* 29.2 (Summer 1987): 46–66, p. 65.

64. Lowell, *Selected Poems*, p. 73.

65. See, for example, Bedford, "The Morality of Form," p. 4, and DeSales Standerwick, "Pieces too Personal," in *Profile of Robert Lowell*, ed. Jerome Mazarro (Columbus: Charles E. Merrill, 1971), p. 15.

66. Perloff, *Poetic Art of Robert Lowell*, pp. 87–93.

67. Williamson, *Introspection*, p. 16.

68. Adrienne Rich, *What Is Found There* (New York: W. W. Norton, 1993), p. 49; hereafter abbreviated as *WFT*; emphasis in original.

69. Adrienne Rich, *Blood, Bread, and Poetry* (New York: W. W. Norton, 1986), p. 123.

70. *WFT*, p. 52; emphasis in original.

71. Adrienne Rich, *The Fact of a Doorframe: Poems Selected and New 1950–1984* (New York: W. W. Norton, 1984), p. 20; hereafter abbreviated as *FDF*.

72. Ibid., p. 20.

73. Ibid., pp. 20–21.

74. Ibid., p. 329.

75. Ibid., p. 225.

76. Ibid.

77. Ibid.

78. Ibid.

79. Robert Lowell, Foreword to *Ariel*, by Sylvia Plath (New York: Harper & Row, 1966), vii–ix, p. viii.

80. A. Alvarez, "Sylvia Plath," in *The Art of Sylvia Plath*, ed. Charles Newman (Bloomington: Indiana University Press, 1970), 56–68, p. 67.

81. Alicia Ostriker, "The Americanization of Sylvia," in *Critical Essays on Sylvia Plath*, ed. Linda W. Wagner (Boston: G. K. Hall, 1984), 97–109, p. 98.

82. See, for example, Alvarez's "Postscript" to his original review, also reprinted in *The Art of Sylvia Plath*, and Ostriker's ironic perspective on her initial reaction to *Ariel*. Jon Rosenblatt provides the helpful reminder that "Plath had been suicidal long before she dived into her unconscious through extremist poetry. In 1953 she attempted suicide . . . yet at that time she was composing poems that Alvarez has characterized as 'formal' and 'elegant,' devoid of any commitment to personal risk" (*Sylvia Plath: Poetry of Initiation*, p. 11).

83. Linda Bundtzen observes that Plath is viewed "as a woman who played with death as other writers play with images, metaphors, and symbols" (*Plath's Incarnations: Woman and the Creative Process* [Ann Arbor: University of Michigan Press, 1983], p. 1). I counter this view by suggesting that Plath explores the difference between real and metaphorical death. In doing so, I follow in the footsteps of Plath's recent critics who work "not to

repeat the closed circle which makes Plath and her problems—or the critic's own version of them—stand in for the problems of her texts but to attempt to explore the problematic of her writing itself" (Linda Anderson, *Women and Autobiography in the Twentieth Century: Remembered Futures* [New York: Prentice-Hall, 1997], p. 103); see particularly Jacqueline Rose's excellent study *The Haunting of Sylvia Plath* (Cambridge, Mass.: Harvard University Press, 1992).

84. Quoted in Kenner, "Sincerity Kills," p. 35.

85. Quoted in Murray M. Schwartz and Christopher Bollas, "The Absence at the Center: Sylvia Plath and Suicide," in *Sylvia Plath: New Views on the Poetry,* ed. Gary Lane (Baltimore: Johns Hopkins University Press, 1979), 179–202, p. 198.

86. Lowell, for example, writes of "the macabre gaiety of her control" (Foreword, p. viii), and M. L. Rosenthal writes of her "sheer wild leap of absolute mastery" (*Our Life in Poetry* [New York: Persea Books, 1991], p. 199). Stephen Spender writes that, in Plath's poetry, "the miracle is an effect of controlled uncontrolledness" ("Warnings from the Grave," in *Sylvia Plath: The Critical Heritage,* ed. Linda W. Wagner [New York: Routledge, 1988], 69–73, p. 70), and A. Alvarez attempts to capture this quality as well: "the whole book of technique is thrown at situations and feelings that otherwise seem to overbear all technique" (*Beyond All This Fiddle* [New York: Random House, 1968], p. 16). Helen Vendler concurs: "Poems like 'Daddy' and 'Lady Lazarus' are in one sense demonically intelligent, in their wanton play with concepts, myths, and language, and in another, and more important sense, not intelligent at all, in that they willfully refuse, for the sake of a cacophony of styles (a tantrum of style) the steady, centripetal effect of thought" ("An Intractable Metal," in *Ariel Ascending,* ed. Paul Alexander [New York: Harper & Row, 1985], 1–12, p. 11).

87. Kenner, "Sincerity Kills," p. 42; emphasis in original.

88. Rosenthal, *Our Life in Poetry,* p. 199.

89. Quoted by Ted Hughes in his Introduction to the *Collected Poems* (New York: HarperPerennial, 1992), 13–17, p. 13.

90. Nancy Hargrove reports that the earthenware head is based on a model of Plath made by her roommate during her junior year at Smith (*The Journey Towards Ariel: Sylvia Plath's Poems of 1956–1959* [Lund, Sweden: Lund University Press, 1994], p. 110).

91. Plath, *Collected Poems,* p. 69.

92. Ibid., p. 70.

93. Hargrove contends that the head represents the poet's evil double, and that it will lead to the destruction of the poet if she is not able to destroy it (*Journey Towards Ariel,* p. 111). But the inconclusiveness of both the poem's narrative and its tone suggests a wider range of possibilities.

94. Plath, *Collected Poems,* p. 69.

95. Ibid., pp. 69–70.

96. Ibid., p. 69.

97. "Edge" has a complicated place in the Plath canon. Hughes, Plath's husband and editor, made "Edge" the penultimate poem in *Ariel,* which was

published after her death. He also chose to position "Edge" as the final poem in Plath's *Collected Poems,* although the more life-affirming "Balloons" was written on the same day and, chronologically, would make an equally appropriate ending. A. Alvarez introduced Plath to the British reading public with the same poem a few days after her suicide, under the headline, "A Poet's Epitaph" (*The Observer Weekend Review,* February 17, 1963, p. 23). What is remarkable about all this is that Plath herself did not include "Edge" in *Ariel* at all. The publication and placement of her poem give it a career-defining weight that Plath herself did not necessarily intend.

98. Plath, *Collected Poems,* p. 272.
99. Ibid.
100. Ibid., p. 273.
101. Ibid.
102. For this reason, it is wrong to read this poem as being literally about the poet's own death (as Peter Dale does when he claims that here, Plath "imagines herself dead" ["O Honey Bees Come Build," in *Sylvia Plath: The Critical Heritage,* ed. Wagner, 62–68, p. 67]; and as A. Alvarez does when he writes that the poem "is specifically about the act [of suicide] she was about to perform" [*A Savage God* (New York: Random House, 1970), p. 36]). In every way, the poem depends upon the poet's aliveness.

3. Sincerity and the Staged Confession

1. See, for example, W. K. Wimsatt and Monroe C. Beardsley, "The Intentional Fallacy," in *The Verbal Icon* (Lexington: University of Kentucky Press, 1954); and C. S. Lewis and E. M. W. Tillyard, *The Personal Heresy* (New York: Oxford University Press, 1939).
2. E. R. Harty, "Voice and Enunciation in the Dramatic Monologue and the Lyric," *Unisa English Studies* 28.1 (April 1990): 14–21, p. 14; emphasis in original.
3. A. Dwight Culler gives the details of the history of the term, explaining that it "did not come to be generally employed until the very end of the nineteenth century, and it was not firmly established as the name of a genre until the beginning of the twentieth century." The term seems to have first been used by George Thornbury in an 1857 poetry anthology ("Monodrama and the Dramatic Monologue," *PMLA* 90.3 [May 1975]: 366–385, p. 366). Systematic attempts to define the dramatic monologue began in the early twentieth century, the most influential early attempt being Ina Beth Sessions's "The Dramatic Monologue," *PMLA* 62.2 (June 1947): 503–516.
4. Megan Gribskov Painter gives a useful overview of the critical disagreements about whether or not "Ulysses" is a dramatic monologue (*The Aesthetic of the Victorian Dramatic Monologue* [Lewiston, N.Y.: Edwin Mellen, 2000], pp. 8–9).
5. Harty, "Voice and Enunciation," p. 21.
6. Wordsworth himself would no doubt put this poem in the class of the "Idyllium," which according to him is "descriptive chiefly . . . of characters, manners, and sentiments . . . The Epitaph, the Inscription, the sonnet, most

of the epistles of poets writing in their own persons, and all loco-descriptive poetry belongs to this class." In contrast, Wordsworth would put what we call the dramatic monologue in the dramatic class, "consisting of Tragedy, Historic Drama, Comedy, and Masque, in which the Poet does not appear at all in his own person, and where the whole action is carried only by speech and dialogue of the agents . . . The characteristic and impassioned Epistle, of which Ovid and Pope have given examples, considered as a species of monodrama, may, without impropriety, be placed in this class" (Preface to the 1815 Edition of *Lyrical Ballads, The Prose Works of William Wordsworth,* vol. 3, ed. W. J. B. Owen and Jane Worthington Smyser [Oxford: Clarendon, 1974], pp. 27–28). Although Wordsworth makes clear distinctions here, we can anticipate the possibility for confusion between idyllic poems that describe characters and "characteristic and impassioned" monodrama.

7. *Lyrical Ballards and Other Poems, 1797–1800,* ed. James Butler and Karen Green (Ithaca: Cornell University Press, 1992); lines 36–42.

8. Herbert Tucker, "Dramatic Monologue and the Overhearing of Lyric," in *Lyric Poetry: Beyond New Criticism,* ed. Chaviva Hošek and Patricia Parker (Ithaca: Cornell University Press, 1985), 226–243, p. 228.

9. Tucker himself raises questions about the supposedly demystifying work of the dramatic monologue, but in different terms. He writes of "the mystification inherent in the critical fiction of the speaker and . . . its collusion with the mysteries of the subjectivist norm it was designed to supplant" ("Dramatic Monologue," p. 241). But while I would locate this mystification in the assumptions about the recoverability of authorial intention that the dramatic monologue entails, Tucker suggests that the idea of the speaker is itself ahistorical in a suspect way (p. 242). Although I disagree with Tucker's assumption that we need "history" to destabilize the claims of a unified, authoritative subjectivity (self-consciousness is a sufficiently destabilizing force in itself), I agree with his underlying suggestion that "while texts do not absolutely lack speakers, they do not simply have them either; they invent them instead as they go" (p. 243).

10. While "My Last Duchess" is a favorite example of the dramatic monologue for critics, to the extent that it seems to be uniquely exemplary of the genre, its atypicality is exposed by the lengths to which critics must go to categorize dramatic monologues that deviate from its parameters. In an early article on the dramatic monologue, Ina Beth Sessions distinguishes between the "perfect" dramatic monologue, represented by "My Last Duchess," and other "imperfect" types. Critics ever since have rebelled against the value judgment implied in this categorization, but "My Last Duchess" has retained its status as a synecdoche for the genre as a whole. See Linda K. Hughes, *The Manyfacèd Glass: Tennyson's Dramatic Monologues* (Athens, Oh.: Ohio University Press, 1987), pp. 5–9, for an overview of "exclusive" versus "inclusive" definitions of the dramatic monologue. She comments that "somehow the exclusionists' dramatic monologue is always distinctly Browningesque" (p. 6).

11. *The Complete Works of Robert Browning,* vol. 3 (Athens, Oh.: Ohio University Press, 1971); lines 1–2.

12. Lines 52–53.

13. Lines 2–13.

14. Lines 22 and 25–26.

15. Lines 31–43.

16. Lines 25–26.

17. Lines 360–363.

18. Alan Sinfield offers one theory of this progression: "Dramatic monologue and allied forms may be employed by the [modern] poet . . . as provisional languages through which he may gradually develop a first-person voice which does not suffer the disadvantages the Victorians sought to avoid. If the poet can cultivate a poetic 'I' which is sufficiently elusive and impersonal to suggest the mysterious and incalculable nature of the human psyche; which heads off the Romantic assumption that the poet's self may be encapsulated, and truth with it, in a single language act; which possesses an ironical self-awareness but does not inhibit commitment, then he will no longer need dramatic monologue" (*Dramatic Monologue* [New York: Barnes & Noble, 1977], p. 71).

19. T. S. Eliot, "Tradition and the Individual Talent," in *Selected Essays: 1917–1932* (New York: Harcourt Brace, 1932), p. 8.

20. T. S. Eliot, *On Poetry and Poets* (Boston: Faber and Faber, 1957), pp. 95–96.

21. The incompleteness of the poem's commitment to the dramatic monologue form has created a great deal of critical debate: to whom the "you" refers, and which, if any, of the poem's actions take place outside the confines of Prufrock's own mind. Elisabeth Howe observes that "the first line suggests that Prufrock is addressing another person; yet he appears to be alone throughout the poem" (*The Dramatic Monologue* [New York: Twayne, 1996], p. 75). Manju Jain concludes that, unlike Browning's dramatic monologues, in this poem "it is difficult to determine when, where, and to whom the persona speaks" (*A Critical Reading of the "Selected Poems" of T. S. Eliot* [Delhi: Oxford University Press, 1991], p. 36). The closeness of Eliot to Prufrock is noted by many critics of the poem: for example, an early commentator on Eliot, George Williamson, recognizes Eliot's "assumption of an ironic mask or attitude, mock-heroic in effect and wit," but suggests that we should understand this irony as having a personal motive and therefore personal meaning: "This irony is also the reticence of a sensitive man, and satire its revenge. It would be possible to treat his changing method, which emerges from the *personae* or attitudes objectified in his poems, as an evolution or attainment of greater and greater psychological directness" (*A Reader's Guide to T. S. Eliot* [New York: Noonday Press, 1953], pp. 51–52).

22. Robert McNamara, "'Prufrock' and the Problem of Literary Narcissism," *Contemporary Literature* 27.3 (Fall 1986): 356–377, pp. 358–359.

23. Ibid., p. 366.

24. T. S. Eliot, *The Complete Poems and Plays 1909–1950* (New York: Harcourt Brace, 1980), p. 7. As we saw in the previous chapter, Eliot later identifies Hamlet as a dramatic character who is not a satisfyingly "objectified" character. In retrospect, Prufrock might be understood similarly as a character who fails to be a full character, because he is not appropriately (in Eliot's terms) separated from the motives of his creator.

25. McNamara, "'Prufrock' and the Problem of Literary Narcissism," p. 370.

26. Still more telling is the conclusion of McNamara's essay, in which the distinction between Victorian narcissism and Modernist objectivity (the central distinction of McNamara's argument) breaks down. As McNamara puts it, Modernism "can analyze romanticism, narcissism, and bourgeois evasiveness . . . but what can it offer as an alternative? Only more analysis. As such, it seems, it becomes one more form of paralysis, repeating the problem of the Victorian discursivity it sought to replace" (ibid., p. 377). Self-consciousness produces not a saving objectivity, but yet more self-consciousness.

27. Eliot, *Complete Poems*, p. 4.

28. Ibid., p. 5.

29. Ibid.

30. Translation from B. C. Southam, *A Guide to the "Selected Poems" of T. S. Eliot* (New York: Harcourt Brace, 1968), p. 33.

31. Eliot, *Complete Poems*, p. 7.

32. Ibid., p. 3. If this were a strict dramatic monologue, limited to a specific exchange between a speaker and a particularized auditor, we could safely interpret this "overwhelming question" as the proposal or proposition that Prufrock later attempts to make to his chosen lady. But the decontextualization of the question, as well as the poem's interest in perplexities beyond those of romantic love, suggest that the "overwhelming question" is an existential one.

33. Eliot, *Complete Poems*, p. 6.

34. Ibid.

35. Ibid., p. 4.

36. Ibid., p. 8.

37. Southam, *Guide*, p. 37.

38. Eliot, *Complete Poems*, p. 10.

39. These were the words Conrad Aiken used to describe the lady upon whom the poem is supposedly based. Aiken suggests that Eliot means to ridicule the lady but also "his own pose" (quoted in Southam, *Guide*, p. 36).

40. By extension, as Elisabeth Howe argues, the speaker "may have the upper hand in the complex game that they are playing, but he seems constantly afraid that he might lose that advantage; [the lady] obviously exerts some kind of fascination that draws him to her at the risk of losing the independence he values so highly" (Howe, *Dramatic Monologue*, p. 79).

41. Eliot, *Complete Poems*, p. 11.

42. Ibid., p. 9.

43. Ibid., p. 11.

44. *The Poems of Matthew Arnold,* ed. Kenneth Allott (London: Longmans, 1965); lines 4–7.
45. Ibid., line 86.
46. John Berryman, *The Dream Songs* (New York: Noonday Press, 1969), p. 64.
47. See A. R. Jones's article on Browning for an overview of this somewhat contradictory contemporary view of Browning's achievement ("Robert Browning and the Dramatic Monologue: The Impersonal Art," *Critical Quarterly* 9.4 [Winter 1967]: 301–328, pp. 303–304).
48. Berryman, *Dream Songs,* p. vi.
49. Ibid., p. 16.
50. Ibid.
51. Ibid., p. 83.
52. Speaking in blackface is one of the complicated localized ways in which Berryman assumes masks. As Eric Lott describes it, minstrelsy involves a "mixed erotic economy of celebration and exploitation" (*Love and Theft: Minstrelsy and the American Working Class* [New York: Oxford University Press, 1993], p. 6). By taking on this particular mask, Berryman perhaps intends a complex mixture of self-deprecation and self-aggrandizement.
53. William Martz, *John Berryman* (Minneapolis: University of Minnesota Press, 1969), p. 40; emphasis in original.
54. Sharon Bryan, discussing Berryman's poetry, argues that "persona poems provide the valuable focus of first person, but declare themselves to be spoken by someone other than the author and so offer an escape—not from personality, but from self-consciousness" ("Hearing Voices: John Berryman's Translation of Private Vision into Public Song," in *Recovering Berryman: Essays on a Poet,* ed. Richard J. Kelly and Alan K. Lathrop [Ann Arbor: University of Michigan Press, 1993], 141–152, p. 144). But I would argue that if Berryman's use of a persona lets him "escape" self-consciousness, it is only by naturalizing it. A number of readers have made similar observations. For example, Helen Vendler captures this effect when she writes of the *Dream Songs,* "a new multiple-Berryman appeared in uninhibited dialogue with himself and his possible selves, a straight man in his own minstrel show, conducting his dreams in public, taking his pills and drinks onto the printed page with him, disavowing his creations all the while, making not confessions but harangues over his private-public address system, all in an eloquent lingua franca" (*Part of Nature, Part of Us* [Cambridge, Mass.: Harvard University Press, 1980], p. 119). Or as Robert Lowell puts it, "Henry is Berryman seen as himself, as *poète maudit,* child and puppet. He is tossed about with a mixture of tenderness and absurdity, pathos and hilarity that would have been impossible if the author had spoken in the first person" (*Collected Prose,* ed. Robert Giroux [New York: Farrar, Straus, & Giroux, 1987], p. 108). Edward Mendelson argues that while the poems look like "a transparently autobiographical series of dramatic monologues," they are actually "a verbal corporation whose members are uncontrolled responses to—and translations from—the world of

experience" ("How to Read Berryman's *Dream Songs,*" in *American Poetry Since 1960,* ed. Robert B. Shaw [Cheadle, U.K.: Carcanet Press, 1973], 29–44, p. 30).

55. Berryman, *Dream Songs,* pp. 3, 60, and 74.
56. Martz, *John Berryman,* p. 37.
57. *Complete Works of Robert Browning;* lines I.395–401.
58. Robert Langbaum, *The Poetry of Experience: The Dramatic Monologue in Modern Literary Tradition* (Chicago: University of Chicago Press, 1985). Originally published: Random House, 1957.
59. Ibid., p. 27.
60. Ibid., p. 83. Langbaum repeatedly reminds us that his understanding of the dramatic monologue depends upon a tension between sympathy and judgment, but his readings tend to favor sympathy, mentioning judgment as an afterthought. A more recent argument in favor of the open-endedness of the dramatic monologue is set forth in W. David Shaw's *Origins of the Monologue: The Hidden God* (Toronto: University of Toronto Press, 1999). Shaw's argument is genealogical, locating the origins of the dramatic monologue in the "subversive traditions" of Kantian agnosticism, the idea of the unconscious, Socratic irony, and Romanticism (p. 3).
61. Robert Lowell, "Anne Sexton," in *Anne Sexton: The Artist and Her Critics,* ed. J. D. McClatchy (Bloomington: Indiana University Press, 1978), p. 71.
62. Harty, "Voice and Enunciation," p. 17.
63. This idea of the "plumb line" comes from another comment about Sexton, this one from Helen Vendler, who suggests that "only rarely can she include a plumb line by which to estimate her own slant out of equilibrium" (*The Music of What Happens* [Cambridge, Mass.: Harvard University Press, 1988], p. 308).
64. Hallam Tennyson, *Alfred, Lord Tennyson: A Memoir* (New York: Macmillan, 1898), p. 196.
65. *The Poetic and Dramatic Works of Alfred, Lord Tennyson,* ed. W. J. Rolfe (Boston: Houghton Mifflin, 1898); lines 18–21, 30–32, and 66–70. For examples of this type of reading, see Tony Robbins, "On the Poem's Focus on Mood," in *Alfred, Lord Tennyson,* ed. Harold Bloom (Broomall, Penn.: Chelsea House, 1999), 40–42, p. 41; A. Dwight Culler, *The Poetry of Tennyson* (New Haven: Yale University Press, 1977), pp. 89–98; and Hughes, *Manyfacèd Glass,* pp. 94–97.
66. See E. J. Chiasson, "Tennyson's 'Ulysses'—A Re-Interpretation," in *Critical Essays on the Poetry of Tennyson,* ed. John Kilburn (London: Routledge & Kegan Paul, 1960), pp. 164–173.
67. "Ulysses," lines 1–5.
68. Line 43. For examples of this type of reading, see Chiasson, "Tennyson's 'Ulysses'"; Kenneth M. McKay, *Many Glancing Colours: An Essay in Reading Tennyson* (Toronto: University of Toronto Press, 1988), pp. 115–122; and Arthur Ward, "On Ulysses's Shortsightedness," in *Alfred, Lord Tennyson,* ed. Bloom, pp. 35–37.
69. Lines 31–32.

70. W. W. Robson makes this case, pointing out the parallels between Ulysses' speech urging his companions to undertake further journeys in the *Inferno* and Ulysses' speech in Tennyson's poem ("The Dilemma of Tennyson," in *Critical Essays on the Poetry of Tennyson,* ed. Kilburn, 155–163, p. 156).

71. David Goslee, *Tennyson's Characters: Strange Faces, Other Minds* (Iowa City: University of Iowa Press, 1989), p. xii. James Kincaid reads the dramatic monologue similarly when he describes it as the form "where the removal of context makes it extremely difficult not only to know how to judge but to be certain if one should judge at all" ("Rhetorical Irony, the Dramatic Monologue, and Tennyson's *Poems* (1842)," *Philological Quarterly* 53.2 [Spring 1974]: 220–236, p. 221). He defines "the rhetoric of the dramatic monologue" as "the uncertainty of context, the demand for judgments, and the absence of ingredients that would make judgments mean anything" (p. 222). But at the same time, Kincaid finds himself capable of arguing that "Ulysses is not condemned nor attacked; he is fully accepted. It is just that we cannot finally be him" (p. 229)—in other words, his solution to the problem of life is admirable but a solution available only to him. This argument depends upon either (1) assuming that Tennyson's intention is recoverable, so that we know he does not condemn Ulysses, or (2) assuming that we can access Ulysses directly, suspending our awareness of Tennyson's possible intentions in constructing his voice. Neither assumption is admissible, but their role in Kincaid's argument illustrates the fantasy of recovering (and/or completely dissolving) authorial intention that the dramatic monologue form makes possible. W. David Shaw makes a parallel attempt to account for Ulysses' contradictions by suspending the question of authorial intention, suggesting that "we hear Ulysses hovering between a stable moral self and a histrionic self that dangerously detonates, splitting into fragments" (*Alfred, Lord Tennyson: The Poet in an Age of Theory* [New York: Twayne, 1996], p. 72), but he concludes that Ulysses' "moments of deception are also our moments of greatest intimacy with [him]" (p. 75). I would counter that to the extent to which we can understand Ulysses to be deceiving himself, we are distanced from him, not made intimate with him, unless we imagine that Ulysses' self-deceptions are Tennyson's self-deceptions (or even our own) and therefore amenable to our sympathy instead of our judgment.

72. "Ulysses" is not the only poem in Tennyson's oeuvre that creates this kind of confusion: critics also debate whether or not "Locksley Hall" is a dramatic monologue (see, for example, Harty, "Voice and Enunciation," pp. 17–18).

73. It is just possible that the reader might encounter "Lady Lazarus" outside the context of Plath's biography, in which case the tension I describe here would not apply. But perhaps more than any other American poet, Plath's poetry is inextricable from what we know about the circumstances of her life.

74. Sylvia Plath, *The Collected Poems,* ed. Ted Hughes (New York: HarperPerennial, 1992), p. 244.

75. Jon Rosenblatt makes somewhat the same point when he observes, "We can easily forget that [the poem is] a dramatic monologue in which the persona plays out various fantasies of suicide . . . Plath's poem breathes in an atmosphere of a heightened personal myth, yet it generates disturbing responses that are more appropriate to realistic accounts of suffering. The reader can legitimately wonder whether Plath is the speaker in her poem or whether she has created a fantasized self-dramatization" (*Sylvia Plath: The Poetry of Initiation* [Chapel Hill: University of North Carolina Press, 1979], p. 145).

76. M. D. Uroff, "Sylvia Plath and Confessional Poetry: A Reconsideration," *Iowa Review* 8.1 (Winter 1977): 104–115, pp. 111–112.

77. The following critics read "Lady Lazarus" as transparently confessional: Jan Gordon, "'Who is Sylvia?': The Art of Sylvia Plath," *Modern Poetry Studies* 1.1 (1970): 6–33, pp. 22–23; Robert Phillips, *The Confessional Poets* (Carbondale: Southern Illinois University Press, 1973), p. 146; Isaac Sequeira, "From Confession to Suicide: The Poetry of Sylvia Plath," in *Studies in American Literature: Essays in Honour of William Mulder*, ed. Jagdish Chander and Narindar S. Pradhan (Delhi: Oxford University Press, 1976), 232–242, p. 235; Murray M. Schwartz and Christopher Bollas, "The Absence at the Center: Sylvia Plath and Suicide," in *Sylvia Plath: New Views on the Poetry*, ed. Gary Lane (Baltimore: Johns Hopkins University Press, 1979), 179–202, p. 187; Elizabeth Hardwick, "On Sylvia Plath," in *Ariel Ascending*, ed. Paul Alexander (New York: Harper & Row, 1985), 100–115, p. 106; Peter Dale, "O Honey Bees Come Build," in *Sylvia Plath: The Critical Heritage*, ed. Linda Wagner (New York: Routledge, 1988), p. 67; P. N. Furbank, "New Poetry," in *Sylvia Plath: The Critical Heritage*, ed. Linda Wagner (New York: Routledge, 1988), 73–74, p. 73. Rarer are the critics who insist that Lady Lazarus is a speaker who must be understood as distanced from the poet; these include A. E. Dyson, "On Sylvia Plath," in *The Art of Sylvia Plath*, ed. Charles Newman (Bloomington: Indiana University Press, 1970), 204–210, p. 210; Mary Lynn Broe, *Protean Poetic: The Poetry of Sylvia Plath* (Columbia: University of Missouri Press, 1980); Sylvia Lehrer, *The Dialectics of Art and Life: A Portrait of Sylvia Plath as Woman and Poet* (Salzburg: Institut für Anglistik und Amerikanistik, 1985), p. 13; Stanley Plumly, "What Ceremony of Words," in *Ariel Ascending*, ed. Alexander, 13–25, p. 16.

78. Harty, "Voice and Enunciation," p. 17.

79. Irving Howe, "The Plath Celebration: A Partial Dissent," in *Sylvia Plath: The Woman and the Work*, ed. Edward Butscher (New York: Dodd, Mead, 1977), 225–235, pp. 229–230.

80. Ibid., p. 230. Dorothy Merwin describes the historical condition in which the dramatic monologue becomes a dominant form as one in which sincere poetry "was vulnerable to attack on two opposite fronts: for being aware of an audience, and for not responding to the audience's needs" (*The Audience in the Poem: Five Victorian Poets* [New Brunswick, N.J.: Rutgers University Press, 1983], p. 7). Plath seems to be caught in a similar double

bind here, which suggests that the dramatic monologue, at least in modern hands, deepens rather than solves this problem of audience.

81. Phillip Hobsbaum, "The Temptation of Giant Despair," *The Hudson Review* 25.4 (Winter 1972–1973): 597–612, p. 606.

82. Uroff, "Sylvia Plath and Confessional Poetry," p. 112.

83. Ibid., p. 113. Steven Gould Axelrod makes a similar point when he argues that, with her suicide, Plath's personae "captured her person" (*Sylvia Plath: The Wound and the Cure of Words* [Baltimore: Johns Hopkins University Press, 1990], p. 236).

84. Joyce Carol Oates, "The Death Throes of Romanticism: The Poetry of Sylvia Plath," in *Sylvia Plath: The Woman and the Work,* ed. Butscher, p. 206.

85. Ibid., pp. 206–207.

86. Ibid., p. 210.

87. Calvin Bedient makes a judgment similar to that of Oates when he writes that "Plath's is a tragedy of weakness, of fatal vulnerability to the sense of injury . . . We feel pity and even terror before such sensitivity, but it has nothing to teach us. It looks like an accident in the scheme of things, a senseless failure. Yet with its extremes of feeling, its spasms, barbarism, surprises, her tragedy has romantic power . . . her imagination startles her experience into drama. She wrote as if vividness itself could soothe suffering, as if she could escape pain by increasing its intensity" ("Sylvia Plath, Romantic . . .," in *Sylvia Plath: New Views on the Poetry,* ed. Lane, p. 15).

88. A number of critics have made this connection: for example, Mary Lynn Broe writes, "'Lady Lazarus' is a peculiarly futuristic indictment of all those critics, editors, and collectors who promote the Plath legend, guest editor to ghastly suicide. As if predicting the lurid approach to her life, not her art, she mocks the glitter-seduced participants in the spectacle of her annihilation. This shoving crowd paws among the poetic ruins, reading and rereading for scraps of sensory details of her foreclosed end. Plath is their 'opus' or 'valuable,' their classic archetypal victim reduced to a shriek . . . Hence, she eludes them and predicts her own marketability as a consumer product of the suicide enterprise. Plath is having her last laugh, a terribly sophisticated and ironic one, at the expense of those who are blind and deaf to her blatant self-exhibitionism in 'Lady Lazarus.' Oblivious to her poetic control and her sense of camp, they react only to the themes of negation and death and mythical rebirth. They do not perceive the rearranging, controlling, and freeing art" (*Protean Poetic,* p. 178). See also M. D. Uroff ("Sylvia Plath and Confessional Poetry," p. 111) and Pashupati Jha (*Sylvia Plath: The Fear and Fury of Her Muse* [New Delhi: Creative Publishers], 1991, p. 91).

89. Plath, *Collected Poems,* p. 245.

4. The Drama of Breakdown and the Breakdown of Drama

1. The past decade has seen an explosion of interest in Byron's celebrity as it was constituted outside the boundaries of his individual poems—for exam-

ple, there has been research into the ways in which Byron's women read-
ers (and lovers) defined his public persona, including Nicola Watson's
"Trans-figuring Byronic Identity," in *At the Limits of Romanticism,* ed.
Mary Favret and Nicola J. Watson (Bloomington: Indiana University Press,
1994), pp. 185–206, and, in extended treatment, James Soderholm's *Fan-
tasy, Forgery, and the Byronic Legend* (Lexington: University Press of Ken-
tucky, 1996). The most recent collection of essays published on Byronic
charisma, *Byromania,* states explicitly that "[i]n order to understand some-
thing of the peculiar violence caught in his shifting reputation and represen-
tation, the contributors to this collection of essays on Byron also [as preced-
ing studies have done] leave out the poems" (Frances Wilson, Introduction
to *Byromania,* ed. Wilson [New York: St. Martin's Press, 1999], 1–23, p. 3).
Undoubtedly an explanation of Byron's and Sexton's charismatic effects
must be sought beyond the boundaries of their poems, in the voluminous
extra-poetic records of their lives they left in their letters, and in the records
we have of readers' responses to their work. I propose here to supplement
the analysis of these materials by seeking traces of charisma in the poems
themselves.

2. For example, Northrop Frye writes, "Byron's life imitated literature: this is
   where his unique combination of the poetic and the personal begins" (*Fa-
   bles of Identity* [New York: Harcourt Brace, 1963], p. 175).

3. Jerome Christensen, *Lord Byron's Strength* (Baltimore: Johns Hopkins Uni-
   versity Press, 1993), p. 22.

4. In J. L. Austin's terms, it could be said that sincere poetry is fundamentally
   constative, working to describe the experiences of a pre-existing self, while
   charismatic poetry is fundamentally performative, concerned with acting
   upon an audience (*How to Do Things With Words,* ed. J. O. Urmson and
   Marina Sbisà [Cambridge, Mass.: Harvard University Press, 1975]).

5. Jean-Jacques Rousseau, *The Confessions,* trans. J. M. Cohen (New York:
   Penguin Books, 1953), p. 17.

6. Ibid.

7. While here I am contrasting charisma to moral sincerity, "charisma" and
   "sincerity" did not always function in opposition to each other. When
   traced to their original Christian associations, and with God as the ultimate
   guarantor of truth, they are complementary ideas: "sincerity" connotes the
   purity or integrity of sacred writ, and "charisma" means a gift of grace
   from God, as shown by the definitions and examples in the *Oxford English
   Dictionary* (2nd ed.). For example, a 1583 theological work was entitled *A
   Defense of the sincere and true Translations of the holie Scriptures into the
   English tonge.* The progression of examples in the *OED* suggests that "sin-
   cerity" transferred its application from objects to people through its textual
   connotation, so that those who believed in an uncontaminated or "sincere"
   doctrine became known as "sincere" themselves. For example, one writer
   assures us regarding a translation of the Bible: "If some few . . . copies had
   been corrupted . . . the sincere number would have detected the corrupt."

But while sincerity was originally associated with textual objects, charisma was originally associated with speech. An example from 1852 states: "The gift of prophecy was the *charism* which enabled its possessors to utter, with the authority of inspiration, divine strains of warning"; and one from 1920 reads, "He himself had the *charisma*, or spiritual gift of utterance." These connotations underline a contrast between the writerly textual complexity that constitutes the sincerity of a poet like Wordsworth and the provocatively staged speech acts that constitute the charisma of a poet like Byron or Sexton.

8. *From Max Weber: Essays in Sociology*, trans. and ed. H. H. Gerth and C. Wright Mills (New York: Oxford University Press, 1946), p. 245.

9. Ibid., p. 262.

10. Christensen, *Lord Byron's Strength*, p. xvi. Christensen's study of Byron in fact champions him as an opponent of both economically deterministic theories of history in the nineteenth century and historically deterministic theories of Romantic poetry in the twentieth. He opposes what he calls Byron's "strength" to the explanations of his appeal that can be derived from historical context. While my analysis is in the spirit of Christensen's study, I prefer Weberian "charisma" to Christensen's "strength" because it can account for Sexton's impact as well as Byron's. Sexton's example serves as a useful corrective to the masculinist connotations of Christensen's terminology—if Byron's assertiveness disrupts normative methods for relating the individual to historical influence and change, then so does Sexton's vulnerability, as can be seen by the problems she poses for feminism (see Ostriker later in this chapter). Christensen defines "strength" as unilateral (p. xvi), but Weberian charisma is relational: the leader's "charismatic claim breaks down if his mission is not recognized by those to whom he feels he has been sent. If they recognize him, he is their master—so long as he knows how to maintain recognition" (p. 246). In poetic terms, the charismatic claim must be staged in relationship to a responsive audience.

11. Richard Howard approaches this definition when he writes that Sexton is "both more and less than a mere 'person,' something beyond a 'character' . . . [She is] what we call a *figure*, the form of a tragic function" ("Anne Sexton: 'Some Tribal Female Who Is Known But Forbidden,'" in *Anne Sexton: The Artist and Her Critics*, ed. J. D. McClatchy [Bloomington: Indiana University Press, 1978], 193–203, p. 194; emphasis in original).

12. Plath, as much as Sexton, qualifies as a charismatic poet in my terms. I focus on Sexton here because, to my mind, she spends the majority of her poetic career in the position of Lady Lazarus, whereas for Plath, the stance she develops in "Lady Lazarus" is only one of a number of possible poetic positions available to her.

13. A. R. Jones, "Necessity and Freedom: The Poetry of Robert Lowell, Sylvia Plath, and Anne Sexton," *Critical Quarterly* 7.1 (Spring 1965): 11–30, p. 14.

14. Quoted in Wilson, *Byromania*, p. 10.

15. Frye goes on to point out that understanding the impact of Byron's personality in his poetry "is crucial to our understanding not only of Byron, but of literature as a whole" (*Fables of Identity,* p. 174).
16. William Pritchard, "The Anne Sexton Show," *Hudson Review* (Summer 1978): 387–392, p. 390.
17. Robert Lowell, "Anne Sexton," in *Anne Sexton: The Artist and Her Critics,* ed. McClatchy, p. 71.
18. Byron allegedly was sexually molested by his nurse at age ten (see, for example, Phyllis Grosskurth, *Byron: The Flawed Angel* [Boston: Houghton Mifflin, 1997], pp. 27–28). Although there is no firm evidence that Sexton was sexually molested by her father, she produced memories of this abuse in therapy. Sexton, her confidants, and her psychologist all were ambivalent about the reliability of these memories. Sexton's biographer concludes, "The veracity of the incest narrative cannot be established historically, but that does not mean that it didn't, in a profound and lasting sense, 'happen.' It is clear from many sources that Sexton's physical boundaries were repeatedly trespassed by the adults in her family in ways that disturbed her emotional life from girlhood onward" (Diane Middlebrook, *Anne Sexton: A Biography* [New York: Vintage, 1992], p. 59). It is tempting to speculate that these life experiences directly bear on the poetic stances these two poets develop. According to Sexton's biographer, some of the symptoms of sexual abuse detectable in her behavior included "her tendency to sexualize significant relationships, and the fluidity of boundaries she experienced between herself and other people" (Middlebrook, *Anne Sexton,* p. 57). These characteristics also apply to the charismatic position as I define it. The idea that childhood sexual abuse produces particular aesthetic effects seems morally dangerous to me, but a more biographically focused project than this one might follow up the connection with interesting results.
19. Matthew Arnold is an important exception.
20. Pritchard, "The Anne Sexton Show," p. 387.
21. Byron has been attacked for his lack of sincerity from the beginning of his career (see, for example, the quotation from *London Magazine* earlier in this chapter), and strangely enough, in response to this line of attack, he has sometimes been claimed as a sincere poet in the naive sense by critics wishing to argue for his value. Matthew Arnold endorses Algernon Swinburne's notion that Byron is valuable for "the excellence of [his] sincerity and strength" (*Essays in Criticism,* 2nd Series [London: MacMillan, 1915], p. 193). As recently as 1993 a critic suggests that we look for Byron's "deepest beliefs and feelings . . . in his poetry . . . [in] the poetry we get an insight into the Byronic mind that comes nearer to the truth of his attitudes and his honest thought than in the playful quips of his immensely entertaining letters" (Leslie Marchand, "Byronic Attitudes," in *Rereading Byron,* ed. Alice Levine and Robert N. Keane [New York: Garland, 1993], 239–251, p. 239). In the most naked plea for our moral approbation, the jacket copy of the 1993 Book-of-the-Month Club edition of Byron's work proclaims that "his poetry resonates with as much sincerity as his fatal decision to

travel to the Mediterranean to fight for the liberty of Greece" (*Lord Byron: Selected Poems* [New York: Softback Preview, 1993]). The "confessional" label has ensured that critics have closely scrutinized Sexton's sincerity.

22. Byron, *The Complete Poetical Works,* vol. 2, ed. Jerome J. McGann (Oxford: Clarendon Press, 1980), *Childe Harold's Pilgrimage,* lines iii.70.662–663.

23. Ibid., lines iii.10.84–87.

24. In this way, in Robert Langbaum's terms, they act like characters in a dramatic monologue (*The Poetry of Experience* [New York: W. W. Norton, 1957]).

25. Anne Sexton, *The Complete Poems* (Boston: Houghton Mifflin, 1981), p. 63.

26. Ibid., p. 484.

27. A gentler, perhaps more successful version of this transaction is proposed in "For John, Who Begs Me Not to Enquire Further," which tentatively suggests that Sexton's private experience could be relevant to her addressee's: "sometimes in private, / my kitchen, your kitchen, / my face, your face" (*Complete Poems,* p. 35). See Alicia Ostriker's "Anne Sexton and the Seduction of Audience" for a detailed examination of the dramatic context that Sexton creates to make this connection possible (*Sexton: Selected Criticism,* ed. Diana Hume George [Chicago: University of Illinois Press, 1988], pp. 3–18).

28. Byron, *The Complete Poetical Works,* vol. 5, ed. Jerome J. McGann (Oxford: Clarendon Press, 1986), *Don Juan,* line xvi.2.16.

29. Ibid., line xi.37.270.

30. Ibid., line ix.26.201–208.

31. Soderholm, *Fantasy, Forgery,* p. 5.

32. Thomas McDonnell, "Light in a Dark Journey," in *Critical Essays on Anne Sexton,* ed. Linda Wagner-Martin (Boston: G. K. Hall, 1989), 40–44, p. 43.

33. *Don Juan,* lines xvii.12.96.

34. Sexton, *Complete Poems,* p. 160.

35. Ibid., p. 174. As Alicia Ostriker puts it, "She had committed herself to an erotic view of art and life and remained committed to it" ("Anne Sexton and the Seduction of Audience," p. 7).

36. Joyce Carol Oates, "Anne Sexton: Self-Portrait in Poetry and Letters," in *Critical Essays on Anne Sexton,* ed. Wagner-Martin, p. 53.

37. Ostriker, "Anne Sexton and the Seduction of Audience," pp. 16–17.

38. Ibid., p. 14.

39. Neil Myers, "The Hungry Sheep Look Up," in *Critical Essays on Anne Sexton,* ed. Wagner-Martin, p. 19.

40. Ibid., p. 21.

41. James Dickey, "On *To Bedlam and Part Way Back,*" in *Anne Sexton: The Artist and Her Critics,* ed. McClatchy, p. 117.

42. Byron, *Childe Harold's Pilgrimage,* lines iii.33.290–292.

43. Lines iii.73.691–693.

44. Lines iii.7.55–60; emphasis in original.

45. Lines iv.122.1090–1091.
46. Lines iii.69.655–658.
47. Lines iii.4.32–35.
48. Lines iii.111.1032–1037.
49. Lines iii.15.132–135.
50. Lines iii.84.790–793.
51. Line iii.3.25.
52. Lines iii.36.317–320.
53. Lines iii.38.338–341.
54. Lines iii.43.386–387.
55. Lines iii.77.725–728.
56. Line iii.77.729.
57. Lines iii.77.729–733.
58. Lines iii.84.789–790.
59. Byron, *Complete Poetical Works,* vol. 2, p. 122. This preface anticipates John Berryman's preface to his *Dream Songs,* in which he discourages his readers from identifying him with Henry, the poems' speaker. But while Berryman explicitly suggests that the speaker and poet should be kept separate while implicitly suggesting that it does not much matter if they are confused, Byron explicitly gives up his attempts to keep his speaker and poet separate, while implicitly suggesting that their separation matters very much. Berryman can afford to have a relaxed attitude about the relationship of Henry to himself because both parties are part of a bigger, naturalized function of self-consciousness. Byron refuses self-consciousness as a natural, shared condition: he can deploy it only as a function of his own terrible individuality.
60. Sexton, *Complete Poems,* p. 15.
61. Ibid., p. 16.
62. Ibid., p. 6.
63. Helen Vendler, *The Music of What Happens* (Cambridge, Mass.: Harvard University Press, 1988), p. 308.
64. Sexton, *Complete Poems,* p. 319.
65. Ibid., pp. 319–320.
66. Ibid., p. 320.
67. Ibid.
68. Ibid., p. 319.
69. As Martyn Corbett puts it, "Each encounter follows a similar pattern in which an offer of help is rejected because it would need to be paid for by the submission of Manfred's proud spirit . . . [The dynamic of the play] is arrested by repeated assertions of Manfred's indomitable and inflexible pride. This movement may be characterized as a study in impasse" (*Byron and Tragedy* [London: MacMillan, 1988], p. 20).
70. Byron, *The Complete Poetical Works,* vol. 4, ed. Jerome J. McGann (Oxford: Clarendon Press, 1986), *Manfred,* lines I.i.5–8.
71. Lines I.i.124–128.
72. In this condition, Manfred's position is not unlike that of Browning's Duke,

who is frustrated by the redundancy of asserting the power of his name, a power that should have already been taken for granted. But rather than looking upon this predicament with ironic detachment, Byron here considers it with deadly seriousness.

73. *Manfred,* lines I.i.137–138.
74. Line I.i.139.
75. Line I.i.158.
76. Lines I.i.159–160.
77. Lines II.ii.244–245.
78. Lines II.ii.249–254.
79. Lines II.ii.211–215.
80. Lines II.iv.501–502.
81. Line II.iv.521.
82. Lines II.ii.199–201.
83. See lines I.i.148–163.
84. Lines III.iv.342–343.
85. Line III.iv.399.
86. Sexton, *Complete Poems,* p. 37.
87. Ibid., p. 38.
88. Margaret Honton elaborates on this logic of guilt: "In Sexton's double image of the devouring mother myth, the speaker accepts blame from her predecessor as well as guilt concerning her successor. Moreover, she equates *blame* with *guilt* in some sort of inverse functioning, never quite stated, but throughout this poem implied: As my mother's sufferings were caused by me, so I am the cause of my daughter's sufferings. With this distorted perception, she encounters the double terror of likenesses and unlikenesses, of reflections and foreshadowings, of apparent answers to *how* and *why* mother and daughter are so much alike, without asking the proper antecedent question *if* the mother's and daughter's 'smiles held in place' are really, or even symbolically, matching smiles" ("The Double Image and the Division of Parts: A Study of Mother-Daughter Relationships in the Poetry of Anne Sexton," in *Sexton: Selected Criticism,* ed. Diana Hume George [Chicago: University of Illinois Press, 1988], 99–116, p. 100; emphasis in original).
89. Sexton, *Complete Poems,* p. 42.
90. Ibid., p. 37.
91. Ibid., p. 38.
92. Ibid., p. 41.
93. Ibid., pp. 38–39.
94. Ibid., p. 40.
95. Ibid.
96. Ibid., p. 41.
97. Ibid.
98. Ibid., p. 37.
99. See ibid., p. 35.
100. Ibid., p. 36.

101. Frye writes, "There is hardly any characterization in the poem: even Don Juan never emerges clearly as a character" (*Fables of Identity*, p. 184).

102. As Jean Hall puts it, "Juan learns very little from his experience, which is why he can happily continue his experiencing" ("The Evolution of the Surface Self: Byron's Poetic Career," *Keats-Shelley Journal* [1987]: 134–157, p. 146).

103. Byron, *Don Juan*, lines x.23.179–184.

104. Line x.24.185.

105. Lines xii.49.387–392.

106. Lines ii.190.1513–1520.

107. Line vi.60.473.

108. Harold Bloom suggests that Juan's "disinterestedness" gradually transforms into "the sickness of uninterestedness" (Introduction, *Lord Byron's "Don Juan,"* ed. Harold Bloom [New York: Chelsea House, 1987], 1–14, p. 9). Frye argues that, in *Don Juan*, "the gloom and misanthropy, the secret past sins, the gnawing remorse of the earlier heroes is finally identified as a shoddier but more terrifying evil—boredom" (*Fables of Identity*, p. 184).

109. Byron, *Don Juan*, lines iii.12.89–96.

110. Lines xiii.96.763–764.

111. Lines v.2.9–14.

112. Lines xv.57.449–454.

113. In making this argument, I follow Philip Martin, who writes, "Few would deny that *Don Juan* is Byron's finest poem, but the way in which it is commonly related to his earlier works—as a document which undermines them and thereby demonstrates an intellectual transcending of their bombast and limitation—is manifestly unsatisfactory . . . *Don Juan* proceeds from the same kind of consciousness that informs the earlier works" (*Byron: A Poet Before His Public* [Cambridge: Cambridge University Press, 1982], p. 6).

114. Byron, *Childe Harold's Pilgrimage*, lines iii.6.46–54.

115. Helen Vendler argues that the *Transformations* exhibit "an extremity of nonparticipatory vision" (*Music of What Happens*, p. 305).

116. Sexton, *Complete Poems*, pp. 233–234.

117. Ibid., p. 234.

118. Ibid., p. 293.

119. Ibid., p. 294.

120. Ibid.

121. Ibid., p. 293.

122. Ibid., p. 294.

123. Ibid., p. 295.

5. Agnostic Sincerity

1. Letter to J. H. Reynolds, 22 November 1817, in *Letters of John Keats,* ed. Robert Gittings (Oxford: Oxford University Press, 1970), p. 43.

2. Letter to Richard Woodhouse, 27 October 1818, p. 157.

3. Ibid.

4. Letter to J. H. Reynolds, 3 May 1818, p. 96.

5. Letter to Benjamin Bailey, 22 November 1817, p. 36.

6. Quoted in David Kalstone, *Five Temperaments: Elizabeth Bishop, Robert Lowell, James Merrill, Adrienne Rich, and John Ashbery* (New York: Oxford University Press, 1977), p. 15. The quotation comes from an unpublished letter Bishop wrote to Anne Stevenson.

7. Quoted in Judith Moffett, *James Merrill: An Introduction to the Poetry* (New York: Columbia University Press, 1984), p. 8; emphasis in original.

8. "Elizabeth Bishop (1911–1979)," in *Recitative: Prose by James Merrill,* ed. J. D. McClatchy (San Francisco: North Point Press, 1986), p. 122.

9. James Merrill, *Collected Poems,* ed. J. D. McClatchy and Stephen Yenser (New York: Knopf, 2001), p. 353.

10. Keats, Letter to Benjamin Bailey, 22 November 1817, p. 37.

11. Letter to the George Keatses, 16 December 1818–4 January 1819, p. 187.

12. Letter to Benjamin Bailey, 22 November 1817, p. 38.

13. Or again, "axioms in philosophy are not axioms until they are proved upon our pulses," Letter to J. H. Reynolds, 3 May 1818, p. 93.

14. Letter to the George Keatses, 19 March 1819, p. 230.

15. Harold Bloom, Introduction, in *Modern Critical Views: James Merrill* (New York: Chelsea House, 1985), 1–7, p. 2. Merrill himself worried about the coldness of his personae, for example in the poem "Dream (Escape from the Sculpture Museum) and Waking," but he seems to have understood this problem as one inherent to self-consciousness in general as much as a potential defect in his particular personality. Thomas Travisano makes the useful observation that something that Bishop and the "confessional" poets share is a "frequent, skilled, and dramatic use of factual or emotional material that is *withheld*" (*Midcentury Quartet: Bishop, Lowell, Jarrell, Berryman, and the Making of a Postmodern Aesthetic* [Charlottesville: University of Virginia Press, 1999], p. 51; emphasis in original). But I would argue that Bishop withholds personal information not in a calculated attempt to enhance the mystique of her persona, but as the result of uncertainty about the usefulness or relevance of "personal" information more generally.

16. Critics have indeed done so—for example, Bishop's reticence and indirection have been understood as a defense against the judgment the world might pass upon her private life as a woman and a lesbian (see, for example, Adrienne Rich, "The Eye of the Outsider: *Elizabeth Bishop's Complete Poems 1927–1979,*" in *Blood, Bread and Poetry* [New York: W. W. Norton, 1986], 124–135).

17. As Earl Wasserman puts it, "Forces contend wildly within the poem, not only without resolution, but without possibility of resolution" (*The Finer Tone: Keats' Major Poems* [Westport, Conn.: Greenwood Press, 1983], p. 178. Originally published by Johns Hopkins University Press, 1967). Though Wasserman does not explicitly name these forces as consciousness and unconsciousness, he suggests that the poet's self-consciousness is one reason for the poem's instability: the poem "is synthetically fashioned: in-

stead of operating within its own framework, it functions only because the poet intervenes and cuts across the grain of his materials to make them vibrant" (p. 179).

18. John Keats, *Complete Poems,* ed. Jack Stillinger (Cambridge, Mass.: Harvard University Press, 1982); lines 1–4.

19. Lines 5–10.

20. Surprisingly, critics have tended to accept Keats's explanation of his condition. See, for example, Wasserman (*Finer Tone,* p. 180); Christopher Ricks (*Keats and Embarrassment* [Oxford: Clarendon Press, 1974], p. 150); Morris Dickstein ("The Fierce Dispute: The 'Ode to a Nightingale,'" in *The Odes of John Keats,* ed. Harold Bloom [New York: Chelsea House, 1987], 29–40, p. 30); Harold Bloom (Introduction, *The Odes of John Keats,* ed. Bloom, 1–23, p. 8); Stuart Ende ("Identification and Identity: The 'Ode to a Nightingale,'" in *The Odes of John Keats,* ed. Bloom, 65–74, p. 66); and James O'Rourke (*Keats's Odes and Contemporary Criticism* [Gainesville: University Press of Florida, 1998], p. 13). It is frequently explained that Keats's empathy with the nightingale accounts for his drowsy numbness. But numbness is not a feeling generally associated with empathy, and it makes little sense for a human being to empathize with a being that lacks human consciousness. To the extent to which Keats is interested in the nightingale at all, he seems interested in its non-humanlike characteristics.

21. Line 20. O'Rourke offers a plausible alternative explanation: "By the outset of the second stanza the speaker is trying to reestablish a link to the nightingale, a connection that seems to have fallen away somewhere in the ellipsis between stanzas. That such a significant event in the poem's plot, namely, a separation of the nightingale from the speaker, should occur only elliptically establishes the ode's texture as a stylized stream of consciousness" (*Keats's Odes,* p. 14).

22. Line 11.

23. Line 23.

24. Lines 31–35.

25. This troublesome phrase is a well-known interpretive crux of the poem. Some readers judge "Already with thee" as an unmitigated success—for example, Bloom (Introduction, p. 9) and John Minahan (*Word Like a Bell: John Keats, Music, and the Romantic Poet* [Kent, Oh.: Kent University Press, 1992], p. 173); others consider it a failure (see, for example, Wasserman, *Finer Tone,* p. 198, and Dickstein, "Fierce Dispute," p. 32). According to my interpretation, "Already with thee" initiates a new kind of conscious unconsciousness (or negative capability) for the poet, perhaps resulting from a partial adoption of the limited consciousness of the nightingale, but this mixture proves as unstable and unsustainable as the poem's other versions.

26. Lines 35–50.

27. In its self-blinding movement, the Ode becomes Keats's anti-visionary poem. As Helen Vendler puts it, "Keats had been . . . a visual poet, imagining scenes of encounter, stationing figures in processions, and giving his gar-

dener Fancy free rein to produce a sumptuous and varied landscape. The imaginative scheme for *Nightingale* forbade, as it turned out, the central visual exercise of his powers" (*The Odes of John Keats* [Cambridge, Mass.: Harvard University Press, 1983], p. 96).

28. Lines 57–58.

29. Line 71.

30. Lines 80–81.

31. It is traditional to read these closing stanzas as introducing new controversy into the poem rather than merely repeating a problem already stated. O'Rourke summarizes: "Whether the 'Nightingale' ode presents the 'it' of its penultimate line as a vision or as a mere daydream, and whether the return to the everyday world at the poem's close is a gain or a loss in perceptual clarity, have been the central concerns of the ode's reception history to the present day" (*Keats's Odes*, p. 2). But if the poem as a whole is read as an attempt to sustain the state between waking and sleeping, and the nightingale is read as a mere vehicle for achieving this state, then the final stanza holds few surprises. In general, I follow Dickstein's reading of the "Ode to a Nightingale" as "a tragic poem rather than a visionary one, founded like so many of the best Romantic poems not on imaginative flight but rather on the dialectical tension of the poet's divided self" ("Fierce Dispute," p. 38).

32. Elizabeth Bishop, *The Complete Poems 1927–1979* (New York: Noonday Press, 1983), p. 159.

33. Ibid.

34. Ibid.

35. Ibid., p. 160.

36. Marjorie Levinson, "Picturing Pleasure: Some Poems by Elizabeth Bishop," in *What's Left of Theory?* ed. Judith Butler, John Guillory, and Kendall Thomas (New York: Routledge, 2000), 192–239, p. 215. While in many ways inspired by Levinson's article, my reading of Bishop is less interested in applying new interpretive grids (for example, psychoanalysis) to the poems than in tracing the questions her poetry raises about the viability of interpretation itself.

37. Bishop, *Complete Poems*, pp. 160 and 161.

38. Ibid., p. 161. Anne Colwell elaborates: "'Unlikely' . . . creates levels of contradiction. It is an ironic word for an experience of a shared sameness. By its emotional flatness it expresses the speaker's feeling of disconnection yet also communicates an intellectual engagement . . . 'Unlikely' is a scientist's word, and its appearance in the mouth of a fainting six year old risks undermining the serious incident with a comic tone. But this risk in itself reinforces the paradox, the dichotomy, the ever-multiplying questions the poem explores" (*Inscrutable Houses: Metaphors of the Body in the Poems of Elizabeth Bishop* [Tuscaloosa: University of Alabama Press, 1997], p. 200).

39. Merrill, *Collected Poems*, p. 127.

40. Ibid.

41. Ibid., pp. 127–128.

42. Ibid., p. 128.

43. Ibid., p. 313; emphasis mine.

44. Mutlu Blasing reads "self-knowledge" here as the "knowledge of pervasive textuality," the knowledge that life is always already literature. If we accept this reading, then "self-knowledge" is simply the knowledge that we are all readers, that we do not have the authority of saying finally what anything means, including our own experiences ("Rethinking Models of Literary Change: The Case of James Merrill," *American Literary History* 2.2 [Summer 1990]: 299–317, p. 310).

45. Moffett reports, "Merrill said once in an interview that, having come this far, he had no idea how to finish the poem" (*James Merrill*, p. 48).

46. Merrill, *Collected Poems*, p. 129.

47. Ibid.

48. Bishop herself creates a precedent for this kind of reading when, in "Poem," she writes, "Our visions coincided—'visions' is / too serious a word—our looks" (*Complete Poems*, p. 177). This emphasis on looks is confirmed by C. K. Doreski (*Elizabeth Bishop: The Restraints of Language* [Oxford: Oxford University Press, 1993], p. 3) and by Kalstone, who comments on "her apparent lack of insistence on meanings beyond the surface of the poem" (*Five Temperaments*, p. 14). But as Bonnie Costello suggests, "What has not been sufficiently explored is the complex, unresolved relationship in this poet's images between observation and metaphor" (*Elizabeth Bishop: Questions of Mastery* [Cambridge, Mass.: Harvard University Press, 1991], p. 3). Doreski elaborates: "Resistance to language that attempts to delve into the psyche or the world of the spirit characterizes her poetry. The process of resistance itself, however, constitutes a powerful rhetorical structure that shapes much of her best work" (*Elizabeth Bishop*, p. 34). It is this complex, unresolved relationship, this powerful rhetorical structure, that my readings will attempt to flesh out.

49. Costello, *Questions of Mastery*, p. 133.

50. Keats, "Ode on Indolence," lines 1–9.

51. Lines 11–15.

52. Lines 15–20.

53. Lines 24–30.

54. Bishop, *Complete Poems*, p. 64.

55. This multiplication of silver surfaces suggests a world made of tiny mirrors, but Bishop notably ignores the possibility that this world could return her reflection to her. This simultaneous courtship and avoidance of the world's reflectiveness parallels her simultaneous courtship and avoidance of epiphany.

56. Bishop, *Complete Poems*, p. 65.

57. Ibid., pp. 65–66.

58. Mary J. Elkins draws a helpful comparison to Frost's "For Once, Then, Something," in which water rebukes water's own clarity: for both poets, "water is both 'dark' and 'clear,' withholding as well as revealing" ("Elizabeth Bishop and the Act of Seeing," *South Atlantic Review* 48.4 [November 1983]: 43–57, p. 53).

59. As Doreski puts it, "Not even the language of transcendence . . . can generate a fiction adequate to both the senses (the physical self) and the psyche (which finds its analogue in the sea). Knowledge, that troubling abstraction, leads beyond metaphor, beyond the apprehensible world. The poet cannot follow . . . yet it is precisely the act of discovering this limitation that is 'historical,' accretive, 'flowing,' organic, and 'flown,' perishing" (*Elizabeth Bishop,* p. 68; see also Colwell, *Inscrutable Houses,* p. 122). Moreover, "This educational disclosure is locked in the language, which reveals itself to be nonrepresentational after all, but a code. Here lies the unnerving power of the reticence that requires interpretation through recognition that language *is* experience" (Doreski, *Elizabeth Bishop,* p. 5; emphasis in original). I would substitute "reading" for Doreski's "language." Kalstone makes a similar point in different terms: it is "impossible—and unnecessary—to distinguish *knowledge* from the *sea* . . . With a final fluency she leaves her declarative descriptions behind and captures a rhythm at once mysterious and acknowledging limitations" (*Five Temperaments,* p. 21). Jeredith Merrin describes Bishop's resistance to epiphany in metrical terms: "Here [at the end of "At the Fishhouses"] the verse flirts with pentameter, but resists that stately regularity." Bishop uses "metrical variation to mute the Romantic horn" (*An Enabling Humility: Marianne Moore, Elizabeth Bishop, and the Uses of Tradition* [New Brunswick, N.J.: Rutgers University Press, 1990], p. 93).

60. Seamus Heaney eloquently describes the shape of this poem: "What we have been offered, among other things, is the slow-motion spectacle of a well-disciplined poetic imagination being tempted to dare a big leap, hesitating, and then with powerful sureness actually taking the leap" (*The Government of the Tongue* [New York: Noonday Press, 1988], p. 105). But to my mind, this leap is equivocal, self-thwarting—Bishop's insight is into the problems of ascribing metaphorical significance to sensory observation, not into "knowledge" as something which transcends individual observations.

61. Merrill, *Collected Poems,* p. 3.

62. Ibid.

63. Keats, "Ode to Psyche," line 67.

64. Bishop, *Complete Poems,* p. 92.

65. Merrill, *Collected Poems,* p. 261.

66. Ibid.

67. Ibid.

68. See Richard Sáez, "James Merrill's Oedipal Fire," for a comparison of this poem with others that have an Oedipal theme in *Modern Critical Views: James Merrill,* ed. Harold Bloom (New York: Chelsea House, 1985).

69. Merrill, *Collected Poems,* p. 261.

70. Ibid.; emphasis in original.

71. Ibid.

72. Bishop, *Complete Poems,* p. 92.

73. Ibid., p. 159.

74. As Blasing's explication demonstrates, the reference to *The White Goddess*

is complex: "The 'huge crane' brings to mind Graves' *White Goddess,* presumably because cranes were sacred to the goddess," who represents an Orphic model of poetic language, but also (at the end of the book) brings about the destruction of irreligious man. To complicate things further, the crane is also linked to the invention of writing. As Blasing points out, the reference to Graves is not direct but is effected through a punning connection between the mechanical crane and the mythical bird/goddess. This "nonhierarchical synchronic duplicity" does not permit us to feel that we have definitively "read" this moment in the poem once we have traced its reference; instead, searching for the reference's origins only multiplies the kinds of reading to be done ("Rethinking Models," pp. 306–307).

75. Bernard Blackstone writes that of Keats's odes, this one is the "most familiar, the richest in texture, the most obscure" (*The Consecrated Urn: An Interpretation of Keats in Terms of Growth and Form* [New York: Longmans, Green, 1959], p. 329). This obscurity comes in part from the ambiguous status of the object the ode addresses.

76. Keats, "Ode on a Grecian Urn," lines 5–10.

77. Lines 11–12.

78. Lines 31–37.

79. Helen Vendler, for example, suggests that this vision, in which "the audience, prompted by the visible artifact, engages by its interrogation in an act of cooperative mutual creation with the artist," is an improvement upon the poem's earlier imaginings of art as historical documentation and art as the presentation of an ideal (*Odes of John Keats,* pp. 122–123).

80. Doreski marks "The Monument" as the point in which "the shifting stance [vis-à-vis experience] becomes a central strategy in Bishop's work" (*Elizabeth Bishop,* p. 24).

81. Bishop, *Complete Poems,* p. 23.

82. Colwell, *Inscrutable Houses,* p. 53. The title of the wood rubbing is "False Positions," which suggests the contorted positions Bishop's readers must adopt to try to see what she describes in her poem.

83. Bishop, *Complete Poems,* p. 23.

84. Colwell, *Inscrutable Houses,* p. 54.

85. Bishop, *Complete Poems,* p. 23.

86. Doreski, *Elizabeth Bishop,* p. 29.

87. The poem never designates a gender for the speaker's companion; here I use the female pronoun for convenience of exposition.

88. Bishop, *Complete Poems,* p. 23.

89. Ibid.

90. Kalstone, *Five Temperaments,* p. 28.

91. Bishop, *Complete Poems,* p. 24.

92. Ibid.

93. Ibid., p. 25.

94. Merrill, *Collected Poems,* p. 362.

95. Ibid., p. 365.

96. Ibid., p. 363.

97. In Stephen Yenser's words, "We are reminded of the elusiveness of a 'source.' Is the poem's real source the relationship with Mademoiselle? Or is it indeed Valéry's lyric? Life or literature?" (*The Consuming Myth: The Work of James Merrill* [Cambridge, Mass.: Harvard University Press, 1987], p. 13). Jeff Westover points out that Merrill tends to approach the past as a multilayered palimpsest rather than through a Freudian binary of manifest versus latent content. The poem simply adds another layer, "an elegant overlay upon the texts of the past" ("Writing on the (Sur)face of the Past: Convival Visions and Revisions in the Poetry of James Merrill," in *Critical Essays on James Merrill,* ed. Guy Rotella [New York: G. K. Hall, 1996], 215–230, p. 217).

98. *Collected Poems,* p. 363.

99. Ibid., p. 364.

100. Ibid., p. 362.

101. Ibid., p. 366.

102. Ibid., pp. 366–367.

103. Ibid., p. 367.

Conclusion

1. An early version of this kind of self-consciousness can be found in the German Romantic writer Novalis's "Monologue": "The particular quality of language, the fact that it is concerned only with itself, is known to no one. Language is such a marvelous, fruitful secret—because when someone speaks merely for the sake of speaking, he utters the most splendid, most original truths. But if he wants to speak about something definite, capricious language makes him say the most ridiculous and confused stuff" (*Novalis: Philosophical Writings,* trans. Margaret Mahony Stoljar [Albany: State University of New York Press, 1997], p. 83).

2. Jean-Paul Sartre, *"What Is Literature?" and Other Essays* (Cambridge, Mass.: Harvard University Press, 1988), p. 49.

3. Bob Perelman, *Ten to One: Selected Poems* (Hanover, Conn.: Wesleyan University Press, 1999), p. 57.

4. Ibid.

5. Ibid., p. 58.

6. Ibid., p. 57.

7. Ibid., p. 58.

8. Ibid., p. 57.

9. Bob Perelman, *The Marginalization of Poetry* (Princeton: Princeton University Press, 1996), p. 12.

10. Alice Fulton, *Feeling as a Foreign Language: The Good Strangeness of Poetry* (St. Paul, Minn.: Graywolf Press, 1999), p. 282; emphasis in original.

11. Ibid., p. 283.

12. John Ashbery, *Selected Poems* (New York: Penguin, 1985), p. 202.

13. Eve Kosofsky Sedgwick, *A Dialogue on Love* (Boston: Beacon Press, 1999), p. 31; emphasis in original.

Index

Arnold, Matthew: "The Buried Life," 97, 100

Ashbery, John, 191; "Self-Portrait in a Convex Mirror," 195

Authorship, theories of, 3, 82–83, 85–86

Berryman, John, 101–107; naturalization of dramatic monologue, 101–103; device of Henry, 102–103, 104–105; naturalization of self-consciousness, 105–107; self-exposure, 106

    WORKS: *Dream Songs,* 101–107; Dream Song 14, 103; Dream Song 57, 101–102; Dream Song 76, 103–104; Preface to *Dream Songs,* 102–103, 230n59

Biographical information, relevance to poetry, 4–5, 108, 110–115, 116

Bishop, Elizabeth, 152–156, 160–163, 167–168, 170–173, 174, 177–178, 181–184, 189; on poet as observer, 152–153; reticence, 155, 189, 233nn15,16; resistance to metaphorical interpretation, 170–174, 236n48; disorientation of reader, 178, 181–184

    WORKS: "At the Fishhouses," 170–173; "Brazil, January 1, 1502," 174, 177; "In the Waiting Room," 160–163, 178; "The Monument," 181–184

Browning, Robert, 83, 85–86, 86–91, 91–92, 100–101, 107, 108; artists as protagonists, 90–91; Eliot on, 91–92; colloquial speech, 100–101

    WORKS: "Bishop Blougram's Apology," 107; "Fra Lippo Lippi," 83, 90–91; "My Last Duchess," 85–86, 86–90, 108

Byron, Lord (George Gordon), 115, 118–119, 120–130, 134–138, 142–146, 149–150; problem of evaluation, 120–121, 124; relationship to moral sincerity, 121, 122, 228n21; relationship to audience, 122–124, 144–145; self-consciousness as sin, 125–127; courting forgetfulness, 126–127, 135–136, 143; world-weariness, 127–128, 144; nonrecognition of doubles, 128–130; distinction between narrator and protagonist, 130, 142–143, 144–145; entrapment in soliloquy, 134–138

    WORKS: *Childe Harold's Pilgrimage,* 124–130, 145–146, 149–150; *Don Juan,* 122, 123, 142–145; *Manfred,* 134–138, 149–150; Preface to Canto IV of *Childe Harold's Pilgrimage,* 130

Charisma: defined by Max Weber, 118–119; against theorization, 119, 150; etymology, 226n7

Charismatic poetry, 116–150; definition, 116–118, 119–120, 150; role of audience, 121–124; role of moral judgment, 121–123; role of sexuality, 123–124; power relationships, 123–124; problem of evaluation, 124

Coleridge, Samuel Taylor: "Dejection, an Ode," 1–3, 5; on organic form, 51–52; on self-consciousness, 199n17